A Practical Guide to Budgetary and Management Control Systems

A Practical Guide to Budgetary and Management Control Systems

A Functional and Performance Evaluation Approach

Lewis Daniel Houck, Jr.

LexingtonBooks
D.C. Heath and Company
Lexington, Massachusetts
Toronto

658.15
H 835

Library of Congress Cataloging in Publication Data

Houck, Lewis Daniel.
 A practical guide to budgetary and management control systems.

 Includes index.
 1. Managerial economics. 2. Managerial accounting. 3. Budget in business. I. Title.
HD30.22H68   658.1'5   78-14716
ISBN 0-669-02705-7

Copyright © 1979 by D.C. Heath and Company

Published simultaneously in Canada.

Printed in the United States of America.

International Standard Book Number: 0-669-02705-7

Library of Congress Catalog Card Number: 78-14716

To James Samuel Lanham, educator and executive, who has made substantial contributions to the professional field of management control systems and whose inspiration led the author to undertake this work.

Contents

List of Figures

List of Tables

Preface

At no time in our recent industrial history since the Great Depression of the 1930s has there been a more critical need for effective activity planning and budgeting and for the skillful allocation of manpower, material, and financial resources available to alternative and often competing operating uses or projects undertaken by profit-seeking manufacturing and service companies. Furthermore, there is an equally critical need among firms in the United States and abroad for effective management procedures to control the uses of these resources in terms of conserving their financial cost and for the purpose of yielding maximum benefits from their use. Our recent economic experiences characterized by dangerously high rates of inflation and periods of severe recession have directly magnified this need for better methods of short-term planning and budgeting as well as more adequate guidelines for the efficient use and financial control of available resources by the firm.

This presentation addresses the subject of short-term quantitative activity planning, budgeting, and evaluation of operating efficiency for manufacturing companies with the overall goal of optimum profit achievement. These topics are discussed according to the primary functions of production, marketing, and administration within the product manufacturing firm and are treated from the standpoint of the relationship they bear to each other in planning and control of functional operations. Parallels are cited throughout the book on specific points of application that are deemed appropriate for profit-seeking, service-type firms. The scope of this presentation includes every managerial level in the organization from production foreman through middle management to senior-executive levels. Both theoretical concepts and formal technical illustrations of budget procedures, control measures, and financial performance reports are used generously throughout this presentation. They are also carefully examined in the discussions as to their use in decision making toward effective quantitative planning for the main functions of the manufacturing enterprise and toward maintaining efficient operations and optimum control of resources and costs.

The book is arranged in two parts. Part I draws on the principles and concepts of managerial and engineering economy, cost and management accounting, together with principles of functional planning and organization structure. These aspects are used to set forth activity planning guidelines and financial control measures for the manufacturing firm. Part II builds on the conceptual and technical foundations established in part I and presents a comprehensive set of illustrations of performance reporting by the primary functions of production, marketing, and administration. Part II emphasizes formal preparation, analysis, and interpretation of short-term operating performance reports. Considerable attention is devoted to guidelines and recommended uses for managerial decision making as it pertains to disclosure and correcting operating inefficiency, evaluating profit contribution for organizational units in the company, and effective planning and budgeting for future operations. A unique feature of the book is that a model company, which I have called the Dynamic Power Tool Corporation, is introduced in the early chapters and followed throughout the text as a means of presenting a single integrated system.

The most significant conclusions reached as a result of the discussions are:

1. Activity planning and budgeting for functional operations in manufacturing companies and the appraisal of operating results at the end of a short-term period are related to each other within the same financial and organizational system.
2. The contribution to total company profitability can be measured by separate functional areas of activity within the company and also according to formal organization structure by levels and departments.
3. Decision-making for activity planning and management control from one operating period to the next will always be implemented according to the authority and responsibilities assigned to organization levels and departments within the company.
4. Analyses for performance evaluation and control are undertaken at the end of the period and broadly represent a quantitative comparison between the results of operations and the formal statement of plans approved by senior management prior to the operating period.
5. There are two types of managerial decision making that follow from analyses of performance. One is to take corrective action based on the interpretation of the analyses toward more efficient performance in future operating periods and increased profit contribution by organizational units within the company. The second type of decision making involves the use of performance results for activity planning and budgeting in future periods.

This book is intended primarily as a guidebook for use by industrial practitioners to include corporate controllers, financial planning and budget executives, and by nonfinancial managers involved in operations planning, budget preparation, and performance evaluation in their own functional areas of responsibility. It is also well suited as an auxiliary text in management courses and management accounting courses at undergraduate and graduate business schools.

Acknowledgments

This work is a synthesis of my experiences over a period of more than fifteen years in academic and business settings. While the main perspectives and points of interpretation are my own, acknowledgment is hereby given to my mentors, associates, and colleagues at universities and industrial organizations who provided me with the background and incentive necessary to produce this work. I would like to extend special thanks to Mrs. Sandra Cotter for her patience and meticulous effort in typing the entire first draft. I am also very grateful to the National Association of Accountants for permission to use table formats in the preparation of tables 8-7, 8-11, 8-14, 8-17 through 8-22, 9-9, 9-12 through 9-20, and 9-23.

Part I
Behavior, Control, and the Design of Management Control Systems

1 Introduction

Financial control of the internal operations of a profit-seeking business enterprise has been included as a subject in accounting and management curriculums of university business schools for many years. The modern term for this field of professional practice is "management control." While much of the literature on this subject has been confined to academic journals and textbooks, there has been a growing need for comparable presentations directed to professional managers who must use control reports in their functional operating areas for financial evaluation, planning, and decision making. The need for control systems and performance reports has become even more critical in very recent years as the result of a severe national economic recession. Tight money markets and the drying up of working capital have caused excessive budget restrictions even for the most vital production or marketing operations of many manufacturing and service organizations.

Control of the functional operations of any business enterprise depends on certain essential elements:

1. An information system that records the progress of an activity or group of activities for a specific length of time. The information system must include a description of activity steps or phases and a quantitative or qualitative measure for tracking the progress or achievement level of the activity.
2. A structural organization element to which the activity is assigned.
3. A formal reporting document for generating "feedback" of achievement levels to the supervisor or manager of the organization unit.
4. A planned or predetermined activity measure against which actual achievement measures can be compared.
5. A decision-making capability that exists within the organization element or unit to take action that will bring the achievement level in line with the planned level.

The preceding five elements are vital to the concept of control and how it can be used appropriately in the manufacturing or service enterprise. First the information system provides a formal documentation of data, which is the basis for presenting and analyzing performance results for any functional activity. This system is simply a set of records on (a) the planned activity and (b) the actual activity for a given period of time. An example would be the company sales volume plan and customer orders for a given month. The plan would

3

include sales quotas for each product line or type of service, which would perhaps be designated by territories and salesmen or classes of customers. The activity documentation would record customer orders for the month according to the preceding classifications. The sales orders then represent performance that can be compared with quotas established at the beginning of the month (the plan). Second the organization element would be the sales department, a designated component of the company organization chart.

Third the formal reporting document would be the master sales report for the department. This report might summarize sales quantities based on customer order with order dates, sales shipments against orders, unit prices, and dollar volume. This information would also be provided in the master document by territories and by salesmen or classes of customers. Fourth, the measures of activity would include the unit price for each product or service taken from the sales plan and the volume quotas. In this way the information contained in the formal reporting document could be compared with planned activity levels and corresponding data.

The fifth element is really the focal hub in control of functional operations. It represents the implementation of control based on the other four as necessary ingredients. In order to have "decision-making capability . . . to bring the achievement level in line with the planned level," there must be a single manager responsible for all sales activity and personnel in the sales department. For purposes of implementing control, the sales manager analyzes the data provided by the information system (elements 1-4). It is his responsibility to take whatever action indicated to correct the achievement level whenever in his judgment it is sufficiently out of line with the sales plan to warrant such action. If the monthly sales volume achieved in territory A is 20 percent below the planned level, the sales manager must first determine what caused the drop. If the order prices for product X are 20 percent below the price established by the company, he must determine why the established price has not been met. The causes for these variations provide the key to the appropriate action to be taken that will bring performance back in line with the established plan.

These same concepts of control can be applied to many different kinds of functional activities in many types of organizations, both profit-seeking enterprises and nonprofit organizations. However, this book focuses on monitoring and controlling financial aspects of functional operations.

Modern management control concepts and practice did not evolve within the accounting or finance professions per se. Rather, they resulted from the arduous and creative efforts of the pioneers of the scientific management school and industrial engineers during the late nineteenth century. Names such as David McCallum, Henry R. Towne, Capt. Henry Metcalf, Frederick W. Taylor, and Henri Fayol come to mind as being perhaps the most prominent contributors to the development of scientific management thought and applications.

Although McCallum's contributions to management viewpoints and practice were made just prior to the Civil War, he saw the major problem as being one of control of operations. Having served as superintendent of the Erie Railroad, he observed first-hand an emerging characteristic of the large railroads, which was that geographical dispersion of operations provided a barrier to close supervision:

> Most railroad managers at that time . . . saw the larger railroad complexes as necessarily inefficient and incapable of profitable operations.
>
> Essentially, McCallum's managerial approach to running the Erie was one of system, common sense, reports, and control. He . . . insisted that those in charge of specific operations were both responsible and accountable for their successes and failures.[1]

The early writings of scientific management thought and applications were confined to engineering publications. Henry R. Towne, president of Yale and Towne Manufacturing Company in the late 1800s, was praised by the editors of *Industrial Management: the Engineering Magazine* as being the first prominent person to contribute to the field of scientific management:

> As early as 1870 Towne began the systematic application of efficient management methods. . . . His paper, "The Engineer as an Economist," delivered to the American Society of Mechanical Engineers in 1886, probably inspired Frederick W. Taylor to devote his life's work to scientific management.[2]

Towne visualized the significant problems existing at that time as pertaining to labor wage rates and worker productivity and efficiency in relation to profits.

> He advocated the determination of the cost of each element of production. Then what the employees of one department gained could be returned to them according to their merit.
>
> Towne's plan guaranteed a definite rate to each employee, with the gain that each department made above the scientifically determined standard split fifty-fifty between employer and employee.[3]

Metcalf, a contemporary of Henry R. Towne, believed that the managerial methods he encountered (as head of Frankford Arsenal) were wasteful and ineffective. His view of management stressed systematizing functional operations and controlling their results.

> The Metcalf theory of management was based on system and control. He visualized and insisted that all authority should emanate from a given source, with a flowback to that source of detailed information concerning expenditures and accomplishments.[4]

Frederick W. Taylor is considered to be the most significant figure in the scientific management movement. He devoted his life to that field of study, and together with the important contributions of a Frenchman named Henri Fayol, he produced a set of principles for management practice including the planning, the organization, the control, and the establishment of work standards against which the efficiency of workers' performance could be measured.

Taylor's major work, *Principles of Scientific Management,* was published in 1911. He devoted much of his initial study to factory activities and processes and to setting standards for the length of time that it would require a particular piece of equipment or worker to complete a given operation. He was a pioneer in the development of work-flow methods, inventory, control, and worker supervision. In the area of worker supervision, he advocated replacing the prevailing practice of rigid regimentation of workers with a system of pay incentives for levels of shop output above standard:

> He saw . . . that management apparently disregarded the obvious truth that excellence in performance and operation would mean a reward for both management and labor.
>
> . . . Taylor saw the need for equally good supervision of an employee and his working conditions. From this need he developed his concept of functional foremanship, with specialists employed in every phase of supervision to insure excellence of operation.
>
> He coordinated and organized the total operation of the shop to the point where working conditions, materials and methods of work flow were standardized so as to make standards of worker performance possible and meaningful.[5]

Interdepartmental organization of work flow, the matching of worker skills and experience with appropriate job assignments, and the establishment of standards for machine and worker output and achievement levels for specific time periods were perhaps Taylor's most significant contributions to factory operations management. He established worker pay-incentive plans for above-standard performance and was the creator of "functional foremanship," a plan for factory supervision that attempted to subdivide supervisor-worker organization and relationships according to specialization of shop activities. He also advocated a clear delineation of management and worker responsibilities and stressed that specific responsibilities belonging to management include planning, organizing, and controlling production activities:

> He (Taylor) championed the use of standards in every phase of management, always driving hard the need for standards of consistency as a prelude to high standards of operation and product quality. . . . Taylor gave to management the collective concept of control—control as a sensing mechanism to maintain established procedures, standards,

conditions, and the like, necessary for the effective and total operation of the system.[6]

Henri Fayol may well be the most influential figure in the scientific management movement after Taylor. His work during the early decades of this century was published in a book in English (1929) entitled *General and Industrial Management*.[7] Like Taylor, Fayol looked on planning, organizing, coordinating, and controlling as being essential responsibilities of management:

> In Fayol's scheme, the work of an administrator involved five facets: planning, organizing, commanding, coordinating and controlling. Planning effort was described largely in terms of decision-making, goal setting, developing policy, and allocating functions to organizational components. Fayol thus reasoned that planning led to organizing, because to allocate functions management would of necessity have to identify and properly arrange (i.e. organize) the units or components of the undertaking.[8]

Fayol was the first prominent leader in the field of management to set forth the notion that quantitative forecasting should be incorporated as part of management planning since planning necessarily involved looking into the future and developing a concrete and actionable program of operations based on a forecast. Controlling then consisted of simply seeing that the specifications and the planned program were met.

C.S. George, Jr., has made a further and most important observation:

> One obvious contribution of scientific management was the overall improvement in factory management. As soon as it opened the way for improvements in the shop, it pushed into sales, general administration and other facets of the enterprise. It brought a more effective utilization of equipment, labor and materials. It spurred the development of more accurate controls, routing and planning. . . . For management, it has pointed the way to a more effective organization, a more reliable product, a better work force, a better understood customer, an improved corporate image, and a more effective profit position.[9]

The historical foundations of modern management planning and more particularly management control, which is the subject of this book, can be traced directly to the concepts and practices founded in scientific management. While the field of industrial engineering and particularly the development and application of production standards may be regarded as the initial outgrowth of scientific management, accounting really did not become actively included in the control function until the industrial boom of the 1950s. Prior to that time, "cost accounting," as it was known, was primarily confined to determining end-product unit cost of production and, with the exception of product-market pricing, was not otherwise used extensively in any systematic way for management planning and control of functional operations. Since then, however, the field of "management accounting" has gained widespread acceptance and application for financial decision making and capital-investment planning, as well as for management control of internal corporate operations.

The most important contribution the scientific management movement and the subsequent engineering studies made to quantitative measurement for management control was the development of activity standards for shop or departmental operations. Determination of standards originally focused on direct inputs, that is, materials and parts for processing or assembling and labor, at the factory shop level. Materials standards were usually set for each product type on the basis of the number of units of the part or material that one unit of the product type required based on specifications for the department.

For direct labor standards, two factors had to be considered: One was the type or grade of labor that would be required to perform a given activity since each labor grade would have a different hourly payment rate. The second factor was labor time in hours and minutes necessary to complete an activity. Extensive production shop research involving time-and-motion study (to which much of F.W. Taylor's work was dedicated) had to be conducted to establish time standards. If more than one grade of labor was applied to a particular production activity, then a standard "labor mix" was established specifying each grade with the standard hourly rate and the standard time for each grade.

Basic standard costing was simply an extension of these engineering standards. The accountant would prepare estimates by applying procurement costs per unit of material to the standard quantity specifications in each production department and by applying the labor rates for each grade to the standard hours specified. The final step in the accountant's estimates was to prepare a production cost plan for each operating time period using the itemized cost standards for material and labor and applying them to the product volume scheduled for the period. The only difference between the cost standard and the cost plan was that the former involved only the individual unit of material or labor input while the latter applied these values to the planned volume of production. Both sets of measures are estimates.

Cost assignment is one of the central and vitally important areas of consideration to the cost accountant and is equally important for management control, performance measures and evaluation. In our discussions of cost assignment in subsequent chapters in part I, we will see that the appropriateness of any particular method or procedure for assigning an increment of financial cost depends on two factors: One is the unit to which the cost increment is assigned, and the other is the purpose or use for which the cost information is intended. We will use the term "unit" in reference to an individual item count for production inputs such as material or labor, to an item of physical product either in semifinished or finished form, or to an organizational department or other subdivision within one of the company's functional areas of operation.

Cost assignment from the standpoint of its purpose or the intended use of such information will result not only in differing amounts but also in differing procedures for making the assignment. We usually think of three major classifications of cost information in terms of use. The first is product costing and inventory valuation; the second is management control of operating activities; and the third is frequently called "special-purpose analysis."

The first purpose, cost assignment to units of product, is one of the oldest and perhaps best known in the cost-accounting and internal corporate financial-management profession. Major portions of chapters 3, 4, and 6 are devoted to this subject. The costs involved pertain only to the functional area of production. As the product changes form in the plant or factory from raw materials or semifinished parts to a finished product, the costs of production activity will include not only raw materials or parts but also labor, service, and maintenance of plant facilities and the use of machinery. The costs of these items are accumulated during the plant production cycle or scheduled period of time and are then assigned to the "batch" of finished product. This accumulation of "flow of costs" and their assignment to individual product units has as its primary purpose the determination of the value of inventories of finished goods and providing an answer to the question, "How much does it cost to make a unit of product X?"

Second, management control of operating activities makes use of internal cost data not only in the production function but in the areas of marketing and administration as well. For this purpose, the unit to which the accumulated costs of operations are assigned is not the good or service that the company produces but the organizational unit or department that is charged with the task of performing specific activities. These activities may be plant assembling operations for a specific product line or a geographic sales territory or a company payroll administration. The important requirement for management control, as the subject is developed in parts I and II, is that a specific set of identifiable and recurring operations are performed that incur costs and are identified with a specific department or manned unit on the company's organization chart. A further requirement is that the operations and personnel assigned to the manned unit are supervised by only one individual; that he also has the decision-making capability and responsibility for the conduct of those operations and people assigned to him.

The third purpose or use of cost assignment is for special decisions. While this subject is beyond the scope of our discussion, we will briefly mention a few of the important aspects of special-purpose analysis. Almost every profit-seeking manufacturer or service company is involved periodically in making decisions as to alternative commitments of financial capital that are essential to the enterprise, although they are indirectly related to normal operations. These special decisions may involve the replacement of existing equipment and facilities whose depreciable life will soon be expired, buying or leasing such equipment, adding or discontinuing specific product lines, or the selection and financing of a new plant site or marketing facility. The feasibility of any of these special-purpose decisions must be based on forecasts of future income returns resulting directly from the decision compared to future costs of the venture.

Each of these decisions then has two essential components: One is the future increase in profits, and the other is the level of future resources required. The financial investment represents the future cost of undertaking the venture. The criterion of relevancy is most important in making an appropriate decision based on a target net return from the venture. Only those items of cost that are incremental, that is, will change or will be different as a result of the decision, are relevant to that decision. Similarly, only the income return that is incremental or will result directly from taking the particular course of action is relevant to that decision.

The contribution-margin concept will be one of the most important aspects of our discussions on management performance reporting and evaluation in part II. The contribution margin (or "marginal income," as it has often been called) is the difference between sales revenue and all variable costs that are related to the dollar revenue figure; the meaning itself is implied by the word "contribution." It is the amount of revenue in excess of variable costs and expenses that contributes toward the coverage of fixed costs and the earning of profit. This contribution would apply either to the company as a whole or to a main segment of the company's operations for which some portion of dollar operating costs or expenses and dollar sales revenue can be identified.

In the marketing function, segments for which a company may want to provide internal financial reports for the purpose of appraising operating performance can readily make use of the contribution-margin approach. Such segments would include geographic sales territories, product lines, organizational sales divisions, or other segments for which both operating costs and dollar revenues can be identified. On the other hand, it is not logical to assume that the same concept and corresponding measurements will apply exactly in the same way in the functional areas of production and administration. This is the case simply because organizational units in these areas do not "produce" sales revenue. Even so, we will see in later chapters on production and administration that management techniques for financial control of operations are not only vital to appraising the efficiency or effectiveness of a unit's performance but will in turn and as a consequence have an ultimate impact on company profits for a reporting time period.

The notion of the relationship between performance efficiency and profits is brought to light more clearly through the concept of a contribution margin. The contribution approach to management control is also historically a fairly recent addition. During the earlier decades of this century and largely as a result of the dedicated efforts of F.W. Taylor, industrial engineers, and advocates of "scientific management," the advent of quantitative work standards and efficiency measurements was confined to the production function. The development of cost-accounting techniques paralleled the former movement, but it was viewed more as an adjunct to stewardship accounting and the preparation of financial reports to stockholders and other publics outside the company. Management accounting (or cost accounting) during this period focused primarily on unit product cost of production for valuing inventories of finished goods. A secondary use of financial information provided by cost accountants was for "cost-plus" market pricing of finished products.

The early 1950s witnessed an expansion in the uses of financial data provided by cost accountants for making decision as to plant and equipment purchases, cost-volume-profit analysis (breakeven analysis), tools and equipment "make-or-buy" decisions and other special-purpose decisions for which management needed the financial data that cost accountants could provide. It was not until the latter part of that decade that the notion of a "contribution margin," in concept and in application, began to appear on the professional scene as manufacturing companies became more profit conscious. What is today called "bottom-line sensitivity" characterized this period and has continued to the present time. Considerable testimony to this trend is evidenced by the fact that following a decade of rapid economic growth and market expansion in the United States after World War II, multiple-product-line companies became profit-center oriented, pursuing a direction of greater decentralization in their organization structure and greater managerial profit responsibility in terms of both functional organization units and product lines.

Our treatment of management control will have a functional orientation and is intended to serve as a guide to line-middle-management groups who must use internal financial reports toward the successful conduct of their operations and the attainment of concrete and realistic profit objectives. Underlying any effective system of report preparation and presentation is the design of the system itself. The design and installation of a quantitative information system that must serve as the foundation for internal reports is a formidable task for any organization. It requires great skill and competence on the part of corporate accounting and finance professionals charged with its development and working in close harmony with those members of senior management who are responsible for developing the organization structure itself. Such a system is ultimately tailored to the organization structure if it is to be a responsibility-reporting system. Further, it must be a multiple-purpose system serving not only management control of operations but the budget-planning and overall cost-accounting phases of the business as well.

Figure 1-1 illustrates a functionally structured organization chart for the hypothetical Gadget Corporation. The chain of command below the executive vice president follows two main paths, one for operations and one for corporate administration. Operations are headed by three corporate vice presidents in charge of production, marketing, and technical services, respectively. Technical services includes all engineering and research and development for the company.

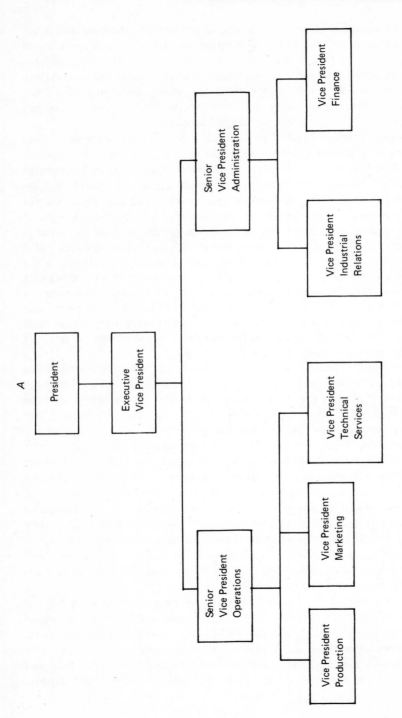

Figure 1-1. Line and Staff Organization, Gadget Corporation

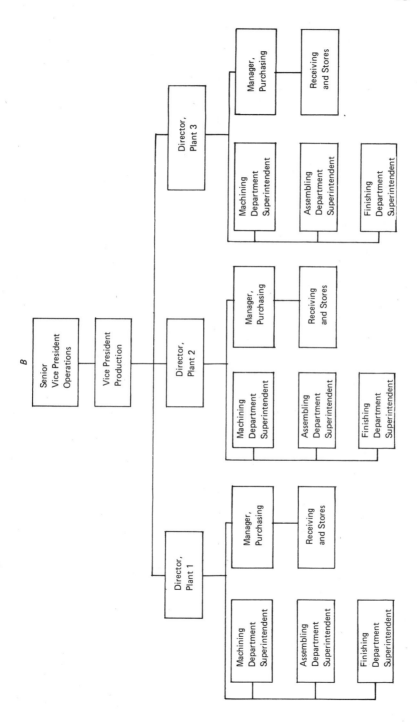

B

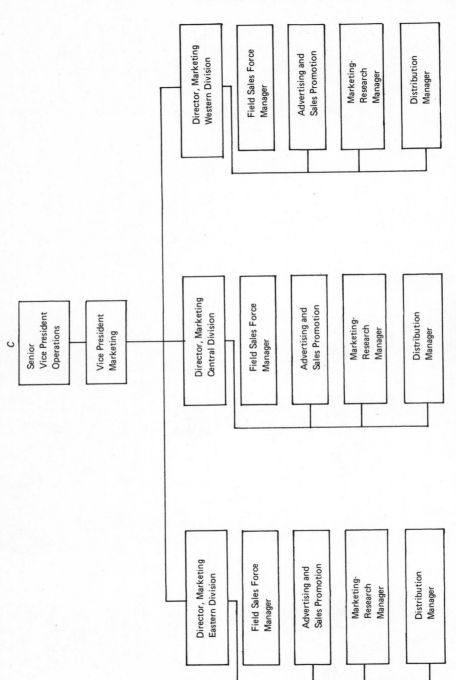

Figure 1-1 continued

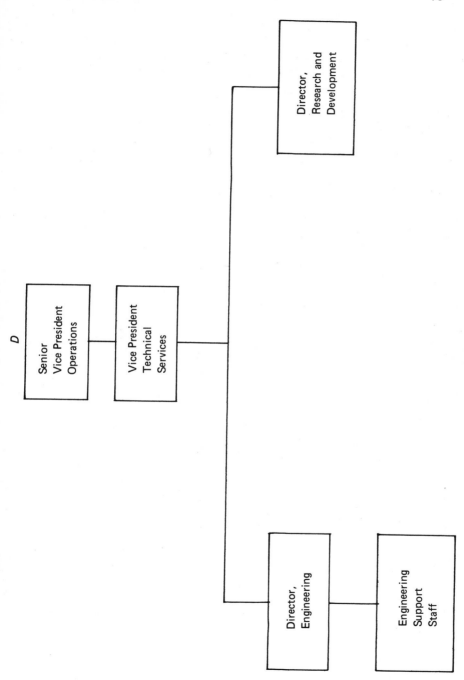

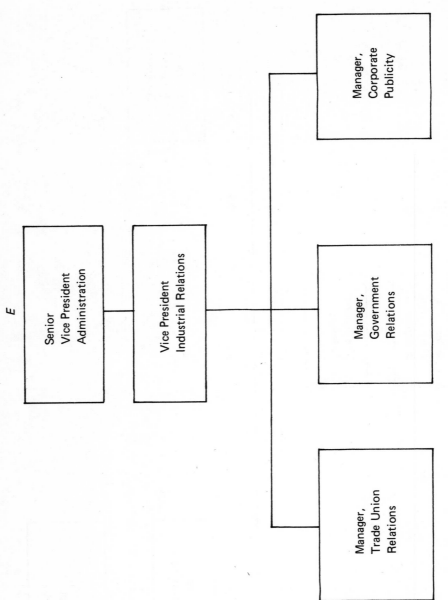

Figure 1-1 continued

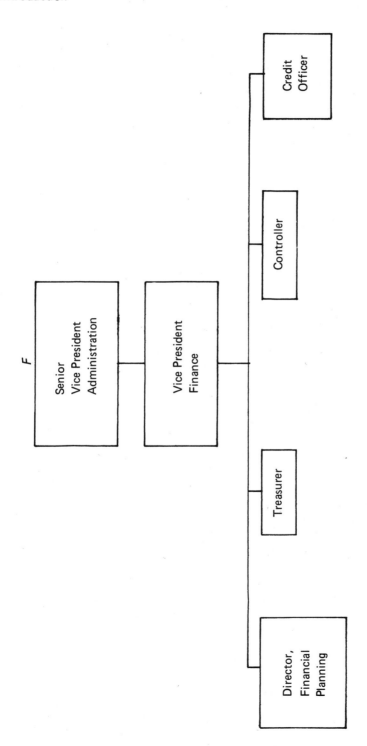

Although the corporate structure is not decentralized according to product grouping or other delineation having all three main functions, the production and marketing operations for all products are mutually supportive based on three geographical locations. Thus plant 1 serves as the production arm for the Eastern Marketing Division, plant 2 for the Central Marketing Division, and so on.

Lines of authority and responsibility are set forth by way of a formal chain of command beginning with the chief executive officer or the chief operating officer and continuing down to the superintendent for plant 1 or the distribution manager of the Eastern Marketing Division. Ideally, for purposes of management control, periodic responsibility—reporting formats would be developed for each unit on the organization chart for which the following conditions apply:

a. The unit is headed by only one officer or manager.
b. The activities of the unit are self-contained.
c. A dollar cost figure either originates from each operation or activity for which the unit is responsible or can be traced to that activity.
d. Controllability is always defined in terms of the degree to which the manager's decision-making authority and capability can affect changes in the cost of an activity assigned to his unit and for which he has performance responsibility.
e. Each manager reports to only one superior above him in the chain of command.

Controllability in terms of operating performance is frequently a point of controversy in establishing and maintaining clear lines of responsibility in the organization's hierarchy. For it is frequently the case that volume levels and costs for a given operation are approved and authorized at one organizational level, but the assignment for which the costs are incurred or the expenditure of funds is made is carried out at a lower level in the hierarchy. For purposes of control and performance appraisal, which level has the "responsibility"? It may at first appear that there is a joint responsibility. Actually, however, there is a different responsibility at each level of the organization.

Let us take an example. The superintendent of the assembling department in plant 1 is responsible for product-assembling operations in his unit in the plant. These responsibilities include meeting production-volume schedules at the close of each quarter, scheduling and assigning manpower to meet standard labor requirements for the volume of assembling output scheduled, setting timetables for equipment usage, and setting requirements for maintenance and services.

The formal procedure followed is this: Each quarter for each of the three plants, the vice president, plant 1, sets production and inventory levels based on sales forecasts. Next the director, plant 1, prepares an activity plan for each of his department superintendents. He confers with each superintendent, and together they reach agreement on that activity plan in accordance with the plant inventory and volume levels that have been set. The director then prepares a budget based on standards for labor, materials, and overhead at the planned volume level. The budget for each department is submitted to the department superintendent, and a less detailed master budget is sent to the vice president, production.

In the preceding example, three levels are involved in the budget plan, and each has a definite responsibility in terms of performance and management control at the end of the quarter based on that plan.

1. The assembling department superintendent, plant 1, is responsible for meeting cost standards for materials, labor, and overhead with the activity plan agreed on by the director, plant 1, at the actual volume achieved for the quarter.
2. The director, plant 1, is responsible for the achievement of planned production and inventory volume levels for each department in the plant. He is responsible to his immediate superior and for explaining any achievement deviations from planned volume levels.
3. The vice president, production, is responsible for monitoring the master performance reports for each of the three plants. If in his judgment there are any material deviations in either plant budget commitments or in plant volume achievement, he will confer with the director of the plant in question.

Since management control is an integral part of functional activities in addition to its significance in relation to organization structure, what is the distinction between planning and control? What are the similarities? How is the functional approach to each handled in terms of the objectives of this book?

It is important to understand at the outset that financial control of functional operations and performance evaluation for any firm that produces and sells goods and services is inseparably related to and dependent on the quantitative planning for those operations. The essential difference is time. The forecasting of sales volume, planning of production schedules, and budgeting for marketing and production activities to achieve planned sales and inventory volume are all interrelated components of planning and must be set forth at the beginning of the fiscal year, quarter, or other time segment within the year.

Analyses for control and performance evaluation are undertaken at the end of the period and broadly speaking represent a quantitative comparison between the results of operations and the formal statement of plans approved by senior management prior to the operating period.

What then do standards provide, and how do they relate to what we have said? Standards essentially represent acceptable levels of any aspect of production or marketing activity within an organizational unit, which we have also called a "responsibility center." A "standard cost" is simply an arithmetic translation of the standard measure for an activity into a monetary value. Since beginning-of-period forecasts and plans are recast in terms of budgets, these budgets are really a presentation of standard or acceptable cost levels at the volume of sales that were forecast and the consequent levels of inventory and production that were scheduled. Performance evaluation then is an appraisal of actual activities experienced at the end of an operating period.

Table 1-1 illustrates the approach: The machining department in plant 1 of the Gadget Corporation has set a production schedule of 10,000 gadgets for the first quarter based on a sales volume forecast of 8,000 and an opening inventory of 1,000 gadgets. The production schedule is a plan, the sales forecast is a plan, and the quarter-end inventory is also a plan, in this case 3,000 gadgets. In addition, engineering studies have been conducted, and on the basis of their results, a standard labor time in the machining department has been set at 1.5 hours per gadget. The current labor rate is $3.00 per hour, which is also a standard. A gadget consists of material A, 2 units, and material B, 3 units. The standard cost of a unit of material A is $1.00, and for a unit of material B, it is $2.00. Assuming that only direct labor and materials are relevant to the production plan, we can compare a production schedule for the first quarter as shown in table 1-1.

Table 1-1
Production Schedule and Budget for Plant 1, Machining Department

First-quarter Production Schedule

Production volume: 10,000 units
Standard labor (at planned volume in units): 15,000 hours
Standard materials:
  Material A: 10,000 @ 2 units = 20,000
  Material B: 10,000 @ 3 units = 30,000

First-quarter Budget

Labor budget:	
15,000 hours @ $3.00 per hour	$45,000
Materials budget:	
Material A: 20,000 units @ $1.00	20,000
Material B: 30,000 units @ $2.00	60,000
	$125,000

First-quarter Operations

Units completed: 10,000 units	
Labor cost of production	$50,000
Materials cost of production:	
Material A: $25,000	
Material B: 60,000	
	85,000
	$135,000

The production budget for the quarter is simply a matter of assigning standard costs to the labor and materials specifications in the production schedule.

We can quickly determine from the information in table 1-1 that performance is in line with standard as to volume of gadgets completed for the period and for the cost of material *B*. However, labor costs and material *A* are over budget in the amount of $5,000 each, indicating a need to investigate plant operations to determine causes for deviations from budget.

The use of standards and standard costs for the preparation of budgets and for financial control and performance evaluation were solely the province of the functional area of production for most comparisons in years past. However, one of the primary objectives of this book is to set forth ways and means for adopting similar concepts and measurements in other activity areas, particularly marketing and administration.

The subject of planning for product-market composition and for production and marketing operations is not intended to be treated as a primary topic. However, since operating control of functional activities and performance evaluation of financial results for any given period of time is dependent upon and interrelated with product-market and functional activity planning, some discussion of the latter is indeed warranted. This will be readily apparent in our discussions on the marketing area. Fiscal or periodic functional planning for operations and primarily in relation to production and marketing is introduced at the beginning of chapter 5. Here we present an overview of operations planning, which we view as consisting of two main types: project planning and period planning.

The view presented in this manuscript is that planning for functional area operations begins with the development of specifications for product-line composition and a blueprint for marketing activities before consideration can be given effectively to scheduling plant operations and inventory volume levels. Twenty years ago the corporate philosophy of many companies ran something like this: "The sales department will deliver whatever the factory produces for inventory. We are in the business of running our factories as efficiently as possible and producing a quality product with the best engineering talent available to us. Selling is a matter of course then, although we do expect our sales force and advertising people to keep pace with our competitors." This viewpoint has changed during the past two decades as product planning has become more market-demand oriented with extensive use of economic and consumer-behavior research techniques to serve as the basis for planning product-line composition. For many companies, the perspective toward functional operations planning following the determination of product-line composition is that it must reflect an integrated combination of market-demand analysis, marketing activities, inventory levels, production scheduling, and financing. They are not independent or self-contained areas of corporate operations planning, nor is one area necessarily dominant while the others take a more passive back seat.

Control of operating costs is the primary technical application of management control for the ongoing activities of any organizational unit within a business enterprise. "Cost behavior" simply means the change in the level of cost experienced that corresponds to (or results from) a change in the level of activity or input associated with the cost. If production volume of gadgets (activity) in the machining department changes from 10,000 to 12,000 units in the first quarter, then the expected change in material A (input) would be:

$$12,000 \text{ (actual)} - 10,000 \text{ (planned)} = 2,000 \times 2 \text{ units, material } A$$
$$= 4,000 \times \$1.00$$
$$= \$4,000$$

The cost of material A then is variable since it varies with changes in the production volume. The superintendent of this department has a salary of $4,500 for the first quarter, which is also part of the departmental operating costs. However, his salary remains the same regardless of how many gadgets are produced and is thus a fixed cost. The most important distinction in cost-behavior analysis as it is used in management control is to separate those costs that change (called *variable costs*) and those that do not change (called *fixed costs*). As we shall discuss in part I, the majority of cost items or classifications that are variable with changes in the volume or levels of operating activity for short-run planning and performance evaluation time periods are those that are also controllable. In this example, the superintendent of the machining department is responsible for all operating activities in his organizational unit. He has the decision-making capability to control both the volume of production (activity) and the amount of material A (input) consumed during the first quarter. Thus he can control the variable input costs of material A. However, since he does not have decision-making authority to change his own salary (a fixed cost of his organizational unit), that is not a controllable cost at his level of responsibility in the company. There are several feasible approaches to determining the behavior of costs for a particular activity by account classification, and they are taken up in the appendix. Our immediate task ahead is to discuss data-reporting systems and measures that provide the foundation for performance evaluation.

Notes

1. Claude S. George, Jr., *The History of Management Thought* (Englewood Cliffs, N.J.: Prentice-Hall, © 1972), pp. 82-83. Reprinted by permission.

2. Ibid., p. 84.

3. Ibid., p. 85.

4. Ibid.
5. Ibid., p. 90.
6. Ibid., p. 97.
7. Ibid., p. 111.
8. Ibid., p. 114.
9. Ibid., p. 96.

2 Designing a Standard-Cost System

In recent decades there has been a sharp divergence of theory and practice within the accounting profession. This divergence pertains to the CPA-oriented financial accounting and preparation of reports for audiences outside the manufacturing firm, on the one hand, and accounting concepts and practices oriented to the use of financial data by line operating managers and senior management of the manufacturer for various internal purposes, on the other hand. These purposes essentially include the planning and valuation of finished-goods inventories, cost preparation and analysis for pricing product lines, as well as cost estimation and financial planning for the acquisition of plant and facilities, and for the planning of future operating projects such as new product research and development or product-line additions in production and marketing. With regard to this dichotomy, two points are essential for our purposes. First we will focus on the second area of this dichotomy and will not concentrate on those objectives just mentioned. Rather, we will explore the design of systems for reporting historical operating financial data, the analysis, use, and interpretation of such data for the management and financial control of operations and for evaluating operating performance in three major functional areas. These areas are production, marketing, and administration. Second there is always an important relationship between the two parts of this dichotomy, and we will point up the nature of this relationship from time to time.

Accounting and financial terminology has been virtually flooded with concepts and definitions surrounding the single word *cost*. Cost has been described in terms of "fixed costs," "variable costs," "out-of-pocket" or "cash costs," "book" or "historical costs," "incremental costs," "sunk costs," "replacement costs," "traceable costs," "common" or "allocated costs," "direct costs," "indirect costs," "full costs," and so on. These terms are often confusing to the layman, although differences in their meaning and appropriate application are quite familiar to members of the financial and controllership professions. The use of these terms as well as the methods of constructing and presenting cost data must always depend on their appropriateness for specific purposes such as financial reporting to stockholders, financial analysts, and other "outsiders"; or internal management decision making for current operating activities or long-term investment; or management control and performance appraisal of the company's operations. This book will define and use those terms and cost concepts that are specifically intended for purposes of management control.

It is virtually useless to attempt to define any financial input to a manufacturer's functional operations as a "true" or "valid" cost. Any valid cost measurement will be quite different in meaning and definition in accordance with the specific use for which the measurement of cost is intended. As an example, if we consider costing finished products in order to value inventories, there are those who believe that the only true measure for the cost of a product is total or fully allocated production cost incurred that was necessary to convert raw materials or component parts into final units of product for a specific time period of past production activity.

On the other hand, there are accountants and plant managers who assert that the only valid measure of production cost is what a finished product "should" cost, meaning a constant standard measurement based on previous experience with different levels of production volume; hence the term "standard cost." If we were to accept the latter definition that the standard represents the true cost of manufacturing a finished product, then inventories would be valued at a constant standard or "normal" cost per unit for any given product line, and the variance or difference between the standard measure and the actual operating cost incurred would bypass the finished-goods inventory account. Assuming that the variance is "unfavorable" or in excess of the standard valuation, this increment for ordinary financial reporting would be treated as a loss from operations charged against revenue in determining net income for that period in which the production cycle or conversion process was completed. Conversely, a positive or favorable variance from standard production would reflect a gain over and above the anticipated normal level of accrued costs for production operations and would be treated as an increment to profit on the quarterly or annual income statement. It would in fact "mean" an increment to income resulting from increased efficiency of manufacturing operations.

The foregoing illustration is vitally important for periodic financial reporting on both the balance sheet and the income statement. Thus the consequences of these alternatives, as they affect the reporting of balance-sheet and profit information to stockholders and other external publics, must be examined.

For purposes of income determination and the preparation of financial statements for external publics, both the standard-cost and variance components of production activity are relevant and must be used to measure income. This will always be the case because the two components combined will be the actual or full production cost incurred regardless of whether they refer to specific aspects of production activity such as labor, materials and component parts, or factory overhead. However, the essential distinction to be made for quarterly or annual reporting of company profits and financial position is the treatment given to the variance component of actual production cost incurred at any given volume level of production activity.

It can appropriately be argued that the aggregate of standard costs for labor, materials, and overhead in production are the only components of actual costs that may be considered "what the cost of production ought to be" under normal conditions of plant operations and barring any significant changes in labor-rate contracts or in economic conditions of the company's supply or procurement markets. Thus when referring to the "actual" cost of a manufacturer's production operations or to a component of operations we are considering two segments of the cost. Taking the cost of materials used in production as an example, we would have the following:

1. *The standard-cost segment* would be the standard price paid for a particular material multiplied by the quantity of the material used in production for a given period of time in the past.
2. *The variance-from-standard-cost segment* would be the difference between the actual cost incurred for the material and the standard cost for that quantity of material.

In preparing periodic statements of the company's financial position and income or profit, both the standard cost and the variance are relevant. They must be used to measure the value of products manufactured (finished-goods inventory) on the balance sheet (that is, charges against sales revenue) when the products are sold.

For reporting the value of finished goods on the company's balance sheet, the financial accounting profession including both corporate accountants and external auditors have traditionally reported inventories at their full actual production cost. However, if we view the normal standard segment of production cost to be the appropriate measure for valuing final-product inventories, then inventories will tend to be understated during periods of production-cost overruns. In these situations it will always be necessary to report a separate balance-sheet asset account such as Overrun Variance from Standard Cost of Inventories.

Similarly, the income statement will reflect a lower stated valuation of Cost of Goods Sold when balance-sheet inventories are credited at the time of sale. This will also create an overstated amount for the company's gross profit since the variance segment of manufacturing cost was not reflected in Cost of Goods Sold. However, since a variance account for cost overruns was set up on the balance sheet, before arriving at a net profit figure, these increments would have to be reported as an operating loss on the income statement when products are sold.

This procedure has not been accepted in the past by auditors and corporate accountants for reporting periodic financial position and profitability to the financial community, stockholders, and other external publics. It is our view that the treatment just described is a preferred means of communicating quarterly financial position and profitability to top management within medium-sized and large manufacturing companies in which standard-cost systems have been established. In fact, for conglomerate enterprises with highly diversified or essentially unrelated production and marketing operations, it would be most beneficial for top-management review to replicate this procedure for each distinct area of corporate operations where there is a final product or service sold to outside markets.

Although our primary concern in this book is the development, analysis, and interpretive use of financial information for internal corporate control of operating activities, the use of standard costs and cost deviations from standard can be incorporated in the preparation of ordinary annual and quarterly statements of financial position and income. They are also equally applicable to companies' manufacturing inventories of physical product or companies' marketing services. The important requirement in any case is that the financial management of these companies possess the capability to set cost standards objectively and fairly for the major components of their operations.

Further, as stated earlier, a "cost standard" represents what a given component of operating activity (such as production plant labor or materials) "ought to cost" under current economic conditions and normal levels of operating volume or activity. Then the variance segment of actual costs incurred, by definition, would reflect either the cost of operating inefficiency or efficiency that is greater than planned or standard. The essential point in this regard is that these efficiency measures can be readily incorporated in a company's ordinary financial reports. Therefore, the first consideration for adoption of these measures should be given to the inclusion of them in quarterly financial reporting to top management since they serve as summary indicators of changes in the firm's efficiency for plant operations over and above the changes in balance-sheet and income statement accounts that top management usually receives for quarterly review. We also see no important objection to a policy of disclosing these same measures in ordinary financial reporting to stockholders and outside financial analysts should the management members on financial reporting policy within a company's senior management group choose to adopt this additional disclosure.

The actual costs incurred are accumulated on the books of account for most companies, and the use of standard costs does not mean that they can serve as substitutes for actual costs.

When considering the design of a cost-accounting system that is appropriate for periodic appraisal of performance and management control of a manufacturing company's operations or activities, as stated earlier, this book will focus on the major functional areas, namely, production or plant operations, marketing function, and administrative activities. In addition, the accounting, reporting, and financial evaluation of a given functional area should have as a basis for control the formal organization of each area by departments. From a practical standpoint, these departments are the areas that incur or "accumulate" costs of the activities for which they are responsible and over which they have operating control. Thus we will approach the subject of developing a standard-cost system for management control in terms of manufacturing operations and organization.

Historically the phrase "standard cost of products" has usually been used in reference to manufacturing or production costs that were accumulated on the company's books of account. Then in arriving at a valuation for finished-goods inventory at the end of a production cycle, these costs were assigned to the completed units of physical product together with all other costs and expenses for plant operations. The reason plant operations represented the only focal area for management control based on a standard—cost system was the fact that standards for operating activities and physical inputs such as plant labor, materials, depreciation on facilities, plant maintenance, and other indirect costs could be set fairly and objectively for different levels of production volume by means of labor time-and-motion studies and other techniques used by industrial engineers.

There are three major component classifications in production operations that accumulate costs during the process of converting raw materials or semifinished parts into final products: (a) raw materials, (b) direct labor, and (c) manufacturing overhead. The costs of raw-material inputs are also considered "direct costs of production" in the sense that they can be traced directly to the units of finished product manufactured. "Direct labor" refers to the wages of employees who work directly on the production line to convert raw materials into finished products. These costs are also traceable and variable as are the costs of raw materials. They are "traceable" in the sense that they are incurred only for the purpose of converting materials or component parts into finished products for final inventory and sale. Both materials and labor employed on the production line are frequently referred to as "prime costs." They will be "variable" since the quantities of these product inputs and attendant costs will vary as the volume of production fluctuates from one quarter to the next within the year.

"Manufacturing overhead" will include all those items of plant cost that are not directly incurred in the product-conversion process. Such overhead costs arise in both production and service departments. Most of the latter department costs are overhead since they are not traceable to units of final product and do not vary with fluctuations in volume of physical-product output. For production departments, manufacturing overhead essentially includes depreciation on equipment and facilities used in the conversion cycle. Other examples of production overhead would be rental charges, property taxes, and the salaries of foremen and supervisors who do not work directly on the production line. For service departments this classification would include all costs of maintenance materials and supplies and maintenance labor as they are used in production departments as well as depreciation charges and expenses for service-department building and facilities.

For example, assume that a particular company manufactures a single product and has the following departmental organization within its plant operations:

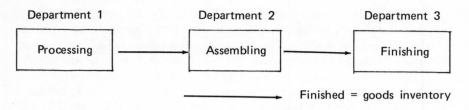

Each department in the plant performs a certain operation on the flow of product from the procurement inventory of raw materials or component parts to finished-goods inventory. We call this flow of product through production departments "the conversion process" since materials and parts are being "converted" to the final product for sale to customers. For the purpose of costing the product and of ultimately determining valuation of finished-goods inventory, each department or organizational unit in the plant is called a "cost center." In other words, as production takes place, both direct variable (prime costs) and indirect costs will accumulate in each department and add to the value of the product as it is being converted to a finished good.

The essential task in accounting for the cost of a product in conversion is to determine the cost per unit as the units of product are passed along from one department to another. For example, table 2-1 shows production operations for a single product and for each of the previously mentioned departments with the accumulated information for volume of production and department costs.

The determination of direct variable or prime cost per unit during conversion is a fairly straightforward arithmetic calculation.

Total direct variable costs/number of units produced in each department
= direct variable cost per unit

Thus

Processing department: $\dfrac{[\$9,000 \text{ (DM)} + \$13,000 \text{ (DL)}]}{850 \text{ units}}$

= $25.90 prime cost per unit

Assembling department: $\dfrac{[\$3,000 \text{ (DM)} + \$6,000 \text{ (DL)}]}{850 \text{ units}}$

= $10.59 prime cost per unit

Finishing department: $\dfrac{[0 \text{ (DM)} + \$4,000 \text{ (DL)}]}{850 \text{ units}}$

= $4.70 prime cost per unit

Table 2-1
Volume of Production and Department Costs

Processing Department

Month: January
    Units started: 850
    Units completed: 850

Direct variable (prime) costs accumulated for the month:
    Direct materials: $ 9,000
    Direct labor: 13,000

Overhead (indirect and constant or fixed) costs for the month:
    Department supervisor's salary
        (indirect labor) $1,600
    Depreciation on
        processing equipment   2,300
    Other depreciation   900
        Total overhead $4,800

Assembling Department

Month: January
    Units started: 850
    Units completed: 850

Direct variable (prime) costs accumulated for the month:
    Direct materials (additional parts) $3,000
    Direct labor   6,000

Overhead (indirect and constant or fixed) costs for the month:
    Indirect labor (supervision) $1,400
    Depreciation on assembling
        equipment   1,500
    Other depreciation   1,300
        Total overhead $4,200

Finishing Department

Month: January
    Units started: 850
    Units completed: 850

Direct variable (prime) costs accumulated for the month:
    Direct materials   0
    Direct labor $4,000

Overhead (indirect and constant or fixed) costs for the month:
    Indirect labor (supervision) $1,800
    Depreciation on shaping and
        polishing equipment   1,200
    Other depreciation   400
        Total overhead $3,400

A unit cost of $41.19 for direct variable or prime costs is obtained for the month of January. The treatment of overhead costs for unit cost of production will be considered in depth in chapter 3.

In formal accounting procedures for plant operations, there are three major inventory-account classifications that record "cost flow" in the production-conversion process: (a) Raw-materials or Component-parts Inventory, (b) Work-in-process Inventory, and (c) Finished-goods Inventory.

The account Raw-materials (Component-parts) Inventory is simply an accumulation of the purchase costs of materials and semifinished parts before these materials are put into production. In other words, the monetary valuation of the raw-materials account represents the quantity of materials purchased at the unit prices paid to suppliers by the purchasing department. Work-in-process Inventory is the major account in the production-conversion process and represents an accumulation of all costs incurred in the manufacturing phase of the business. This account is charged with direct labor, direct materials, and manufacturing overhead as production takes place. As units of product are completed and ready for sale to customers, the costs that have been charged to the Work-in-process account are then credited to this account and are transferred to the Finished-goods Inventory account. Then when units of the product are sold, Finished-goods Inventory is credited, and Cost of Goods Sold accumulates these charges for periodic determination of profits for the manufacturing enterprise.

Developing a standard-cost accounting system for the firm will provide the foundation for management control of operations and is the very cornerstone on which the technical presentations, analysis, and discussion throughout this book are based. A standard-cost accounting system should be designed whenever possible using the internal bookkeeping methods that already exist in the company.

In this regard, most manufacturing firms use either a job-order accounting procedure or a process-costing approach in plant operations or both. Further, and of equal importance to maintaining a viable and effective system of management control is the fact that it must be tailored to the specific activities of each of the major functional areas and also to the formal organization structure within each area. Our approach here will be functional for two reasons: First many companies are unfamiliar with formal management control systems based on standard costing, and those that have employed these technical systems have usually applied them in the production area. Second a thorough understanding of the development and uses of management control based on standard costing in the major functional areas of company operations must be gained before considering tailoring these methods to the organizational structure of the individual company.

As stated earlier, the main account in ordinary bookkeeping for the costs of plant operations is Work-in-process Inventory. Before considering the introduction of a standard-cost system, it would be useful to review the two fundamental ways of accumulating costs for work-in-process as production activities take place, namely, (a) job-order accounting and (b) process accounting. A historical cost-accounting system assigns all actual costs incurred in plant operations during a specific time segment (typically a month or quarter within the fiscal year) to the products produced during that period. The job-order and process-costing procedures are the two essential alternatives in accounting for the cost of manufacturing operations. Both approaches will accumulate the "flow of costs" for materials, direct and indirect labor, and manufacturing overhead. The job-order procedure is used by firms that design and produce made-to-order products or equipment whereby each unit of final output has one or more technical elements or components that are unique. Thus a job-order account to accumulate doses or batches of costs for materials, labor, and overhead allocation is established on the company's books for each individual unit of finished product. This procedure is required as a basic or first-level cost-accounting system for plant operations yielding made-to-order units of final product since the cost "bundle" to complete the manufacturing conversion cycle will be different for each unit of finished goods.

It is not only useful to know "how much" each tailor-made unit cost in the plant, the aggregate of which determines the valuation of finished-goods inventory at the end of an accounting period; it is also essential for many firms to maintain a separate set of production-cost records for each unit for purposes of market pricing when prices are determined on the basis of a percentage mark-up over "full" cost per unit.

However, in all cases where units of product are uniform and are not manufactured to a set of individual specifications based on customer order or "batches," this system has certain practical and economic limitations. The bookkeeping detail for each production and service department in the plant is expensive and cumbersome to maintain when a separate set of cost records must be kept up to date for each set of order specifications or batch of finished goods. The duplication of job-order record keeping can be quite cumbersome and costly for both clerical and data-processing time for companies handling several thousand customer orders per month. Also in cases where most units of a given product are uniform, then the job costing within departments does not add to the usefulness of cost accounting for valuing inventories and more particularly for control. This inefficiency exists because in cost accounting for control, the ultimate goal is appraising operating performance for separate areas or departments within the plant rather than appraising performance for separate jobs worked on within a department.

The establishment of a basic job-order procedure can be considered the first stage in designing a standard-cost system for management control. Here the subsidiary accounts to Work-in-process will accumulate materials, direct labor, and overhead costs by individual jobs or orders placed by customers. Figures 2-1 and 2-2 illustrate the job-cost sheet for each individual product specification obtained through specific customer order. That is, the costing unit for a product is based on the plant production order for the unit or batch of final output.

In the example cited earlier for product costing in a plant that utilized three production departments, the cost information pertained to a single product for the month of January. Also records for materials, labor, and overhead were maintained for each responsibility unit of operations in the plant. For determining the direct or prime cost per unit of finished goods for the month, each

Job Order No. 1   Description: Beta

Date Started: January 1   Date Completed: January 31

Quantity Ordered: 10

Materials Cost

Part No.	Unit Price	Quantity
31	$2.50	4
4	4.25	8
28	1.20	14

Unit Materials Cost $60.80

Labor Cost

Operation	Labor Grade Specified	Hours	Rate Per Hour
23	4	4.5	$3.50
14	2	3.0	4.25
7	1	6.5	5.50

Total Labor Cost $64.25

Order Overhead Applied $ 380.00

Order-completion Cost $1,630.50

Figure 2-1. Production Order Cost Sheet, Product Beta

production department was considered a "cost center." In a job-costing system, all labor, materials, and overhead operating costs are further maintained for each product individually as it passes through the conversion cycle. The necessary documents for this procedure are called "job-cost sheets."

In the example, there are two products, beta and delta, passing through each of the departments in January. Figures 2-1 and 2-2 show accumulated production costs for each product. Similarly, job-order sheets would be prepared for products beta and delta as they moved through the assembling and finishing departments. Determining unit prime costs for each product is easy since the record-keeping system itself is a unit-cost system. As the number of order units increases in volume for any given period or conversion cycle, the record-keeping system itself becomes quite cumbersome. Thus it is essential to keep in mind that a job-cost system will best accommodate those plant operations in which units produced are either tailored to individual customer specification or where the production volume in any one product is too small to justify devoting production facilities exclusively to it for any length of time.

Job Order No. 2 _____   Description: Delta _____

Date Started: January 1 _____   Date Completed: January 31 _____

Quantity Ordered: 15 _____

Materials Cost

Part No.	Unit Price	Quantity
8	$ 3.75	3
17	1.20	10
5	16.50	2
9	4.00	8

Unit Materials Cost $88.25

Labor Cost

Operation	Labor Grade Specified	Hours	Rate Per Hour
10	9	7	$3.80
3	2	10	4.25
16	8	2	5.00

Unit Labor Cost $79.10

Overhead Applied $ 400.00

Order-completion Cost $2,510.25

Figure 2-2. Production Order Cost Sheet, Product Delta

After the job-order cost procedure has been established in the producing and service departments for plant operations, a second stage will introduce elementary product standards into the job-cost system. This step can be accomplished by simply taking the unit standard cost of raw materials or component parts and applying it to the volume of physical input for the job as well as the standard rate per hour for direct labor applied to the actual hours of labor time worked. Then as jobs are completed, costs are transferred from the Work-in-process Inventory account to Finished-goods Inventory at standard cost, not at actual cost. Thus

Job Order 1

	Actual	Standard
Direct materials	$ 9,000	$7,200
Direct labor	4,500	1,800
Total	$13,500	$9,000

Work-in-Process is charged at actual cost:

> Work-in-Process $13,500
> > Raw-Materials Inventory $9,000
> > Wages Payable $4,500

Then Finished-goods Inventory is charged with the standard costs accumulated in Work-in-process, and the variance accounts are set up for the difference between the standard cost of the completed unit and the actual cost accumulated in Work-in-process Inventory. In this way, the latter account is cleared as the job or order batch is completed. Finished-goods Inventory is reported on the balance sheet at standard cost, and the variance accounts for direct material and labor are similarly reported on the balance sheet as inventory cost-control accounts or alternatively are charged to the income statement as "operating-loss" accounts for the production cycle period. Thus

> Finished-goods Inventory $9,000
> > Work-in-process (at standard cost) $9,000

and

> Materials variance account $1,800
> Labor variance account $2,700
> > Work-in-process $4,500

The primary advantages of introducing standard costs to the accounting procedures for plant operations are: (a) uniform costing for the valuation of inventories of finished goods for ordinary financial-statement preparation and for management decision-making purposes such as market pricing on a cost-plus-margin basis, and (b) at least a start at breaking out variances for purposes of control and appraising operating performance.

As already mentioned, the main disadvantage to maintaining the preceding approach to accounting for plant activities is the expensive and cumbersome replication in keeping standard-cost and variance records for each job. Also variances are broken out only according to jobs that have been completed and will not be reflected according to time periods. It is essential to understand here that performance evaluation and control relate to time and not to job orders. Another drawback from the standpoint of control is that performance reporting relates to areas of responsibility, which means departments within the business enterprise and not specific job orders or batches of end product. From a decision making standpoint, we can control the amount of inputs to these activities by areas of managerial responsibility but not job-order specifications per se. Managerial responsibility pertains to the span of functional operating control (that is, decision-making latitude) that a manager has within his department or subunit of the functional area.

The next stage in designing the system will be the development and application of cost standards for plant operations. In doing so, our assumption will be that units of a given product are technically uniform. Also per-unit standards can be established for each product manufactured and according to operating activities.

For example, suppose our hypothetical company produces a single product, product delta. Furthermore, there are two departments (or operating areas) in the plant that work on the product, the machining department and the assembling department. The following product-cost card contains standard costs for direct materials, direct labor, and overhead for both departments that work on product delta.

Product Cost Card

Product Delta

	Machining Department	Assembling Department	Total
Direct materials	$0.54	$0.18	$0.72
Direct labor	1.08	0.36	1.44
Plant overhead	0.20	0.05	0.25
Total	$1.82	$0.59	$2.41

Data presented in this way provide product totals per unit for product delta and for:

1. Materials, labor, and plant overhead
2. For each department, and
3. For total product per unit at $2.41.

For our purposes, a "manufacturing operation" may be defined as an activity at the first level of subdivision, which has a known unit of output and a level of costs that differs from other activities. The primary advantages of using this standard-cost presentation are: (a) Standards are now related to departments that have the responsibility for controlling costs, (b) variances can now also be related to the time period in which they occur so that they can be related to income in that period, and (c) both Work-in-process and Finished-goods Inventory can accumulate standard costs.

The one real disadvantage to this stage in the design is the duplication in the bookkeeping for variances since they are broken out on the job-cost sheets and in the Work-in-process account.

In the fourth stage, the duplication in the underlying record keeping is eliminated by dropping job-order costing. In eliminating job costing, the budget allowances for product-cost standards will now be related only to operating departments or responsibility centers according to the volume of units produced in each department, as shown in table 2-2. These department budget allowances are developed for specific periods of time and are determined by applying the standard rates to the actual volume of production for control purposes.

In our view, standard costs that are applied to uniform products are more meaningful for pricing products than job orders because individual job orders and related costs are expected to vary in all cases where job-order specifications are not uniform. Therefore, a separate cost analysis and pricing decision would have to be made for each job order, which is unnecessary and inefficient. The only sound justification for maintaining a job cost-accounting system for purposes of pricing products would be in cases where manufacturing specifications are individually drawn up by product order and where there is substantially a lack of uniformity in individual specifications. Further, as already mentioned, variances should properly relate to responsibility centers or departmental areas of operating activity for control purposes in manufacturing, not to specific jobs. The bookkeeping is then reduced considerably by eliminating cost assignment to jobs.

Table 2-3 states all cost standards with the exception of materials in terms of a common measurement such as direct labor hours. This last stage will be developed using the same standard cost and budget data for product delta but this time using only the machining department to illustrate the procedure. Note, however, that the same steps would apply to any other department in the plant.

Table 2-3 converts the operating standards for direct materials, direct labor, and overhead to department standards for product delta. This format would be replicated for each separate product line and in each department in the plant.

Table 2-2
Department Budget Allowances
(based on standard)

Machining Department: Production Volume (80,000 units)

Direct materials	($0.54 × 80,000 units)	$43,200
Direct labor	($1.08 × 80,000 units)	86,400
Manufacturing overhead	($0.20 × 80,000 units)	16,000
	$1.82	$145,600

Assembling Department: Production Volume (80,000 units)

Direct materials	($0.18 × 80,000 units)	$14,400
Direct labor	($0.36 × 80,000 units)	28,800
Manufacturing overhead	($0.05 × 80,000 units)	4,000
	$0.59	$47,200

Table 2-3
Departmental Budget, Machining Department

	Standard Cost	Budget for Production
Direct Materials:		
Quantity: 2 lb		
per unit @ 27¢ per lb $0.54 per unit		$43,200
Direct Labor:		
	$1.80 per DLH	
6/10 hour per unit		
80,000 × 0.6 = 48,000 DLH @ $1.80		86,400
Manufacturing Overhead:		
Rate per DLH × $0.331/3		
48,000 DLH × 0.331/3		16,000
Total budget		$145,600
Standard output per hour		
	80,000 units	
	48,000 DLH	
	1.67 units per hour	

Also it is most important to note here that the 48,000 standard direct labor hours and the *actual volume* of 80,000 units were the common bases used in preparing the production budget for the period, with the exception of direct materials. First there is really no meaningful way to express a budget standard for materials except on a per-unit basis. Second actual volume produced must be used as the basis for establishing periodic budget standards for the amounts of departmental physical inputs to production. The reason for using the actual volume is that presumably the planned production volume will be the actual units produced for the period barring any "windfall" that would either curtail production and achieve a lower volume output than planned or conversely require additional shifts during the period. Thus the system will provide for the control of the physical inputs to production over which the department manager has decision-making viability, *given* the actual finished-goods quantity level produced.

At this stage, standards are developed for each organizational department in the plant rather than by separate operations within a department. The refinement of separating standard costs by operations within a department is not really necessary for control since causes for variation can be traced to operations whenever necessary. For example, if the assembling department uses two different grades of labor on two separate operations, a standard labor rate would be developed for each grade. The budget report would include itemized subsets or subsidiary schedules for standard rates and hours for each grade at any given volume of actual output. In this way, a labor variance on the department report at the end of a production period can then be identified as to the particular operation that contributed the variance.

When a company chooses to incorporate standard costing procedures in its system of bookkeeping for costs and expenses in plant operations, there are four major alternatives to presenting inventory-control accounts:

1.   Use a single inventory account.

2.   Use three inventory accounts:
     Raw-materials Inventory
     Work-in-process Inventory
     Finished-goods Inventory

3.   Introduce four subsidiary accounts for both the Work-in-process and the Finished-goods Inventory accounts:
     Raw Materials
     Direct Labor
     Variable Overhead
     Fixed Overhead

4.   In addition to presenting Raw-materials Inventory and Finished-goods Inventory accounts as in alternative 2, maintain subsidiary accounts to Work-in-process by the main cost types for operating inputs:
     Raw-materials-in-process
     Direct-labor-in-process
     Overhead-in-process

The first alternative is too abbreviated for any actionable control of production operations, while the second approach follows the traditional bookkeeping procedure that has been most widely used for preparation of ordinary financial statements. The third alternative would make the erroneous assumption that Finished-goods Inventory contains cost elements that are controllable after they have passed through the production operating cycle. It would further involve additional bookkeeping that is unnecessary due to the fact that the Work-in-process Inventory account itself represents departmental operating inputs for control purposes.

In view of these arguments, the fourth alternative would be preferred. If a single Work-in-process account is used with subsidiary accounts to accumulate expenses for Materials, Direct Labor, and Overhead, then each of these accounts may be accompanied by an operating performance variance account. For example, the Direct Labor account underlying Work-in-process Inventory would accumulate actual department costs incurred, subsequently to be transferred to Finished-goods Inventory at standard cost, with the difference being charged to a separate Direct Labor Variance account. For example,

Work-in-process Inventory

| Direct labor at standard | $ 9,000 |
| Direct labor at actual | $10,000 |

This basic information then may be applied in this way:

1. Direct Labor (in-process at actual cost)   10,000
            Wages payable   10,000

2. Work-in-process Inventory (Direct Labor Standard cost)   9,000
            Direct Labor (in-process)   9,000

3. Direct Labor Variance   1,000
            Direct Labor (in-process)   1,000

Since the Direct-labor-in-process account is really an underlying operating control account for Work-in-process Inventory, this procedure can be simplified by setting up the variance account at actual cost and then making all transfers at standard cost:

1. Direct Labor Variance (at actual cost)   10,000
            Wages payable   10,000

2. Work-in-process (Direct Labor at standard cost)   9,000
            Direct Labor   9,000

In this way, all transfers are made to Work-in-process and Finished-goods Inventories at standard cost. Also the differences between actual and standard costs remain in the labor variance account to be transferred to the balance sheet or the income statement at the end of the period. In this example, the amount is $300.00.

To summarize, the two primary methods of accounting for actual costs and standard costs of materials, labor, and overhead, as they relate to Work-in-process are:

Method I: Charge Work-in-process at actual cost.

Method II: Charge Work-in-process at standard cost.

Method I: Using this method, the in-process accounts for raw materials, direct labor, and overhead would accumulate actual costs as they are incurred, which would then have to be removed from these accounts. Thus

Raw-materials Inventory (actual prices and quantities)	11,000	
Accounts payable		11,000
Raw-materials-in-process (actual prices and quantities)	11,000	
Raw-materials Inventory		11,000

If the standard cost of materials put into production was $9,000, then the variance of $2,000 (containing both price and usage variance components) is removed from Work-in-process:

Raw-materials price		
Variance	1,000	
Raw-materials use		
Variance	1,000	
Raw-materials-in-process		2,000

Method II: Using this alternative, the in-process accounts for raw materials, direct labor, and overhead would accumulate only the standard costs of production for any given period of operations. Again using the example for raw materials,

a. When Raw-materials Inventory is carried at actual prices:

1. Raw-materials variance (at actual cost requisitioned from purchasing) 11,000
    Raw-materials Inventory 11,000

2. Raw-materials-in-process (at standard costs) 9,000
    Raw-materials Variance 9,000

b. When Raw-materials Inventory is carried at standard prices:

1. Raw-materials Inventory (at standard prices) 12,000
    Raw-materials price Variance (purchasing) 2,000
    Accounts payable 14,000

2. Raw-materials use Variance (at actual quantity requisitioned) 8,200
    Raw-materials Inventory 8,200

3. Work-in-process (at standard quantity) 7,000
    Raw-materials use Variance 7,000

In the foregoing treatment, the first transaction records the materials price variance at the time the raw materials are acquired from an outside supplier, and this variance is properly carried in the account structure of the purchasing department. The second and third treatments pertain to the transfer of materials as they are requisitioned and used in the plant. Here, the variance account accumulates the cost of materials at the actual quantity requisitioned for production. The Work-in-process Inventory then accumulates the standard quantity of materials as they are used, leaving the quantity variance account at the end of the production cycle when they are transferred to Finished-goods Inventory.

Method II applied to the direct labor input to a production department would similarly be handled on the books this way:

Direct Labor Rate Variance	500	
Direct Labor Efficiency Variance	14,000	
Accrued wages payable		14,500
Work-in-process (Direct Labor at standard time allowed)	12,000	
Direct Labor Efficiency Variance		12,000

Segregating variances is one of the most essential technical operations in a standard-cost system. It is important for ordinary financial reporting and is the cornerstone to the preparation of internal cost reports for purposes of management control of operations. We introduce the subject here by means of a case illustration pertaining to direct materials and labor inputs to production; it is important to keep in mind, however, that this subject will recur at several points throughout this book in connection with production operations as well as the functional areas of marketing and administration.

In setting up a cost-reporting system that will segregate the variance segments of actual cost incurred from the standard-cost segments, we will assume that unit standards have been established by means of an analysis of unit-price behavior in the company's supply markets for machine tool components. We will also assume that production time standards have been developed for each grade of production labor through industrial engineering techniques such as the applications of learning-curve theory or time-and-motion studies and that hourly rate standards for each labor grade were based on contract negotiations between the firm's labor union and its senior management.

For illustration purposes, we will "set up" a hypothetical manufacturing company called the "Dynamic Power Tool Corporation." This company makes a product line of machine tools for industrial markets. We will further assume that there are three products in the line and that each of these products has technically uniform components. We will identify these products as MT1, MT2, and MT3. There are three assembling departments and one service and maintenance department in the plant, identified as follows:

Assembling department A, which works on product MT1 only

Assembling department B, which works on product MT2 only

Assembling department C, which works on product MT3 only

Department *K* provides general factory services and maintenance to the other departments.

Dynamic's marketing operations are conducted in three geographic markets: Eastern, Central, and Western. Prices quoted to industrial buyers are uniform by region, and unit standard market prices have been set for each product:

MT1:$ 5.00
MT2:$10.00
MT3:$50.00

Until recently, the accounting system used in the plant was maintained primarily to facilitate preparation of the company's quarterly and annual financial statements rather than for control of the plant's functional activities. Senior management at Dynamic has recently decided to install and maintain a standard costing system for control using as a basis the direct variable product-cost system already existing in the four assembling departments. In department *K*, all costs are fixed. The company segregates its fixed and variable operating costs for each functional area in preparing quarterly financial statements for submission to top management. Dynamic's income statement for the first-quarter operations ending March 31 appears in table 2-4. Note that what we call marginal income in this presentation is Dyanmic's net sales figure less direct variable costs for the quarter. Production standard costs for the first-quarter operations appear in table 2-5 with all rates stated on a per-unit basis for finished products.

Senior management has requested that the first quarter serve as a trial run for the new standard cost system and that actual operating costs carried on the books be converted to standard costs off the books for this period. They have

Table 2-4
Dynamic Corporation Income Statement, First Quarter

	Budget	Actual	Over (Under) Budget
Net sales	$810,000	$841,500	$31,500
Variable costs:			
Of goods sold	413,505	439,335	25,830
Of marketing	32,400	33,660	1,260
Total direct costs	$445,905	$472,995	$27,090
Marginal income	364,095	368,505	4,410
Fixed costs:			
Of production	$186,300	$184,212	(2,097)
Of marketing	105,300	108,135	2,835
Of general and administration	21,870	22,446	576
Total fixed costs	$313,470	$314,793	$ 1,314
Net income before taxes	$ 50,625	$ 53,712	$ 3,096

Table 2-5
Dynamic Corporation Production Standard Costs, First Quarter

Product	MT1	MT2	MT3
Department	A	B	C
Materials	$0.54	$1.80	$ 5.40
Labor	1.08	1.93	9.00
Overhead	0.18	0.14	0.45
Subtotals	$1.80	$3.87	$14.85
Department	K	K	K
Materials	$0.18	$0.23	$ 0.59
Labor	0.36	0.72	1.80
Overhead	0.05	0.09	0.22
Subtotals	$0.59	$1.04	$2.61
Total	$2.39	$4.91	$17.46

also requested that the quarterly income statement (table 2-4) they are accustomed to receiving be recast in terms of the standard costs for comparative review. Table 2-6 presents the additional information that will be necessary to meet this request.

Dynamic's transactions for the first quarter are listed in the following section. These transactions will be posted to ordinary T-accounts (figure 2-3); the account balance will then be used to prepare an income statement in standard costing form. All beginning inventories have been recast, and the balances are posted at standard cost. The transactions are lettered and corresponding letters are reflected in the T-accounts preliminary to determining the end-of-quarter balances for these accounts.

Transactions
A. The purchase of component parts for the quarter are recorded.
B. Component parts are issued to the plant from the purchasing department during the quarter. These issues are charged directly to the materials quantity or use variance account at standard prices. The Component-parts Inventory is properly carried on the books of the purchasing department.
C. Similar to the manner in which component parts are handled, the Labor Variance account in the plant is charged directly with the labor payroll accrued for the quarter.
D. Variable and fixed manufacturing expenses are posted to the appropriate accounts for all items used in production other than direct variable materials and labor.
E. The overhead variance account for the plant carries the accumulated actual variable overhead in production during the quarter.
F, G, H. The Component-parts-in-process is charged with the standard cost of

Table 2-6
Dynamic Corporation Standard-Cost Data

Beginning Inventory for the Plant (January 1)

	Per Books	*At Standard*	*Difference (Adjustment)*
Component parts	$202,320	$200,250	$2,070
Parts-in-process	86,400	85,914	486
Labor-in-process	102,375	101,592	787
Overhead-in-process	12,240	12,159	78
Finished goods	381,960	380,925	1,035
Total	$785,295	$780,840	$4,456

Component Parts: Purchasing

Purchases	
At cost	$89,955
At standard	88,605
Price variance	$1,350
Issues to plant at standard cost	$100,800
Direct labor payroll, first quarter	$193,743

Plant Overhead, First Quarter

	Fixed	*Variable*	*Total*
Vouchered	$138,006	$25,407	$163,410
Payroll	31,320	0	31,320
Depreciation	14,886	0	14,886
Total	$184,212	$25,407	$209,616

Costs Applied to Production at Standard, First Quarter

Component parts, from physical inventory at standard	$100,125
Labor, from payroll records	$182,538
Overhead	$ 23,445

Products Completed at Standard Cost During the First Quarter

	Units	*Materials*	*Labor*	*Overhead*	*Total*
MT1	81,000	$ 64,800	$129,600	$20,250	$214,650
MT2	20,000	40,600	53,100	4,500	98,100
MT3	2,250	14,958	27,000	1,683	43,650
		$120,358	$209,700	$26,433	$356,400

First-quarter Sales and Cost of Goods Sold

		Sales		*Standard Cost*
	Units	*Standard*	*Actual*	*of Goods Sold*
MT1	85,500	$427,500	$423,000	$226,575
MT2	27,000	270,000	270,000	147,150
MT3	3,150	157,500	148,500	61,110
		$855,000	$841,500	$434,835

Table 2-6 continued

Other Costs and Expenses for Dynamic's First-quarter Operations

Marketing, fixed	$108,135
Marketing, variable (sales	
commissions: 4%	33,660
General and administrative expenses	22,446
	$164,241
Less nonplant depreciation	6,606
Vouchered	$157,635

First-quarter Cash receipts and disbursements

Received on account	$877,860
Paid on account	
Accounts payable	$334,242
Accrued payroll	231,768
Total	$566,010

parts applied to production during the quarter, as are the in-process accounts for labor applied or used during the month and for overhead applied to production at the standard cost of these inputs for the quarter.

J. The standard cost of production imputs for the quarter that have been traced or attached to completed units of each type of machine tool are transferred to Finished-goods Inventory.

K. Completed units sold to industrial customers during the quarter are transferred from Finished-goods Inventory to Cost of Goods Sold (at standard).

L. Variable marketing expenses allowed represent commissions paid to salesmen at the rate of 4 percent applied to unit sales at actual prices in the amount of $855,000.

M. Product sales are recorded at standard prices, and the difference between the standard prices and actual prices paid by customers is carried in the appropriate variance account.

N. Marketing and general expenses for the quarter are recorded in the T-accounts. The standard variable marketing expense of $33,660 is the standard expense for sales commissions.

P, R. Cash receipts and disbursements for the quarter are recorded.

Cash

Beginning balance 326,475	(R) 566,010
(P) 877,860	

Accounts Receivable

Beginning Balance 580,770	(P) 877,860
(M) 841,500	

Component-parts Inventory

Beginning balance 202,320	(B) 100,800
(A) 88,605	

Component Parts in-process

Beginning Balance 86,400	(J) 120,263
(F) 100,125	

Direct Variable Labor in Process

Beginning balance 102,375	(J) 209,700
(F) 182,538	

Plant Overhead in process

Beginning balance 12,240	(J) 26,437
(H) 23,445	

Finished-goods Inventory

Beginning balance 381,960	(K) 434,835
(J) 356,400	

Allowance for Depreciation

	Beginning balance 72,126
	(D) 14,886
	(N) 6,606

Accounts Payable

(R) 334,242	Beginning balance 438,588
	(A) 89,955
	(D) 163,410
	(N) 157,635

Accrued Payroll

(R) 231,768	Beginning balance 38,115
	(C) 193,743
	(D) 31,320

Sales

	(M) 855,000

Cost of Goods Sold

(K) 434,835

Variance in Selling Prices

(M) 13,500

Variable Standard Marketing Expenses

(L) 34,200

Variable Marketing Expenses (Sales Commissions)

(N) 33,660	(L) 34,200

Variable Production Expenses

(D) 25,405	(E) 25,405

Fixed Production Expenses

(D) 184,212

Component-parts Price Variance

(A) 1,350

Component-parts Use or Quantity Variance

(B) 100,800	(F) 100,125

Direct Labor Variance

(C) 193,743	(G) 182,538

Figure 2-3. Dynamic Corporation Transactions, First Quarter

Figure 2-3 continued

Plant Overhead Variance

(E) 25,407   (H) 23,445

Fixed Marketing Expenses

(N) 108,135

General and Administrative Expenses

(N) 22,446

Now that we have converted the first-quarter transactions for Dynamic's operations to a standard-cost basis and segregated the variances resulting from the difference between these standard costs and actual book costs incurred, we can recast the income statement in terms of the results shown in table 2-7.

The following presentation illustrates the kind of operating-statement format that might be prepared for review by top management once a standard-cost system has been developed for the company's functional activities. We have focused initially here on designing the system for plant production operations. However, the reader can also begin to gain a feeling for the applications of

Table 2-7
Dynamic Corporation Income Statement, First Quarter

Sales			$855,000
Standard variable costs:			
Cost of goods sold		$434,835	
Marketing costs		$ 34,200	$469,035
Standard marginal income			$385,965
Variances for the quarter:			
Selling prices		$ 13,500	
Marketing expenses		(540)	
Production costs:			
Materials prices	$ 1,350		
Materials use	675		
Labor	11,205		
	$ 1,960	$ 15,190	$ 28,150
Actual marginal income			$357,815
Actual fixed costs:			
Marketing expenses		$108,135	
Production costs		184,212	
General and administrative expenses		$ 22,446	$314,793
Net operating income before taxes			$ 43,022

standard-cost systems to functional activities in addition to production and may wish to study the income-statement format with a view toward appraising the financial performance for the quarter in which the Dynamic Power Tool Corporation initiated standard-cost accounting.

3 Absorption Standard Costing for Production

An absorption cost-accounting system, often referred to as a "full product-allocation system," attempts to assign all indirect (to product lines) costs of production in each department in the plant to units of product as they are converted from raw materials or parts into finished goods. Overhead costs may be collected and classified by types of expense, some of the more typical identifications being indirect labor, supplies, tools, utilities, and depreciation on equipment. Once classified by type, overhead-expense items are assigned to cost centers (for example, a department or other organizational unit to which they are charged). As the conversion process is completed in each department, three major considerations arise:

1. The assignment of general plant overhead costs to a managerial or operating department—that is, a cost center or responsibility center (as defined in chapter 1). These costs are common to all departments in the sense of not originating in or being traceable to a given department. They would include depreciation or rental charges, utilities, and maintenance on buildings that house several departments whether they are service or operating units in the production organization. Any plant utilities or service operations, the uses of which are shared by all operating departments that are involved in product conversion, would be included in this first category. Their attendant costs therefore would have to be assigned or allocated to those departments that are commonly served by such utilities or services. The quantitative criterion for such allocation is usually based on a measure of the relative use of these facilities or services (in time or amount) by each of the producing departments.

2. The assignment of overhead-expense items that do originate within a department but are not directly traceable to any one product line passing through the department in conversion to each of the product lines. These items would include machinery depreciation and maintenance, department utilities, or the salaries of supervisors and foremen assigned to the operations of a particular department.

3. The determination of the volume to be used in deriving rates for assigning factory overhead to units of each product line as they pass through the operating departments in conversion. This is a critical consideration as the volume selected will greatly affect the unit cost in assigning fixed costs to any given product line, which in turn will affect the valuation of finished-

goods inventories. In those companies for which market pricing policy is based on unit cost of production, the level of unit costs for products will also affect customer contract rates or market prices set for each product line.

In discussing these considerations under an absorption or "full-allocation" product-costing system, we must remember that only plant production facilities or operations are applicable to the assignment of costs to products in conversion and the valuation of finished-product inventories. Costs of operations for any other functional areas within the company (for example, research and development, marketing, administration) are not applicable.

When all these expense items that have either been allocated to (or traced to) the producing departments or originate within departmental operations have been classified so that they may be assigned to each product line for a given period of operations, the problem arises as to the selection of an appropriate level of unit volume in order to arrive at an overhead-absorption rate per unit for each product line. Traditionally, for those companies using an absorption product-costing system, actual unit volume of goods completed in a department was used as the measure for determining an overhead-absorption rate.

In using actual volume of production, the usual method is to divide the total fixed overhead by the actual units produced during a given month or quarter within the year to obtain an overhead rate per unit. Alternately, actual overhead costs can be divided by the actual quantity of a direct conversion input (for example, direct labor or direct materials) to obtain an overhead rate. Then overhead costs are assigned to units of product by applying this overhead rate to the number of units of the direct conversion resource absorbed by each unit of product. This procedure is followed as operations are completed in each producing department to which these overhead costs are assigned.

The use of actual volume in determining overhead-absorption rates has little conceptual or practical validity, particularly for product costing and inventory valuation. It is nearly impossible to compare the unit costs of one period with those of another and make any meaningful evaluation of the changes for any purpose, whether that purpose is the setting of market prices for final products, analysis of inventory flows and values, or control of operations in the plant. When production volume is low, a high unit cost can be a serious distortion when it is due only to the change in production volume per se. Conversely, when monthly or quarterly volume is higher than the annual or longer intermediate term "average" volume, the per-unit product cost will again be distorted in the opposite direction since these same overhead expenses will not have changed, but their absorption or allocation will be over a larger number of units produced.

What are we trying to say here? In essence, the vital issue is that when a company allocates fixed production costs in each department in the plant to physical units produced and does so on the basis of actual unit volume, there will always be erroneous and seriously misleading values for the unit cost of a product from one production period to another. These distortions will always be reflected in the valuation of finished-goods inventories because cost per unit to manufacture a product in the plant is being treated as a function of the physical volume of production rather than as a function of cost levels. Only variable costs of production change with increasing or decreasing levels of physical output, particularly during short periods such as the month or quarter within the operating year. The fixed costs that are allocated to each unit of product do not change. However, when actual volume in units is used as the basis for the absorption of constant overhead for any given period of time, then unit costs of product output will be high during low levels of production volume and low during high levels of production. These results will always occur under such a system even though the overhead costs absorbed remain unchanged since they are fixed by both definition and cost behavior.

Another limitation in using actual units completed as the basis for developing overhead rates is that these rates cannot be calculated until the end of the production period for which the rates apply. When customer billing is determined on the basis of actual costs plus margin, and this is usually the case in a job-order manufacturing and record-keeping system, it would be rather embarrassing to explain to customers that volume differences accounted for identical orders costing different amounts in two successive time periods.

In view of these limitations in using actual volume for the purpose of determining a per-unit absorption rate for constant overhead expenses, the question arises as to what criterion should be used for selecting a production volume in lieu of the actual level of unit output during any given month or quarter within the year. The issue of selecting an alternative volume measure boils down to the fact that it is undesirable for overhead-absorption *rates* per unit of output to change from one production period to another as the sole result of changes in the unit volume of output. What measure of volume should be used then?

There is no simple answer to that question since different industries and conglomerate corporations will have quite dissimilar production operations and will experience quite different patterns for both production volume and cost behavior from one year to another. Even closely competitive companies within an industry whose product lines and plant operations may be quite similar will experience different production volume levels from one month or quarter to another within a given fiscal year. These results might be attributed to company differences in scale of operations or short-term competitive behavior in product markets.

One approach to solving the problems of using actual volume for periods within the year is to make a one-year forecast of production for each product line. While it is true that this procedure would facilitate the development of constant standard absorption rates for months or quarters within the year, the same problem of allocating overhead expenses that remain fixed from one year to the next would remain since our production-volume forecast will change for any two consecutive years. Although the annual forecast of production has been widely used, we still face the problem of comparing unit product costs between two consecutive years that we faced in using actual volume for determining overhead rates for consecutive months or quarters within a fiscal year.

In arriving at a meaningful rule of thumb (and one that is acceptable to management), a company would be wise to select a volume level for *each* product line that can be considered an average (and therefore constant) forecast or projected production volume covering a period of more than one year. Such a measure will then be free of normal seasonal variations in output levels and the effects of random events such as labor strikes or inadequate materials supplies due to shortages in procurement markets.

Our primary objective is to develop standardized absorption rates that are constant and that represent a "normalized" use of plant capacity for a time period that is longer than a single forecast year. In doing so, it is preferable to base this rate on an intermediate-term projection of production volume. This projection in turn should be based on a forecast of sales for the same time period and the expected amount of fixed plant overhead to be absorbed for this period. The projected volume of output is really an average practical utilization of plant capacity for the intermediate period that is forecast. Customer orders will vary for any one product line by months and quarters within the forecast period due to seasonal factors, expansions or deletions within product lines, or the market activities of competitors. Production scheduling will then follow similar patterns of variation in an effort to avoid shortage or overages in finished-product inventories.

In developing constant absorption rates for fixed plant overhead based on (a) an average projected volume of production output for each product line and (b) an expected percentage utilization of plant capacity for each producing department, management must address two considerations: First, management must select a criterion for establishing a forecast period that will exceed one year of operations; second, management must determine the accounting treatment for under or overabsorbed overhead.

The forecast period should equitably comprise that number of consecutive years of operation for which management anticipates no major plans for expansion or deletion of plant facilities. It is also preferable that this time period is one for which no major changes are expected in existing or currently planned product lines or in functional market organization and operations. For many manufacturers with small- or medium-sized product-line sales volumes and whose markets remain fairly stable, this forecast period can be as long as five or seven years. Unless a company's management anticipates highly unstable product-market conditions, the forecast period can rarely be less than three years in order to achieve the foregoing objectives for an absorption-costing system.

With regard to under or overabsorption of overhead for a given measurement and reporting period within an operating year (that is, a month or quarter), these amounts simply mean that normalized practical capacity was underutilized or exceeded and can readily be handled as adjustments to period costs and expenses on the company's profit statement. In this way, per-unit costs for each product line and corresponding inventory values will not vary with changes in the volume of production but only with increasing or decreasing variable costs that result from these volume changes per se.

There are two prominent feasible approaches to setting rates for assigning overhead to units of product:

I.   Use the intermediate-range forecast of production volume previously mentioned for each product line and apply absorption rates directly to units of product as conversion is completed in each department.
II. Select a production measure that is not only variable with volume of product output but also a direct input to each product line in conversion.

Table 3-1 illustrates the application of each of these alternatives for three product lines—MT1, MT2, and MT3—with the following output projections for plant 1 and its two major operating departments, machining and assembling. Table 3-2 shows the annual fixed costs for each department.

For method I, and given the plant production projections based on a three-year forecast, we are confronted with a three-stage allocation procedure in deriving an annual fixed overhead rate per unit for each product:

Stage 1: We must first allocate the share of fixed cost that products MT1, MT2, and MT3 will bear for each department in plant 1.

Stage 2: In this stage we determine the amount of direct fixed costs to be allocated to each product and derive a per-unit rate for MT1, MT2, and MT3.

Stage 3: The final step will be to derive a per-unit rate for common fixed costs for each of the three products.

In the first stage, we consider only those fixed costs that are direct to each department and the percent of capacity utilization for each of these fixed charges. The annualized charges will usually include depreciation on facilities and equipment, supplies and tools expenses, as well as utilities and maintenance costs that are direct in the sense of being traceable to each department or cost center although they are common or indirect to specific product lines.

Furthermore, it is appropriate that absorption rates be determined only to the extent of the capacity utilized for depreciable equipment and facilities. These projected utilization rates are what controllers and cost accountants often

Table 3-1
Annual Projections of Scheduled Production, Plant 1
(production output in units based on sales forecast)

Product MT1

Year	Machining Dept.	% Capacity	Assembling Dept.	% Capacity
1	60,000	60	60,000	50
2	105,000	70	105,000	87.5
3	120,000	80	120,000	100

Three-year average projection in units:

95,000		95,000

Machining department capacity 100,000 units MT1 (year 1).
Machining department capacity 150,000 units MT1 (years 2 and 3).
Assembling department capacity 120,000 units MT1.

Product MT2

Year	Machining Dept.	% Capacity	Assembling Dept.	% Capacity
1	40,000	33	40,000	33
2	60,000	50	60,000	50
3	80,000	67	80,000	67

Three-year average projection in units:

60,000		60,000

Capacity 120,000 units MT2 (both departments).

Product MT3

Year	Machining Dept.	% Capacity	Assembling Dept.	% Capacity
1	35,000	35	35,000	35
2	45,000	45	45,000	45
3	55,000	55	55,000	55

Three-year average projection in units:

45,000		45,000

Capacity 100,000 units MT3 (both departments).

call "practical capacity." To use any higher rates such as those based on optimum capacity would be unrealistic since physical product output and final inventories cannot equitably absorb the costs of unutilized plant facilities that were not involved in conversion. We will now recast the dollar fixed costs in terms of these projected rates of utilization.

In doing so, we must first prorate (stage 1) the proportions of total fixed costs to be absorbed by each of the three product lines by using the relative shares of three-year average output, as shown in table 3-3.

Table 3-2
Annual Fixed Costs by Departments

Depreciation on Equipment

Year	Machining Dept.	Assembling Dept.
1	$20,000	$ 40,000
2	25,000	40,000
3	30,000	40,000
Total	$75,000	$120,000

Three-year average annual projection:

	$25,000	$ 40,000

Common Fixed Overhead

	Year 1	Year 2	Year 3
Depreciation on building	$ 20,000	$ 20,000	$ 20,000
Rent	75,000	80,000	85,000
Total	$ 95,000	$100,000	$105,000

Three-year average annual projection:

	$100,000

The figures in table 3-4 for each year represent the share of depreciation in terms of total capacity that would be absorbed by each product line. Again these figures are based on the average projected output of final product. The next step, table 3-5, will be to convert the figures to the amounts to be absorbed based on projected annual capacity utilization (stage 2).

We have now derived equitably the dollar amounts of fixed overhead to be allocated to each unit of final output for each of the three product lines. With this information, we can determine the absorption rates per unit of output for each product that will be applied during the three-year period for which the projections were made (stage 3). This determination is made by simply taking the projected three-year average output and dividing it into the absorption amounts for each of the three years by department as shown in table 3-6.

Table 3-3
Relative Product-line Shares of Three-Year Average Output, Plant 1

Product	Three-Year Average Output	Percent
MT1	95,000	47.5
MT2	60,000	30.0
MT3	45,000	22.5
Total	200,000	100.0

Table 3-4
Depreciation on Equipment by Departments

Year	Annual Depreciation	MT1 47.5%	MT2 30.0%	MT3 22.5%
Machining department				
1	$20,000	$ 9,500	$ 6,000	$4,500
2	25,000	11,875	7,500	5,625
3	30,000	14,250	9,000	6,750
Assembling Department				
1	$40,000	$19,000	$12,000	$9,000
2	40,000	19,000	12,000	9,000
3	40,000	19,000	12,000	9,000

Since the average three-year projected production volume for MT1 is 95,000 units, the fixed rates for departmental overhead will be as shown below the columns in table 3-6.

All the preceding rates have been rounded to three decimal places. The final consideration here is to determine similar product-absorption rates for common (to departments) fixed expenses for each year. Referring back to the information presented in table 3-2, we simply prorate the annual totals for rent and building depreciation by the same three-year average percentages we used for departmental overhead (table 3-7).

We are now able to summarize the total per-unit product fixed-cost absorption rates as shown in table 3-8.

To simplify the development of these rates, only the combined rates for departmental overhead were presented earlier. However, the individual rates would have to be developed on separate schedules in each department in the plant just as they are presented here in the final summary.

The important point to emphasize (and reemphasize) in using an absorption-cost system is that the unit rate for assigning overhead to products in conversion must be constant for any given year of plant operations as long as the overhead costs themselves remain constant. You will notice that in our illustrations, the absorption rates per unit do differ from one year to the next. Two factors will cause these differences in rates: One factor is the differing percentages of capacity utilization. We do not want to include the cost of facilities that are not used in any given year in the cost of products completed (cf. pp. 55-56). The second factor is that the rates will be different as a result of changes in the dollar amounts of projected fixed overhead. These changes would be due to such managerial actions as renewal of leasing contracts with higher annual rental rates on factory buildings and additional increments to depreciation resulting in planned replacements or new acquisitions of equipment and facilities.

In developing an application for method II, a production measurement is

Table 3-5
Absorption of Depreciation on Equipment

Machining Department

Year	Depreciation Amount	% Capacity Utilization	Depreciation Absorbed
Product MT1 (47.5%)			
1	$ 9,500	60	$ 5,700
2	11,875	70	8,312
3	14,250	80	11,400
Product MT2 (30.0%)			
1	$ 6,000	34	$ 2,040
2	7,500	50	3,750
3	9,000	66	5,940
Product MT3 (22.5%)			
1	$ 4,500	35	$ 1,575
2	5,625	45	2,531
3	6,750	55	3,712

Assembling Department

Year	Depreciation Amount	% Capacity Utilization	Depreciation Absorbed
Product MT1 (47.5%)			
1	$19,000	50.0	$ 9,500
2	19,000	87.5	16,625
3	19,000	100.0	19,000
Product MT2 (30.0%)			
1	$12,000	34	$4,080
2	12,000	50	6,000
3	12,000	66	7,920
Product MT3 (22.5%)			
1	$ 9,000	35	$ 3,150
2	9,000	45	4,050
3	9,000	55	4,950

selected as an intermediate means of deriving the constant per-unit rate of overhead absorbed. Again interperiod-production volume will vary, but since fixed costs remain constant, the overhead rates should change *only* as a function of capacity utilization and any incremental changes that may occur in these fixed costs. The intermediate measure to be selected should be a direct variable input to factory product conversion. The two most obvious inputs would be direct labor and materials. We will use direct labor in our illustrations here. In doing so, the initial objective is to derive an average or standard quantity of labor input for each product line on a per-unit basis.

Using data from table 3-3, the three-year projected average volume per product line and the overhead cost amounts to be absorbed would be developed according to method I (table 3-9).

Table 3-6
Absorption of Depreciation on Equipment, Three-Year Rates

Product MT1

Year	Machining Dept.	Assembling Dept.	Total
1	$ 5,700	$ 9,500	$15,200
2	8,312	16,625	24,937
3	11,400	19,000	30,400

Year 1: $\dfrac{\$15,200}{\$95,000} = \$0.160$ per unit

Year 2: $\dfrac{\$24,937}{\$95,000} = \$0.262$ per unit

Year 3: $\dfrac{\$30,400}{\$95,000} = \$0.320$ per unit

Product MT2

Year	Machining Dept.	Assembling Dept.	Total
1	$2,040	$4,080	$ 6,120
2	3,750	6,000	9,750
3	5,940	7,920	13,860

Year 1: $\dfrac{\$6,120}{\$60,000} = \$0.102$ per unit

Year 2: $\dfrac{\$9,750}{\$60,000} = \$0.162$ per unit

Year 3: $\dfrac{\$13,860}{\$60,000} = \$0.231$ per unit

Product MT3

Year	Machining Dept.	Assembling Dept.	Total
1	$1,575	$3,150	$4,725
2	2,531	4,050	6,581
3	3,712	4,950	8,662

Year 1: $\dfrac{\$4,725}{\$45,000} = \$0.105$ per unit

Year 2: $\dfrac{\$6,581}{\$45,000} = \$0.146$ per unit

Year 3: $\dfrac{\$8,662}{\$45,000} = \$0.192$ per unit

Analysis of engineering manning tables has further indicated the labor-hour requirements per unit of output for each product line by department and labor grade as shown in table 3-10.

Total average annual labor for the three-year projection period cannot be

Table 3-7
Common Overhead, Plant 1

Product	Percent Applied	Year 1	Year 2	Year 3
MT1	47.5	$45,125	$ 47,500	$ 49,875
MT2	30.0	28,500	30,000	31,500
MT3	22.5	21,375	22,500	23,625
Total	100.0	$95,000	$100,000	$105,000

Product MT1

Year 1: $\dfrac{\$45,125}{\$95,000} = \$0.475$ per unit

Year 2: $\dfrac{\$47,500}{\$95,000} = \$0.500$ per unit

Year 3: $\dfrac{\$49,875}{\$95,000} = \$0.525$ per unit

Product MT2

Year 1: $\dfrac{\$28,500}{\$60,000} = \$0.475$ per unit

Year 2: $\dfrac{\$30,000}{\$60,000} = \$0.500$ per unit

Year 3: $\dfrac{\$31,500}{\$60,000} = \$0.525$ per unit

Product MT3

Year 1: $\dfrac{\$21,375}{\$45,000} = \$0.475$ per unit

Year 2: $\dfrac{\$22,500}{\$45,000} = \$0.500$ per unit

Year 3: $\dfrac{\$23,625}{\$45,000} = \$0.525$ per unit

obtained for each department by applying the per-unit hours to the average projected output for MT1, MT2, and MT3 (table 3-11).

The overhead rates applied can now be derived as shown in tables 3-12 and 3-13. Departmental overhead is then absorbed by taking the appropriate hourly rates and applying them to the standard hours for each unit of MT1, MT2, and MT3 as they are completed in each department or cost center.

For common overhead rates, it seems more reasonable to develop product rates as we did in method I since there are no "total standard man-hours" that would logically relate to common plant overhead. It would be possible, however,

Table 3-8
Summary of Total per-Unit Product Fixed-Cost Absorption Rates

Year	Machining Dept. Rate	Assembling Dept. Rate	Common Plant Rate	Annual Absorption Rate
Product MT1				
1	$0.060	$0.100	$0.475	$0.635
2	0.087	0.175	0.500	0.762
3	0.120	0.200	0.525	0.845
Product MT2				
1	$0.034	$0.068	$0.475	$0.577
2	0.062	0.100	0.500	0.662
3	0.099	0.132	0.525	0.756
Product MT3				
1	$0.035	$0.070	$0.475	$0.580
2	0.056	0.090	0.500	0.646
3	0.082	0.110	0.525	0.717

to use the standard man-hours for one of the plant departments if management wishes to use the second method consistently for product overhead absorption (table 3-14).

Method II is clearly more elaborate than method I, although they accomplish the same task under the same concept. It is questionable whether the second approach is worth the additional time and expense involved in clerical and computer record keeping for many medium-sized or small manufacturers. The only difference is that final product is charged with overhead based on a dollar rate for units of a conversion factor (for example, labor as in the preceding example) rather than a rate for units of finished product (as in method I). For companies that manufacture a variety of products passing through the same departments, it may well be necessary to adopt some applied form of the second method.

A word of caution needs to be emphasized regarding the allocation of common overhead to product. First, common overhead may be a very significant amount in plain dollar figures, particularly for companies that own the buildings used to house plant facilities and accrue large sums of depreciation annually. Second, all methods used to allocate such common costs down to units produced within product lines for a given period of measurement are bound to be somewhat arbitrary. There is no single rationale or procedure that is valid to the exclusion of all others, and good human judgment combined with an objective appraisal of a company's particular plant operations and organization must be relied on. It is essential therefore that the criterion selected for such allocation be considered carefully by a company's management as to its

Table 3-9
Annual Depreciation and Overhead Absorbed

Annual Depreciation Absorbed, Machining Department

Year	MT1	MT2	MT3
1	$ 5,700	$2,040	$1,575
2	8,312	3,750	2,531
3	11,400	5,940	3,712

Annual Depreciation Absorbed, Assembling Department

Year	MT1	MT2	MT3
1	$ 9,500	$4,080	$3,150
2	16,625	6,000	4,050
3	19,000	7,920	4,950

Common Overhead Absorbed, Plant 1

Year	MT1	MT2	MT3	Total
1	$45,125	$28,500	$21,375	$ 95,000
2	47,500	30,000	22,500	100,000
3	49,875	31,500	23,625	105,000

objective validity and the appropriateness of the rationale upon which the selection of a procedure is based.

Since "common overhead" refers to all fixed annual costs that are not direct to individual producing or service departments in the plant, an allocation is often made to departments before these costs are assigned further to product lines. A criterion for such allocation must be agreed on by management, which will then serve as the basis for developing a quantitative procedure. We will consider two distinctly different criteria that have been used widely by manufacturers under a full-allocation product-costing system. They are what we may call the "value-added" criterion and the "benefits-received" criterion.

1. The value-added concept arises from the viewpoint that each product line in conversion incurs certain direct inputs (labor, materials, supervision, engineering, and technical expertise) and that these inputs add value from the standpoint of the final utility value or usefulness of the finished product. Thus the allocation method management selects should be some measure of the value-added inputs to each product line.
2. The benefits-received concept maintains that the value of a product should be measured in terms of its revenue-producing capability (for example, percent share of total sales dollars), and that this measure provides a more equitable basis for allocating common overhead amounts in the plant.

If companies elect the first criterion, they must translate "value added" into

Table 3-10
Standard Labor Hours per Unit of Output

Machining Department

		Product	
Labor Grade	*MT1*	*MT2*	*MT3*
4	1.5	—	2.5
8	2.26	1.5	—
17	—	2.5	0.5
3	3.5	—	—
29	—	1.0	4.5
Total hours per unit	7.26	5.0	7.5

Assembling Department

		Product	
Labor Grade	*MT1*	*MT2*	*MT3*
9	3.0	4.5	—
7	—	2.5	—
5	—	—	3.5
14	1.5	—	4.5
Total hours per unit	4.5	7.0	8.0

Total Man-hours

Product	*Machining Dept.*	*Assembling Dept.*	*Total*
MT1	7.0	4.5	11.5
MT2	5.0	7.0	12.0
MT3	7.5	8.0	15.5

a specific measure of production such as the relative plant capacity utilized by each product line or the relative inputs of direct labor or materials. In our illustration, we used the percentage utilization of capacity over the intermediate period for which production volume was projected for MT1, MT2, and MT3 to arrive at an allocation of common overhead by years. We then developed product-line unit rates by dividing the projected average volume into each of the annual dollar amounts to be absorbed.

If we had elected to use the sales-value or benefits-received approach, we would have substituted the three-year average share of dollar sales for the average percent of capacity utilization in assigning common overhead to be absorbed in each of the forecast years. Thus given the information in table 3-15, we can allocate common overhead just as we did previously when we used capacity utilization rates as the basis for absorption (cf. pp. 56 and 60) (table 3-16).

Table 3-11
Standard Annual Labor Man-hours per Product Line

Machining Department

Product	Three-year Average Output	Man-hours Per Unit	Total Standard Man-hours Per Product
MT1	95,000	7.26	690,000
MT2	60,000	5.0	300,000
MT3	45,000	7.5	337,500

Assembling Department

Product	Three-year Average Output	Standard Man-hours Per Unit	Total Standard Man-hours Per Product
MT1	95,000	4.5	427,500
MT2	60,000	7.0	420,000
MT3	45,000	8.5	382,500

The rates and allocated amounts in table 3-16 differ from our previous figures (cf. table 3-6) because the forecast sales volume in units for each product will differ from production projections due to allowances for three-year beginning and ending inventories. These percentages also represent weighted averages based on relative unit-sales prices, as we mentioned.

Now we can take these annual product allocations for common overhead and develop unit-absorption rates as we did before, by dividing the projected

Table 3-12
Overhead-Absorption Rates per Hour of Direct Labor,
Machining Department

Year	Overhead Absorbed	Total Standard Man-hours	Rate Per Hour
Product MT1			
1	$ 5,700	690,000	$0.0086
2	8,312	690,000	0.0125
3	11,400	690,000	0.0187
Product MT2			
1	$2,040	300,000	$0.0068
2	3,750	300,000	0.0125
3	5,940	300,000	0.0198
Product MT3			
1	$1,575	337,500	$0.0047
2	2,531	337,500	0.0075
3	3,712	337,500	0.0110

three-year average output into the annual dollar overhead allocations (cf. table 3-7):

Product MT1

Year 1: $\dfrac{\$43,890}{\$95,000}$ = \$0.462 per unit

Year 2: $\dfrac{\$46,200}{\$95,000}$ = \$0.486 per unit

Year 3: $\dfrac{\$48,510}{\$95,000}$ = \$0.510 per unit

Product MT2

Year 1: $\dfrac{\$20,995}{\$60,000}$ = \$0.350 per unit

Year 2: $\dfrac{\$22,100}{\$60,000}$ = \$0.368 per unit

Year 3: $\dfrac{\$23,205}{\$60,000}$ = \$0.387 per unit

Product MT3

Year 1: $\dfrac{\$30,115}{\$45,000}$ = \$0.670 per unit

Year 2: $\dfrac{\$31,700}{\$45,000}$ = \$0.704 per unit

Year 3: $\dfrac{\$33,285}{\$45,000}$ = \$0.741 per unit

One final note on the use of average volume of production for an intermediate-range forecast period is in order before we turn to the subject of measurements for plant operating control under an overhead absorption system. One of our vital premises in the foregoing presentation on product costing was that standard absorption rates represent a normalized use of plant capacity for as long a period of consecutive years of operation that product-line output in the plant can be feasibly and accurately projected (cf. pp. 54-55). Since the unit volume of production for each product line is in fact an annualized average, the figure may be derived best from the average forecast of sales volume for the same period and adjusted for planned levels of finished-goods inventories at "both ends" of the forecast period. Furthermore, it is best that the fixed-over-

Table 3-13
Overhead-Absorption Rates per Hour of Direct Labor,
Assembling Department

Year	Overhead Absorbed	Total Standard Man-hours	Rate Per Hour
Product MT1			
1	$ 9,500	427,500	$0.0222
2	16,625	427,500	0.0388
3	19,000	427,500	0.0444
Product MT2			
1	$4,080	420,000	$0.0097
2	6,000	420,000	0.0143
3	7,920	420,000	0.0190
Product MT3			
1	$3,150	382,500	$0.0082
2	4,050	382,500	0.0106
3	4,950	382,500	0.0129

head costs in each year of the forecast period not only reflect the percent of plant capacity that the projected volume will use but also be adjusted for normal down-time and "unplanned" idle facilities. A company can readily quantify this factor based on its historical track record for plant operations by departments.

Table 3-14
Common Overhead, Plant 1, Absorption Rates per Direct Labor Hour
(based on machining man-hours)

Year	Overhead Absorbed	Total Machining Standard Man-hours	Rate Per Hour
Product MT1			
1	$45,125	690,000	$0.0679
2	47,500	690,000	0.0714
3	49,875	690,000	0.0750
Product MT2			
1	$28,500	300,000	$0.0950
2	30,000	300,000	0.1000
3	31,500	300,000	0.1050
Product MT3			
1	$21,375	337,500	$0.0633
2	22,500	337,500	0.0667
3	22,500	337,500	0.0700

In other words, we do not want to absorb into products the cost of facilities that are idle and that are not part of planned capacity utilization. Such cost increments can be treated appropriately as "period" charges on the company's earnings statement.

Table 3-15
Three-Year Product Sales Forecast

Product MT1

Year	Forecast Sales in Units	Unit Price	Dollar-volume Forecast
1	50,000	$32.00	$1,600,000
2	95,000	35.00	3,325,000
3	115,000	34.00	3,910,000
Total	260,000		$8,835,000
Three-year average			$2,945,000

Product MT2

Year	Forecast Sales in Units	Unit Price	Dollar-volume Forecast
1	40,000	$25.00	$1,000,000
2	45,000	28.00	1,260,000
3	65,000	30.00	1,950,000
Total	150,000		$4,210,000
Three-year average			$1,403,300

Product MT3

Year	Forecast Sales in Units	Unit Price	Dollar-volume Forecast
1	20,000	$58.00	$1,160,000
2	45,000	50.00	2,250,000
3	50,000	53.00	2,650,000
Total	115,000		$6,060,000
Three-year average			$2,020,000

Products MT1, MT2, and MT3 Combined

Product	Three-year Average Sales Dollars	Percent Share
MT1	$2,945,000	46.2
MT2	1,403,300	22.1
MT3	2,020,000	31.7
		100.0

Table 3-16
Common Overhead, Plant 1, Three-Year Allocation

Product	Percent Applied	Year 1	Year 2	Year 3
MT1	46.2	$43,890	$ 46,200	$ 48,510
MT2	22.1	20,995	22,100	23,205
MT3	31.7	30,115	31,700	33,285
Total	100.0	$95,000	$100,000	$105,000

We will now turn our attention from the first major area of application under an absorption-costing system for plant operations, namely, the costing of products as they pass through conversion and valuation of finished-goods inventory. The latter consideration is really an extension of the subject of product costing, and we will continue our discussion of inventories in chapter 6.

Our major emphasis for the remaining sections of this chapter will be the use and applications of an absorption (full-cost) system for control of operations, and this subject will be vital to our discussions of performance reporting and evaluation in part II. When we consider accounting systems for control of organizational and operating activities, we must keep in mind that our concern is no longer the use of those costs that a system generates for assignment or nonassignment to product lines. Rather, our attention will focus on the association of the system with the activities of these departments that we have called "responsibility centers" and the resource inputs to these departments that make possible the conversion of raw materials into finished products.

In dealing with control of overhead for plant operations, we must keep in mind two things. First, in terms of cost behavior, there are two basic categories of overhead. "Variable overhead expenses," which are directly traceable to the production or to the service departments but not to individual product lines, will tend to increase or decrease with changes in production output. These expenses will include items such as production set-up, materials handling, maintenance labor and operating supplies, power, light, and heating utilities. "Fixed overhead" will comprise mainly depreciation on equipment, taxes, and insurance. These items can be very substantial in amount for any given time period. Some overhead items will be partly fixed and partly variable as we will discover in our subsequent illustrations in this chapter and in chapter 4. Examples of these hybrids might include materials-handling costs and maintenance.

The second point of importance is that most major fixed overhead can rarely be controlled in the particular department charged with its cost. The foreman of the assembling department in the plant cannot make a decision that will alter the amount of depreciation expenses for the factory building or the assembling equipment charged to his department; therefore they are beyond his control in terms of responsibility. Ordinarily, variable overhead can be considered controllable by management at the department level. For example, the department head can alter the quantity of operating or maintenance supplies wherever he believes it is necessary to sustain the production volume scheduled and thereby change the expense amounts incurred for these items from one operating and reporting period to another.

Standards for variable overhead can be set on the basis of engineering evaluation of quantities of each item necessary to complete operations in a department for different levels of product output. Standards for fixed overhead are usually easier to develop. For example, depreciation expenses on productive assets are constant periodic allotments based on the value of the machine or building and the number of projected years or months of useful service life for each asset. Property taxes and insurance are similarly allotted to a department in constant amounts of expense for a particular number of operating and reporting periods.

In our approach to the area of overhead expenses for operating control in production, we find that there are three important technical measures of variation from budgeted overhead based on standard rates and allotments to departments. They are:

1. overhead-spending variance,
2. overhead-efficiency variance, and
3. overhead-volume variance.

Volume variance is the only one of the measures that occurs in reference to fixed overhead but never in reference to the indirect cost items that are variable with increases or decreases in physical volume of product output. The spending and efficiency variances from standard are essentially properties of variable overhead and will be taken up more specifically in chapter 4 on direct-costing systems. Only the spending variance will appear later in this chapter in our discussion of plant service departments. Our purpose in using this order is that the primary consideration in an absorption system is the treatment of fixed overhead for product costing and for control.

How may we describe a volume variance from an established norm or standard of activity? This measure of variation occurs because the level of production for a specific period and expressed as standard hours allowed for the actual volume of production frequently does not coincide with the normal or expected activity level. The latter measure is used as the basis for planning production schedules and for selecting a predetermined product-costing rate for fixed plant overhead, as we have seen. Normal capacity is simply the expected average utilization of capacity for a period of time exceeding one year of operations. In our illustrations on analysis of the results of operations for control, we will use the capacity utilization figures, which we derived previously for product costing.

We may also state our case in this way: The volume variance for fixed overhead in production occurs because of the difference that exists between our applications of absorption accounting for the costing of units of product by means of the predetermined rates and the use of this same system for control of operations through budgets. Perhaps the most important point to understand here is that volume variance will occur in analyzing the results of operations for control because the actual level of activity often does not coincide with projected normal volume of capacity utilization. In addition, our measure of fixed charges for the period we are evaluating in a given department is the same in either case.

Let us now see how the preceding concept might be applied in practice. In our illustration, we will assume that plant 1 of the Dynamic Power Tool Corporation is operating with the same three-year projections of scheduled production for each product line (MT1, MT2, and MT3) and the same capacity utilization percentages we had previously (cf. table 3-3). Further, figures 3-1 to 3-4 pertain to the month of February for the first year in the intermediate-range projection period. *Remember:* Our present concern is the treatment of fixed overhead for control of departmental operations under an absorption system, not the determination of product costs and valuation of finished-goods inventories.

The volume variance is a concept that has caused confusion among both professionals and laymen as it applies in an absorption-costing system. It simply means that a given department operated for the period of measurement at a level of output based on standard hours that was different from normal use of

---

Department: Processing and Machining

Period: February
Measurement Base:
    Direct Labor Hours

Normal Capacity Utilization:
    MT1: 5,750 DLH[a]
    MT2: 2,500 DLH
    MT3: 2,813 DLH

Labor and Parts Standards

Standard materials: $1.70 per unit of MT1
                      2.25 per unit of MT2
                      1.50 per unit of MT3

Standard labor time: 30 minutes per unit of MT1
                      20 minutes per unit of MT2
                      40 minutes per unit of MT3

Standard labor rate (one grade): $2.05 per labor hour

[a]You will recall that our standard man-hours (cf. table 3-14) were 690,000 for MT1 in the first year. One twelfth of this figure would be 57,500 DLH. For purposes of simplification, we have converted this unit to a 1:10 ratio.

Figure 3-1. Dynamic Corporation Departmental Standards Summary

	Rate Per Direct Labor Hour	Fixed Budget Per Month
Supervision	0	$ 925
Other indirect labor	0.15	0
Set-up	0.12	0
Operating materials	0.27	0
Materials handling	0.05	310
Maintenance supplies	0.13	142
Scrap and rejects	0.07	0
Property taxes	0	875
Utilities	0.12	0
Depreciation	0	1,667
Department overhead budget	$0.91	$3,919
Fixed overhead allocated to MT1	0	$ 558
Totals	$0.91	$4,477

Figure 3-2. Variable and Fixed Budget Standards for Overhead Expenses

capacity for that period. Perhaps the easiest way to look at it is this: Fixed costs do not change, and the volume variance arises because the actual production measured in standard hours allowed either exceeded or fell short of the standard hours for normal production volume. Since the latter measure was used for applying fixed overhead in product costing, the volume variance tells us that we have underapplied or overapplied the constant overhead amount.

When production volume is less than projected utilization of capacity for the period, we have an "unfavorable" volume variance because department activity is below the normal or standard volume. This is the situation in our illustration here. Had actual volume exceeded the projected or normal volume, we would have applied more fixed overhead to product than we should have. However, in this case, we would say that department performance for the period

Variable rate per budget	$0.9100
Fixed rate for processing and machining department ($3,919 ÷ 5,750 DLH)	0.0970
Fixed rate for allocation to product MT1 ($558 ÷ 5,750 DLH)	0.3236
	$1.3306

Figure 3-3. Standard Overhead Rates for MT1 in Machining Department Based on Normal Use of Capacity (5,750 DLH)

Department :   Processing and   Period : February
                 Machining

Operating Data for February :

Production :   9,200 units of MT1
              7,500 units of MT2
              6,000 units of MT3

Actual labor hours :   5,200 DLH for MT1
                     2,700 DLH for MT2
                     3,000 DLH for MT3

Actual cost of materials used (MT1) $16,600

Actual overhead expenses :
   Machining department $ 9,125
   Allocated to MT1   558

Volume variance :

= Absorbed at standard overhead rate — overhead
   budget for standard hours allowed for production

= (Standard hours allowed × total overhead rate) —
   (standard hours allowed × variable overhead rate +
   fixed overhead)

= (4,600 DLH × $1.33) — (4,600 DLH × $0.91 + $4,477)

= ($6,118) — ($4,186 + $4,477)

= ($2,545)

Note: 4,600 standard DLH allowed is simply the units of MT1 produced times the hourly rate per unit (9,200 × 30 minutes).

Figure 3-4. Dynamic Corporation Departmental Operations Summary

was favorable because actual production achieved would have exceeded the normal capacity utilization level. There is no volume variance when standard hours for normal use of capacity and standard hours for actual production for the period are the same. This overhead-variance measure causes another problem for us, that is, it is rarely one which is controllable at the department level because most fixed costs cannot be altered by any decision on the part of department supervisors or managers and therefore cannot be the responsibility of the department (cf. pp. 69-70).

Variable overhead as well as direct labor and materials, which we call "prime product costs," not only fluctuate in amounts as production volume changes but in addition, most of these costs can be controlled at the department level. (These topics will be taken up in chapter 4 and in part II.)

One area remains to be considered in absorption costing for control of production-department operations before moving on to direct standard costing systems. Service departments provide an auxiliary function to producing units in the plant. These services include routine maintenance and repair work on production machinery and equipment, as well as professional engineering and technical advisory services that are not organizationally assigned to a line production department. The following statements will generally apply to plant service departments for companies using an absorption-accounting system.

1. The costs of any services provided by an auxiliary department in the plant to one of the producing units are allocated directly to that unit.
2. Expense charges for most of these services provided to a producing unit will become a part of the latter department's common overhead to be absorbed by product lines.
3. Conceptual and technical aspects of financial control of operations in service departments are essentially the same as they are for line operating departments with the major exception that the latter do not have "units of product" since they deal in services. Thus standards can be set for hourly labor rates based on professional salary levels and wage rates for other employees by grade. Budgets based on these standards can be developed directly from the scheduled volumes of the production departments, which in turn determine the materials-usage levels and work loads for service employees for a particular period of plant operations.
4. Financial control of service-department operations will usually involve determination of spending and volume variances when comparisons are made between budgets and actual results of service activities at the end of the month or quarter.

Figure 3-5 provides information for service department A of the Dynamic Corporation for February.

Most manufacturing companies will experience any one of three possible situations in cost behavior for plant service departments:

1. All major classifications of service costs for a particular period are fixed while variable-cost items are not material.
2. Major classifications of service costs are semifixed or fixed while variable costs are not material or there are no variable costs.
3. Both variable and fixed account items are material.

The first situation is the least frequently encountered while the third situation will be experienced by most companies. Using the data presented in figure 3-5 for service department A, we will examine each of these possibilities.

Situation 1. Service departments with predominantly fixed costs would have to be considered the exception rather than the rule for the majority of plant operations in manufacturing companies. These organizational units usually provide professional and staff services where the staff organization of personnel is fairly permanent. Significant operating costs and expenses for these units are

```
┌─────────────────────────────────────────────────────────────────┐
│ Department:  Service, A                        Period:  February  │
│                                                                   │
│ Operating standards                                               │
│   Labor:                                                          │
│     Variable:    $2.40 per machining-department labor hour        │
│     Fixed:       Professional    $2,950                           │
│                  Supervision     $1,300                           │
│                                                                   │
│ Standard hours per month                                          │
│    (service to machining department)           $1,400             │
│                                                                   │
│ Actual labor hours                                                │
│    (service to machining department)           $1,300             │
│                                                                   │
│ Actual service department A labor                                 │
│    expenses for February                       $7,580             │
└─────────────────────────────────────────────────────────────────┘
```

Figure 3-5. Dynamic Corporation Service Department Standards

the salaries of professional employees. Monthly and quarterly charges in constant amounts can be allocated to each production department on a prorata-use basis and included as part of departmental overhead to be absorbed by product lines.

Note that there is no volume variance for these operating units when budgeted service expenses are based on actual hours of production for an operating period. This circumstance exists because the budget will then be equal to the total amount allocated to the line operating departments. The two measures are one and the same. There will be a spending variance for any difference between the actual expenses incurred for the service unit at the end of the period and the budget based on actual hours (cf. chapter 4, pp. 88-89).

Although variable costs are minor relative to fixed costs, it is best to establish a variable rate for these costs, and fixed amounts can be assigned to the machining department considering the relative permanency or stability of these costs. The variable rate is $2.40 per labor hour. Then allocation of the expenses of service department A to the machining department for February would be:

Actual production hours × variable-cost rate + fixed amount for the period

$$(1,300 \text{ hours} \times \$2.40) + \$4,250 = \$3,120 + \$4,250 = \$7,370$$

Spending Variance:

Actual expense − budget for actual production hours

$$= \$7,580 - (1,300 \text{ hours} \times \$2.40 + \$4,250)$$

$$= \$7,580 - \$7,370 = \$210U[1]$$

For control, this spending variance is unfavorable since it exceeded the budget for services provided to the line departments based on actual production hours.

Volume Variance:

Budget for actual production hours — allocation to production departments

$$= (1,300 \text{ hours} \times \$2.40 + \$4,250) - (\$7,370, \text{ as above})$$

$$= 0$$

Situation 2. This situation exists for those service departments in which organizational staff assignments are not permanent. Labor and supervision charges will still be based mostly on salary levels rather than hourly rates, and these charges will not be essentially different as a result of production-volume variations. Such costs are semifixed, and they will vary only when there is a change in the number of employees assigned to the service unit at a given salary level or when a salary level itself changes. In determining production-department allocations for a particular month or quarter and in measuring variances for control of service operations, we will examine two approaches:

a.   Total allocation to producing departments is treated as a fixed amount for the period.
b.   Total allocation to the producing departments is treated as a rate based on the constant service charges and on standard hours for production rather than on actual production hours for the month or quarter.

Here we have two different ways to handle the same amounts of costs and expenses for the service unit, and we assume there are no variable costs. In (a) we simply assign the same fixed amount to each production department prorata in each measurement and reporting period. These charges can then be included in common overhead of the production units. The only variance for control for which the service department need prepare a calculation is the spending variance (cf. p. 75):

$$\$7,580 - \$4,250 = \$3,330U$$

Note that there is no variable rate because there are now no hourly wages in service department A. Suppose professional salaries increased at the beginning of February by $790 and supervision increased by $580 with actual expenses remaining the same. The spending variance would then be:

$$\$7,580 - (\$4,250 + \$1,370) = \$1,960U$$

Alternative (b) converts the fixed amounts to a rate in allocating these costs to line departments prorata. In doing so, determination of the rate has to be based on standard hours of service to each production department so that the rate will remain constant from one period to the next. The rate for fixed costs (all labor in this instance) is determined as follows:

Fixed-cost rate = fixed costs ÷ standard production hours

= \$4,250 ÷ 1,400 hours = \$3.036

Then the allocation of the costs of service department A to the machining department for February would be:

1,300 hours $\times$ \$3.036 = \$3,947

Spending Variance:

Actual expense − budget for actual production hours

= \$7,580 − \$3,947 = \$3,633U

Volume Variance:

Budget for actual production hours − allocation to production departments

(1,300 hours $\times$ \$3.036) − \$3,947 = \$3,947 − \$3,947 = 0

Situation 3. This is the most frequently encountered cost pattern for plant service departments of manufacturing companies. Nonprofessional employees including service maintenance and repair personnel will have hourly wage rates, and service supplies and materials will likewise vary with the output of the line departments. All these items can be treated as a variable rate applied to actual production hours, or actual units of production in the case of service supplies and materials. We will assume the information for service department A as shown in figure 3-6.

For service supplies and materials, the allocation to the machining department would simply be the standard volume for MT1 at \$1.90 per unit, or \$15,042. The actual expense for February was \$15,472.

Materials-use Variance

Actual expense − materials allocation to production departments

= \$15,472 − \$15,042 = \$430U

```
Department: Service, A                          Period: February

Operating standards

   Supplies and Materials:        $1.90 per unit of MT1 in the Machining Department.
                                  7,917 standard units of MT1 per month
                                  (machining-department standard output).
                                  Materials expense for February $15,572.

   Labor:
     Variable:    $2.40 per machining-department labor hour
     Fixed:     Professional      $2,950
                Supervision       $1,300

   Standard hours per month
     (service to machining department)            $1,400

   Actual labor hours
     (service to machining department)            $1,300

   Actual service department A labor
     expenses for February                        $7,580
```

Figure 3-6. Dynamic Corporation Departmental Standards Summary

The labor allocations to the machining department may be handled best by using a rate for both variable and fixed amounts. In establishing a variable rate for fixed labor costs, the rate must be based on standard production hours for service to the machining department for February so that this rate will be constant in successive periods. The variable rate is $2.40 per labor hour as in our previous examples, and you will recall that we had determined the fixed labor rate to be $3.036 (p. 77). Keep in mind that this fixed labor rate is only for allocation of expenses to line departments for services performed, not for control and evaluation of service-department operations. The allocation of the labor charges to the machining department for February can now be made:

Actual production hours × variable-cost rate + actual production hours × fixed-cost rate based on standard production hours

= (1,300 hours × $2.40) + (1,300 hours × $3.036)

= $3,120 + $3,947 = $7,067

We will determine budget variances for service-department operating control as we did in our previous examples, and this time we will have both spending and volume variances for control of operations in service department A.

Spending Variance:

Actual expense — budget for actual production hours

= $7,580 − (1,300 hours × $2.40 + $4,250)

= $7,580 − $7,370 = $210U

Volume Variance

Budget for actual production hours — allocation to production departments

= (1,300 hours × $2.40 + $4,250) − $7,067 = $7,370 − $7,067

= $303U

Here we have a volume variance because service hours were 1,300 during February while standard service hours for product MT1 per month are 1,400 for services to the machining department or 100 hours less than normal monthly service and our fixed rate was based on standard hours. Thus

1,400 − 1,300 = 100 × $3.036 = $303U

Again the volume variance accounts for the difference between actual and standard levels of activity; in this case, the activity is hours of service to a line department.

In this chapter we have discussed the development of an absorption- (often called "full-allocation") costing system for production operations as it may apply to the two most significant areas of use. These areas are the determination of product-line costs for inventory valuation or for product market pricing and the development of operating control measures for fixed plant overhead expenses. We have seen that in the first area of application, absorption methods for cost determination can involve elaborate and expensive procedures for assigning both departmental and common plant overhead to units of each product line. This is particularly true for manufacturers that have included such procedures as part of their formal bookkeeping system for production-department operations.

From the standpoint of developing measures for the control of activities within production departments, we have seen that there is very little a department manager can do to "control" the expenses of significant fixed-overhead items whether they originate within the operations of his department or are common to the plant. We will return to this point again in part II, chapter 8. Based on the foregoing presentation, it should be evident that items of fixed overhead such as depreciation on plant buildings or production machinery and equipment can involve complex allocation procedures in assigning them to units of each product line in conversion.

Furthermore, these expenses are often highly significant in terms of the dollar amounts charged to a period of production activity, and at the same time they are beyond the decision-making influence of the department manager. They arise as the result of top-management financial planning and long-term investment in plant equipment and facilities. The subsequent expense charges based on the investment cost of acquiring these assets are really predetermined from the standpoint of their assignment to any period of production operations or to an organizational unit within the plant. Assignment of amounts of these expenses is made on the basis of depreciation schedules drawn up for the total number of years or time periods of useful life that such assets provide productive services to the company.

An absorption or full-allocation system then is one that provides for the assignment of fixed (or nonvariable) costs and expenses to units within each product line over and above the direct variable production expenses for determination of unit cost of manufacturing and the valuation of inventories of finished products. In our discussion of measurements for control, we have seen how volume variances are the result of differences between normal or standard output levels and actual production volume for a particular period and how they provide little information that will enable managers to exercise operating control over cost items that are constant and beyond decision-making influence at the plant department level.

Note

1. The letter U appears for each formula illustration that results in a negative or unfavorable variance in this chapter and in chapters 4 and 5.

4 Direct Standard Costing for Production

Chapter 3 discussed the development and applications of absorption costing for plant operations, focusing on establishing a system for assigning fixed-overhead expenses to physical units of product as well as developing appropriate control measures for fixed overhead. Chapter 4 addresses the same objectives—namely, product costing and measures for control of production activities—but with respect to direct and variable production expenses. In doing so, we will consider two broad account classifications. The first classification includes direct materials and labor that are traceable to specific product lines in the sense that these items result from the production-conversion process and would not exist otherwise. The second classification is variable overhead, which includes production-department expenses that vary with the level of physical production volume but are indirect in the sense that they are not traceable to individual product lines in the conversion process.

As before, the general plant organization comprises the following three department classifications:

1. production or operating departments,
2. service departments, and
3. administrative and staff departments related to production.

Chapter 2 stated that the primary role of these departments is to convert raw materials and component parts into finished goods for sale to customers. That chapter used hypothetical examples of three organizational units alternately referred to as "cost centers" and "responsibility centers." They were:

a. The materials-processing department where basic raw materials that are purchased from outside suppliers undergo additional processing such as casting or machining before they are ready for assembly. Processing operations are determined either by specification in accordance with individual customer order or in accordance with engineering specifications for mass-produced product lines.
b. The assembling department where various component parts are assembled into finished product as in the manufacturing of machine tools or automobiles.
c. The finishing department, which might include such operating activities as polishing, varnishing, and inspecting, or performing test runs to ensure that performance specifications for the final product are met.

Generally, the level of expenditures for materials and labor in the operating departments is influenced by the volume of production in these departments for any given time period of operations.

Service departments are those that perform auxiliary functions for the operating departments such as maintenance and repair of equipment and facilities in the production departments. The level of expenditures for service activities also varies with production volume, although certain cost items such as the department supervisor's salary would tend to be constant for monthly or quarterly reporting periods.

Administrative or staff departments in the factory or plant incur costs in connection with running the plant manager's office. The incurrence of these costs represents a general administrative and supervisory function for all factory operations, and they tend to be constant with respect to unit volume of production for any time period within the planning year. These costs would include the salaries of the plant manager and his assistants as well as depreciation on office equipment.

Chapter 3 discussed common factory costs and expenses as a subtopic of absorption costing. You will recall that this classification of plant expenses includes general factory depreciation and property taxes or rent. These costs can always be allocated to departments on some equitable basis such as square footage of floor space occupied by each department for allocating depreciation or some equitable measure of benefits received for general services that are provided to all departments such as the services provided by factory personnel management. You will also recall that the allocations of these general expenses does not make them controllable within any operating department to which they are allocated.

Chapter 2 discussed fundamental procedures for costing products under direct costing. In ordinary financial accounting, the ultimate purpose of product costing is inventory valuation and periodic income determination. In this way, product costing relates to the financial statements or end-of-period balance sheet and income statement. This approach is viewed from a financial accounting standpoint, and the costs assigned to each unit of product representing the cost of all operating activities in the factory will be multiplied by the volume of production in units to determine the value of Finished-goods Inventory on the balance sheet. And in that period when units of the final product are sold, this per-unit product cost multiplied by the number of units sold will determine the valuation of Cost of Goods Sold and consequently the value of gross profit.

We also stated earlier that in the plant-conversion process, each department will accumulate both direct costs and overhead costs. We said that the primary components are prime costs or direct materials and direct labor. They are also traceable in the sense that they can be directly traced to or identified with the physical production of the product. Another important characteristic is that these costs are variable, meaning that they will fluctuate in proportion to changes in physical volume of production over time.

It is most important to keep in mind both the meaning of a term such as "direct cost" and the use or purpose of the particular operating cost input as it has been defined. If we consider that our purpose is the assignment of cost in production to product to obtain a valuation of finished-goods inventory, then the term "direct cost" refers to prime costs of materials and labor. Prime costs are always traceable to units of product in conversion. For this reason, they will also always be variable with changes in volume of production for any period of consecutive months or quarters of operation.

Under direct costing of products for purposes of inventory valuation and as these values consequently affect the value of gross profit and net income, all variable prime costs are assigned to physical units of product as they are passed along from one department to another in the plant. The reasoning here is that the level of variable costs is determined by the level of production volume. Thus for product-costing purposes (and only for product costing), we consider direct costs to mean the same thing as variable costs.

Direct costing of finished-goods inventory represents the accumulation of direct materials and direct labor (or prime costs) as a minimum. Furthermore, the question will always arise as to whether those items of overhead that are not prime or traceable to physical units in conversion but that are variable in proportion to changes in physical volume of production should be inventoried. It is our view that there is no clear rationale or guideline on this issue. It is true that in most production situations the allocation of variable rates to product lines for indirect labor and materials may be difficult and simply not worth the additional effort for this purpose. For our illustrations, we have elected to use prime rates for purposes of product costing and inventory valuation.

Direct materials, direct labor, and variable overhead are accumulated in each department or cost center. Since the variable costs of production will fluctuate in direct proportion to changes in production volume, a standard variable rate per unit produced may be determined for each variable cost item in each department. This procedure is followed regardless of whether a prime rate or total variable rate is used for valuation of inventories. Then as the product passes along from one department to another, the variable rate per unit is multiplied by the quantity of product for which each department has completed its operations. In other words, the direct cost of finished-goods inventory is simply the sum of the variable rates (prime or total variable) per unit for all departments multiplied by the quantity of products produced for each product or product line.

In recent decades there have been numerous corporate management groups and members of the controllership profession who persistently advocate absorption or full-allocation costing. These advocates have felt that direct costing will always result in understatement of the value of finished-goods inventories as well as an erroneously inflated gross profit figure on the income statement. It is true that inventories will have a consistently lower value for companies that adopt a direct cost system for product-costing purposes. However, it is really only the gross-profit figure that is affected in this way under a direct product-cost system. Since fixed costs are not allocated to (absorbed by) product lines, they must then appear as an operating expense on the company's periodic income statement. Therefore there will be no material impact on net earnings simply because the company elected to change from a full product-cost to a direct product-cost system. The important criterion in making a choice between the two systems is whether the overall advantages of simplification and applications of direct costing outweigh the more cumbersome and expensive aspects of maintaining an absorption system. We will return to this point toward the end of the chapter.

The second important application of direct costing is for control and evaluation of production operations. The term "direct cost" is used somewhat differently for control than for product costing because costs are now associated specifically with departments or responsibility centers, rather than products. Direct costs for control of departmental operations would always include all materials, labor, and variable overhead costs that arise in each department (or are traceable to a particular department).

This distinction is a most important one not only by way of definition but further by cost classifications included under the alternative definitions. Choosing the right definition as well as that set of input classifications appropriate to the definition will make an important and material difference in the dollars involved for either valuation of inventories or for management control of a department or responsibility center. For control purposes, it is appropriate that cost standards be developed for all variable costs and for all fixed costs that are directly related to each department.

For variable costs, variances from standard include two segments: a spending segment and an efficiency segment.

Variable Materials

a. A variance from standard due to the prices paid for materials is termed the "spending variance."
b. A variance from standard due to the quantity of materials used is termed the "efficiency" or "quantity variance."

Variable Labor

a. A labor-rate variance for the difference between the standard labor rate and the actual wage rate paid is termed the "labor-spending variance."
b. A labor time or use variance representing the difference between the standard hours allowed at the actual volume of production and the actual hours worked is termed the "labor-efficiency variance."

For fixed-overhead costs, as in chapter 3, the overhead volume variance arises as the result of utilizing an amount of plant facilities that differs from the budgeted amount for a given level of scheduled production volume. It is never applicable in a direct-costing system. The concept and measurement of a fixed-cost volume variance arises only under absorption costing. The costs involved represent what we call "non-cash" or "non-working-capital book costs" for current use of operating facilities for which capital-investment outlays were made in some prior years. The overhead-spending variance, on the other hand, may be applicable to control of certain fixed costs under a direct-costing system because such fixed costs represent the use of a company's funds or working capital during that period for which we are measuring and evaluating operating performance.

At this point, let us resume our illustration of plant operations for the Dynamic Power Tool Corporation. We must bear in mind that our concern in this example will be direct-costing measures for performance appraisal and control of operations rather than for product costing and inventory valuation. We will consider the processing and machining department in the plant, and figures 4-1 to 4-2 are the summarization schedules for activities during the month of February.

These summary schedules for standards and for operations during February will enable us to analyze the departmental direct variable cost variances from standard for labor and materials as well as variances for overhead.

Direct Labor Variances

Rate variance = budget for actual hours worked − actual labor cost

$$= \$10{,}660 - \$10{,}720 = \$60U$$
$$[\,\$2.05 \times 5{,}200 \text{ DLH}\,]$$

We have determined that the labor-rate variance in the machining department was over budget by $60. Why did we determine the labor-rate variance based on the budget for actual hours rather than for standard hours allowed for the actual production volume during February? The reason is simply that we are concerned with either hourly rates paid to workers or with grades of labor used that are different from specifications for standard labor rates or grades for any given operating activity. In doing so, it is necessary to hold labor hours constant at the actual hours used for the production period in question. In this case the budget for actual hours worked would be the standard rate of $2.05 applied to the actual hours worked, which is 5,200 DLH.

Quantity or Efficiency Variance

Budget for standard hours allowed at actual production volume − budget for actual hours worked

$$= \$9{,}430 - \$10{,}660 = \$1{,}230U$$
$$[\,\$2.05 \times 4{,}600 \text{ DLH}\,] - [\,\$2.05 \times 5{,}200 \text{ DLH}\,]$$

```
Department: Processing and Machining      Period: February

                                          Measurement Base: Direct labor hours

                                          Normal Capacity Utilization:
                                                  MT1: 5,750 DLH
                                                  MT2: 2,500 DLH
                                                  MT3: 2,813 DLH


Labor and Parts Standards
  Standard materials:   $1.70 per unit of MT1
                        $2.25 per unit of MT2
                        $1.50 per unit of MT3

  Standard labor time: 30 minutes per unit of MT1
                       20 minutes per unit of MT2
                       40 minutes per unit of MT3

  Standard labor rate (one grade):  $2.05 per labor hour

Variable rate and fixed budget standards for overhead expenses:
```

	Rate Per Direct Labor Hour	Fixed Budget Per Month
Supervision	0	$ 925
Other indirect labor	0.15	0
Set-up	0.12	0
Operating materials	0.27	0
Materials handling	0.05	310
Maintenance supplies	0.13	142
Scrap and rejects	0.07	0
Property taxes	0	875
Utilities	0.12	0
Depreciation	0	1,667
Department Overhead Budget	$0.91	$3,919

```
Standard product costs (MT1)
  Materials (prime)      $1.70
  Direct labor (prime)    1.025
  Variable overhead       0.455
                         $3.180
```

Figure 4-1. Dynamic Corporation Departmental Standards Summary

The labor-efficiency variance tells us that we accumulated more actual hours worked in the machining department for the month than the standard hours budgeted at the actual volume of output or 5,200 DLH. In doing so, it was necessary to hold the pay rate constant at $2.05, which is the standard rate for the grade of labor specified. In other words, we are comparing the difference between actual hours worked and standard hours allowed *at actual production volume.* These results show an efficiency overrun of 600 DLH. The 4,600

Department: Processing and machining   Period: February

Production: 9,200 units of MT1
            7,500 units of MT2
            6,000 units of MT3

Actual labor hours: 5,200 DLH for MT1
                    2,700 DLH for MT2
                    3,000 DLH for MT3

Actual cost of materials used *(MT1)* $16,600
  Direct labor cost *(MT1)* $9,260
  Actual overhead expenses $9,125

Summary of direct labor variances:

	Rate	Efficiency
Budget for standard hours		$ 9,430
Budget for actual hours	$10,660	10,660
Actual labor cost	10,720	
	$60	$ 1,230

Summary of overhead expense variances:

	Spending	Efficiency
Budget for standard hours[a]		$8,105
Budget for actual hours[b]	$8,651	8,651
Actual overhead expense	9,125	
	$474U	$546U

[a]4,600 hours @ $0.91.
[b]5,200 hours @ $0.91.

Figure 4-2. Dynamic Corporation Departmental Operations Summary

standard hours allowed for actual volume achieved is easily obtained. For product MT1, 9,200 units were produced for the month, and standard time for the appropriate direct labor grade is 30 minutes.

Direct Materials Variances

Quantity or efficiency variance = cost of materials used
— budget for materials at actual volume of production

= $16,600 — $15,640 = $960U

[$1.70 × 9,200 units]

The materials efficiency or quantity variance accounts for the difference between the cost of materials for product MT1 and the standard or budgeted quantity for the actual volume of output for the month. In determining the efficiency or use variance, we are saying, "how much material input should we have used based on standard quantity allowances and how much did we use?" The price factor is held constant at the standard price.

Although our variance analyses for materials and labor are intended to be used for controlling production activities in the plant in our examples here, we have presented this information in the schedules for each product line. You will recall that prime costs are used for both product costing and ultimately for valuation of finished-goods inventory as well as for management control purposes. It is for this reason that we have presented direct materials and direct labor by individual product lines. While the analyses in this illustration pertain only to product line MT1, the same calculations would be prepared for each of the other product lines.

Examining the budget schedule for overhead expenses, we see that standard variable rates have been prepared for each of the indirect labor, operating materials, utilities, and maintenance accounts. These items are direct to the department's operations for control purposes but are common in terms of the product lines. Supervision, property taxes, and depreciation do not have rates since these expense items do not change in amount with fluctuations in production output.

Conversely, overhead items such as operating materials, scrap and rejects, or utilities, while indirect to product lines, are all variable, and no fixed or constant amounts of expense are applicable to these items. Materials handling and maintenance supplies have both rate and amount figures, which means that they are semivariable (or semifixed). The variable overhead expenses are preset on the basis of annual estimates of production volume and are converted to rates based on annual estimates of man-hours of labor.

Since these fixed rates for variable overhead are based on production projections or forecasts, they are in fact annualized averages set in terms of a per-DLH rate since direct labor hours represent a common variable input for the department. In setting rates for each item of variable overhead, it is a good rule of thumb to use a production-input factor (such as direct labor, materials) or estimated units of product to be worked on which can best satisfy two criteria:

1. an input factor that most closely varies with changes in production volume, and
2. one that is most "common" to all activities and product lines pertaining to the particular department in question.

The information on the schedule quickly tells us that the sum of all variable rates for overhead items is $0.91 per DLH. The two calculations that concern us are the overhead-spending variance (first encountered in chapter 3) and what we call the "overhead-efficiency variance."

Overhead-spending variance = budget for actual hours worked
— actual overhead expense

$$= \$8,651 - \$9,125 = \$474U$$

$$[\$0.91 \times 5,200 \text{ DLH} = \$4,732 + \$3,919]$$

The term "spending variance" means just what it says, although the formula contains two segments. The fixed segment of $3,919 is simply a one-month share of the machining department's fixed overhead. The variable component is $0.91 per direct labor hour multiplied by the actual labor hours worked or 5,200 DLH. The total budget then is $8,651 while the total actual overhead was $9,125 for February. The overhead out-of-pocket expenditures for the department exceeded the budget by $474. The spending variance may be partly variable and partly fixed but will always be a cash or working-capital variance. This is a most important point to understand.

A word of caution regarding the spending variance is in order. Most companies will find that the majority of items and their amounts that are to be included in the spending-variance increment will be variable overhead. Those items that are essentially fixed will not ordinarily include depreciation for equipment and facilities in either the operating or service departments. Depreciable assets are a part of long-term planned capital investment, and depreciation "costs" are allocated over the projected number of years of service life of these facilities. A general rule of thumb for selecting fixed-overhead items to be included as a part of the spending-variance calculation is this:

If the expenditure for the asset is provided for out of the company's current working capital within the same time period for which the spending variance is measured and the services provided by the asset are "used up" within that period, then the portion over standard based on budgeted amounts can be properly considered a part of the spending-variance increment.

Fixed-overhead items that are generally eligible for inclusion in a periodic spending-variance calculation for control might include any unplanned property-tax or insurance increases and salaries for production or service-department supervision that exceed the budgeted amount for the period, based on standard time and wage rates for supervisors in that department. In our illustration, materials handling and maintenance supplies included monthly fixed budgeted amounts, and any working-capital expenditures in excess of these amounts would be considered part of the departmental spending-variance calculation for the month.

Based on the information in the preceding illustration, we would obtain the overhead-efficiency variance as follows:

Overhead-efficiency variance = budget for standard hours allowed
at actual volume — budget for actual hours worked

= \$8,105 — \$8,651 = \$546 U

[\$0.91 × 4,600 DLH = \$4,186 + \$3,919]

The efficiency or use variance will always apply to the variable segment of overhead expenses. In this illustration, the variable rate is based on hours of direct labor that was 600 hours in excess of the standard hours allowed for the actual volume of MT1 produced in the machining department.

We have now presented two alternative approaches to internal cost systems for plant operations—namely, the absorption or full-allocation approach and the direct-costing approach. In formal record keeping for production activities, a direct cost system values work-in-process and finished-goods inventories on the company's balance sheet at variable costs only while fixed expenses are treated as period charges to the quarterly income statement. In concept, the variable items and particularly prime costs really represent the expenditures for production operations per se, while nonvariable or constant costs such as plant depreciation and property taxes are the "capitalized investment" for production rather than the costs of doing business, that is, producing goods or services for a particular period of time.

For control of operations in the plant, a direct costing system will provide for all the important measures of variation from operating budgets based on standard costs. Variations from standard performance of all activities that incur variable and out-of-pocket expenses in both producing and service departments are provided for, and these are the items of expenditure that are subject to decision-making influence by middle management at the line operating or service-department level. Volume variance is the only important performance measure that is unique to an absorption system, and as we have seen, this is not really a measure of cost variation, nor is it one that is controllable by line managers.

We have not yet approached the subject of using the measures developed in chapters 3 and 4 for appraising performance in the plant departments or for evaluating incremental contributions of departmental operations to overall company profitability for a particular reporting period. These important applications of the performance measures we have developed thus far will be taken up in part II.

5 Revenues, Costs, and the Preparation of Performance Standards and Measurements for Marketing

We will introduce the subject of performance measures for the marketing function by way of some pertinent statements about product market planning. Our reason for doing so is that many companies view the planning for company operations as originating in marketing and believe that planning and scheduling for volume and operating levels in production and control of inventory levels must follow. Hence production planning is based on the planning for sales volume levels and operations undertaken by marketing management.

For both manufacturing firms and other types of profit-oriented organizations that provide services rather than physical products to external markets, the planning of operating activities may be defined as encompassing two main types: project planning and period planning. We will consider project planning to include a specific set of work-completion objectives and a set of operating-activity specifications to meet those objectives. The project plan then is an independent and self-contained package.

Top management may look on project planning as being auxiliary to period planning. Examples might include industrial-engineering studies intended to improve the efficiency of parts-assembling activities in the plant, research and development to expand an existing product line, or pilot projects to explore the technical feasibility of manufacturing entirely new products. In the marketing area, economic and psychological studies of market potential, penetration, and field market-acceptance testing among consumers would also come under the general heading of project planning. Each project plan would include estimates of returns or benefits that the company would derive from achieving the stated objectives together with estimates of the financial capital investment or cash flow required to sustain the project for the length of its life. Top management would then review the proposed projects and their rankings in a hierarchy of priorities. Selection among competing projects would be made on the basis of the rankings and capital requirements in relation to the financial resources available that can feasibly be committed to projects. The development of zero-base analysis and budgeting is fairly recent. Although this subject is beyond the scope of our presentations in this book, these methods are particularly suited to company project-planning efforts. The reader is encouraged to examine the current articles and books dealing with zero-base analysis.

While the project-planning package is task oriented and the length cf time required from start-up to completion may vary considerably among competing packages, period planning is distinctly time oriented in accordance with its name. This area of planning deals with the company's normal and on-going operations involving those product lines that have gained acceptance by top management based on market performance and the flow of activities surrounding these products in production, marketing, and administration. In this sector of operations, our thinking is not addressed to self-contained tasks, their resource requirements, and the effectiveness of their implementation, nor is it addressed to weighing the relative merits of task-oriented costs and benefits. Rather, we think in terms of the flow of goods through the functional-area operations of production and marketing. In recent years we have viewed the planning phases of "period planning" as beginning with quantitative forecasts of market demand for a company's products for future and specific time periods. Based on the forecast, quarterly production schedules are drawn up, inventory levels are estimated for the same time segments, procurement plans and schedules are prepared, and marketing operations are blueprinted. Budgets are then prepared in accordance with resource requirements necessary to meet the operating assignments and schedules in each functional area.

When budgets have been approved by top management and operations are under way, the measurement of performance comes into play. Sales results are measured against market forecasts, production turn-out is measured against scheduled quantities, and operating costs are analyzed in comparison to the budgeted amounts for organizational departments within the functional areas. Furthermore, performance by functional areas and by organizational responsibility centers is measured in terms of the contributions that these units make toward the earning of a profit for the company as a whole. This concept is by no means new although it is vital to management's evaluations of the financial performance of units within the company for specific past periods of time, and it is a concept that is central to the material presented in part II.

Period planning and particularly the analysis and appraisal of the results of operations based on plans for specific periods of time are at the core of our discussions in this book. Project planning and its orientation to task goals and assignments will be taken up in specific areas where its application is appropriate, particularly in the function of administration.

Period planning then we will define as the planning of all production and marketing activities or operations to be undertaken for a specific future period of time. Usually this time period is the fiscal year, although evaluation and revision of forecasts and plans can be undertaken at shorter interim periods. Since period planning for quantitative sales targets or quotas, production-volume schedules, and inventory levels are based on a forecast of sales volume for each product line, cost standards can be applied to these projections quite effectively to prepare forecast budgets for marketing and for production. The forecast budget for production would be drawn up by applying rate and quantity standards for materials, labor, and other conversion inputs to the forecast sales volume adjusted for beginning and end of period-planned levels of inventories.

In the marketing area, similar procedures can be applied in preparing the forecast budget once standards have been developed for the marketing function. What types of standards are appropriate to marketing operations? We may group standards according to these main classifications:

1. Standards for product-line selling prices
2. Standards for revenues
3. Standards for costs and expenses relating to field sales operations and sales-promotion activities

Standards for Selling Prices

In establishing standards for selling prices, the relationship between sales price and sales volume is important because the interaction of price and volume can generate different levels of revenue for a specific time period. This is what is referred to by economists as the "price elasticity of demand." As a practical illustration of this economic concept, a price reduction would tend to have the effect of increasing volume and market share whereas a price increase would tend to reduce volume and market share. Obtaining enough field market data to gain a knowledge of the different levels of sales volume that would result at different prices for a product line may not be practically feasible without extensive market testing.

In the absence of accurate and reliable market data that would permit sophisticated demand analysis as an approach to setting target product-line prices, we can set what is called an "internally based" target or standard selling price. The price is obtained by taking the standard unit cost of production and adding a constant or a percentage mark-up or margin. The target price is then applied to forecast sales in units and summed for all product lines to obtain the projected revenue for the planning period. The standard price would take into consideration any differential selling prices within a product line that are based on considerations of technical quality or market price competition and average price differences that may exist according to geographic territories or customer classifications.

Standards for Revenues

We usually think of revenues as being those dollar returns to the company that are generated by the combined efforts within the marketing function including product market pricing, field sales force and personal selling operations, and advertising-media and sales-promotion campaigns. From the standpoint of the reporting of financial results of operations and profitability for a specific past period, revenue is the first item that appears on the company's earnings statement. We can also view the earnings statement as being a postoperating-period "mirror" of the financial operating plan or forecast budget for the company as a whole or for functional areas.

In preparing the planned or forecast budget for marketing, the standards for specific product market selling prices and what we call "sales offsets from revenue" can be used in developing the net-revenue portion of the marketing budget. In doing so, the standard selling prices would first be applied to the forecast sales quantity to derive gross revenues. The gross figure for forecast or budgeted revenues would also take into consideration differential selling prices within each product line. Then similar standards can be prepared for the offsets from gross revenue for each product line in order to arrive at a net-revenue budget for the period. These offsets will ordinarily include the following:

a. Cash discounts that represent a direct reduction in the gross selling price.
b. Quantity discounts that represent price concessions for large-volume orders.
c. Sales returns and allowances to include:
    1. Standards for returns that can be set as an average percentage applied to sales volume based on past experience. Sales returns are properly treated as adjustments to (that is, reductions in) sales volume rather than adjustments to gross selling prices.
    2. Standards for allowances that reflect price concessions for not filling orders properly.

Allowances are reductions in selling prices rather than sales volume. This is the important difference between returns and allowances. Returns may not be a significant percentage of sales volume so as to warrant consideration in making sales forecasts, but they will always affect determination of period performance and contribution to company profitability made by the marketing function. Similarly, the significance or materiality of allowances may not be sufficient to justify making an adjustment in setting standard product-line selling prices, although they will warrant treatment in determining end-of-period market performance and profit contribution.

To illustrate the annual preparation of forecast net revenue, you will recall from chapter 3 that the Dynamic Corporation prepared three-year forecasts for each of the three product lines (p. 68, table 3-15). The standard unit price and forecast sales in units are shown in table 5-1. The forecast or budgeted gross revenue would then be:

Product MT1	50,000 @ $32.00	$1,600,000
Product MT2	40,000 @ 25.00	1,000,000
Product MT3	20,000 @ 58.00	1,160,000
Total forecast gross revenue		$3,760,000

Table 5-1
Dynamic Corporation Standard Unit Price and Forecast Sales

Product	Forecast Sales in Units	Standard Unit Price
MT1	50,000	$32.00
MT2	40,000	25.00
MT3	20,000	58.00

Of the four sales offsets to gross revenues, we mentioned that cash discounts and sales allowances reflect adjustments to target selling prices of products, while quantity discounts and sales returns are adjustments to the forecast product-sales volume in units. In deriving forecast or budgeted net revenue for Dynamic's marketing operations in Year 1, each of these offset items must in fact be projected at the beginning of the year.

The simplest and most direct way to forecast sales offsets is to examine the sales track record for each product line for a series of operating and reporting periods in the past and convert the average trend into a fraction of the product selling price or volume. For cash discounts that are concessions in list or gross product prices offered to customers, it may well be a cumbersome task to track and average discounts for all sales transactions for a series of annual periods or even quarters. A weighted average of the ratio of cash discounts to gross revenues can be converted more easily to a percentage. Thus we will assume the information for four periods prior to the current year (Year 1) to be as shown in table 5-2.

Table 5-3 shows the results of taking the period time series of cash discounts as a percentage of gross revenues. The unit-sales volumes can provide the weights for the individual period percentages and the results averaged to obtain a single percentage for the four periods. An alternative requiring less computation would be to use a simple four-period average applied to the forecast gross revenue and a four-period moving average thereafter. In doing so, we find that the combined estimated cash discounts for Year 1 are as shown in table 5-4.

Table 5-2
Dollar Sales Volume and Cash Discounts by Product Lines

	Product MT1		Product MT2		Product MT3	
Period	Gross Sales Dollars	Cash Discounts	Gross Sales Dollars	Cash Discounts	Gross Sales Dollars	Cash Discounts
4	$1,650,000	$ 66,000	$ 828,000	$66,240	$1,276,000	$89,320
3	1,920,000	115,200	1,000,000	80,000	1,083,000	97,470
2	1,269,000	76,140	805,000	48,300	1,100,000	99,000
1	1,170,000	35,100	828,000	41,400	935,000	74,800

Table 5-3
Period Cash Discounts as a Percentage of Gross Revenues by
Product Lines

Period	Product MT1	Product MT2	Product MT3
4	4%	8%	7%
3	6	8	9
2	6	6	9
1	3	5	8
Average	4.7%	6.7%	8.2%

Sales allowances are also concessions to gross product prices, and a procedure similar to those used for projecting cash discounts may be used. We also stated that quantity discounts and sales returns are adjustments to unit sales. The same procedures may be used in averaging percentages for a series of prior operating and reporting periods although the rates would then be applied to unit sales before the dollar estimates for both items are determined. Again the detailing would properly be developed by individual product lines. The format for forecast or budgeted net revenue for the Dynamic Corporation might be presented as shown in table 5-5.

Standards for Marketing Costs and Expenses

The objectives for establishing standards for the operating costs of marketing activities are essentially the same as they are for production activities:

a. They are used as guides for planning and budgeting marketing activities that are required to produce anticipated sales.
b. They are used for appraisal or evaluation of marketing-activity performance and control of marketing costs and expenses.

We may approach the classification of marketing-acitivity costs either in

Table 5-4
Combined Estimated Cash Discounts, Year 1

Product	Budgeted Gross Revenue		Estimated Cash Discounts
MT1	$1,600,000	4.7%	$ 75,200
MT2	1,000,000	6.7	67,000
MT3	1,160,000	8.2	95,120
Total			$237,320

Table 5-5
Dynamic Corporation Marketing Plan Budget, Year 1

Gross sales revenue		$3,760,000
Forecast adjustments to		
product-line selling prices:		
Cash discounts	$237,320	
Sales allowances	36,000	273,320
		$3,486,680
Forecast Adjustments to Product-line Unit Sales		
Quantity discounts	$75,000	
Sales returns	26,500	101,500
Budgeted net revenue		$3,385,180

terms of the relationship they bear to sales volume or according to patterns of cost behavior.

a. Activity costs that influence or affect changes in sales volume.
b. Activity costs that are incurred as a result of the sales volume generated for the period.
c. Marketing activities that experience different patterns of cost behavior.

Costs that influence or affect changes in sales volume would include all marketing activities pertaining to the direct selling effort. Examples would be the salaries of marketing managers and field sales-force personnel, storage and warehousing, as well as expenditures for all advertising-media and sales-promotion programs.

Certain other costs are incurred in the functional area of marketing that influence sales although they are not directly related to the selling effort. They would include costs incurred to support marketing research and new product feasibility or research-and-development projects. While the latter are not organizationally a part of the marketing function per se, the primary objective of all of these activities is to expand total company sales volume over a consecutive number of years and not necessarily during the short-term planning period.

Technical and engineering product development projects must be "packaged" from the standpoint of planning levels of project activity in each quarter of an operating year. The budgets and cost estimates accompanying each package represent the target levels of expenditure for that period. Although the product being developed may not reach the market for several planning and reporting periods after current-period expenditures for development, the objective of such projects is still the expansion of product sales volume for the company. Similarly, product-market feasibility or economic studies and market testing for advertising and promotion campaigns are all undertaken for the purpose of stimulating sales volume for new products or those that are already on the market.

For other types of marketing activities, the cause-and-effect relationship between costs and sales volume is the reverse. Such marketing costs and expenses are generated by sales or are incurred as the result of producing sales volume. In a classification according to this definition, we would find expenditures for physical distribution and shipping, order filling and collection, salesmen's commissions, together with related expense-account items.

We may also classify the costs of marketing activities according to cost behavior similar to those behavior classifications we encountered for the production function. For the marketing area, we have appropriately chosen to call the main behavioral categories "variable," "programmed-fixed," or "sunk-fixed" costs.

Most marketing activities for which the accompanying expenses directly influence changes in sales volume are either programmed fixed or semifixed costs for the short-term planning period such as a year or a quarter within the year. Salesmen's salaries, advertising expenditures, and marketing-research costs are programmed at the beginning of the period and will not experience any material changes during that period of marketing operations. On the other hand, if quarterly revisions of these costs are made as the result of any changes in the sales forecast, then they would be semifixed or step costs for the year as a whole. Major marketing expenditures that vary with fluctuations in sales volume will be salesmen's commissions, order-filling costs, and shipping charges.

There are few types of expenses in marketing operations that will be directly variable with sales-volume fluctuations, although salesmen's commissions, order-filling costs, and shipping charges will usually follow this pattern of cost behavior.

A knowledge of cost-behavior patterns for various direct selling and promotional activities in marketing can be gained only through experience over a series of operating and reporting periods, although such knowledge will be essential for setting activity cost standards that are realistically attainable.

Our discussion in this chapter began with defining the project and operating-period approaches to product-market activity planning. We also described the first quantitative phase toward implementing the marketing plan and ultimately evaluating financial performance as being the preparation of a net-revenue budget. Accompanying the revenue budget will be an estimation of personal selling and promotional activity costs together with the administrative expenses of marketing required to achieve the targeted revenue. As marketing operations progress during the period, there will be a need for financial monitoring and feedback on the results of these activities in order to evaluate performance for profit control of the marketing function.

By "feedback," we mean the operating results of marketing in terms of sales prices realized and sales-volume levels achieved for each of the company's product lines as well as the relative volume shares or "mix" of unit sales by product lines. Raw data for these feedback measures may be obtained through the field sales-force organization on a weekly or biweekly basis. However, there may be a time lag of two to six weeks before formal analysis of the raw data and interpretation for profit control can be completed. The length of this time lag will in turn depend on the size and complexity of the marketing function in terms of the field sales organization, the number and diversification of product lines, and the number of price differentials involved.

The first important consideration in developing a reporting and analytical system for profit control is to organize the feedback information according to what we might call "marketing-activity points" or "segments." The description or types of segments may vary among companies in accordance with differences in formal marketing organization, the nature and complexity of distribution channels, product lines, and geographic market definition. An appropriate general rule for choosing segments for profit-control analysis is that interpretation of quantitative analyses can lead to corrective action that will directly improve the contribution made by that segment to operating profitability within the marketing function and for a particular time period. Our concern here will be the presentation of suggested guidelines for types of segments and measures for profit control. The subject of formal reporting, analyses, and interpretation of marketing performance based on these measures will be continued in chapter 10, part II.

How may we select "segments" and corresponding measures for marketing operations in such a way that the analyses of data can lead to action for profit control? We can answer this question by first asking, what product-oriented data will contribute to an expansion or shrinkage of dollars in the net-profit figure? Certainly price and volume movements are product-specific measures that affect profitability on the revenue side. However, costs and expenses of activity inputs relate to areas of marketing operation rather than being product-specific measures. These operations include physical distribution, personal selling effort in the field, and mass-media and promotional programs.

We mentioned that the planning and budgeting of net revenue began with forecasts of unit-sales volume for each product line. The projected prices of product lines for the planning period also quite obviously enter into the determination of budgeted net revenue, and these prices can then be used as the standards against which we can measure the performance of product prices realized in the market during the period. Rate and amount standards for marketing costs and expenses based on forecast sales volume can be developed by specific operations and by departments within the marketing organization. There is essentially no difference between procedures that can be used for developing cost and expense standards in arriving at rate and amount budgets in marketing and the procedures we developed in chapters 3 and 4 for production.

Since market-feedback data are mostly identified either by products or product lines (revenue data) or by specific areas of marketing operation (cost and expense data), we can approach the definition of market segments for profit contribution analysis in the same way:

1. Product segments
   a. Individual products
   b. Product lines
   c. Product-marketing divisions
2. Market segments
   a. Salesmen
   b. Sales districts
   c. Sales regions
   d. Product-marketing divisions

In both classifications the specific profit-center (also responsibility-center) segments are identified on the basis of size. The first classification has a product-specific orientation while the second has a geographic-market orientation. The largest segment is the Product-marketing Division. This segment is the same under both definitional classes and would apply only to large diversified manufacturers whose product divisions are themselves self-contained production and marketing organizations. The organizational structure of this kind has at times been called "horizontal integration."

In approaching the subject of appropriate measures to apply to feedback data for market performance and profit evaluation, the planned sales objectives for each product line and for each geographic market may become the standards against which actual market performance is compared at the end of an operating period. The budgeted or "standard" sales for the period are broken down according to the product or market segment definitions the company wishes to use that best meets its needs for performance evaluation and profit control. For purposes of our illustrations here, we will assume that the Dynamic Corporation is not large enough to have a product-division organization. In the examples that follow, the segment definitions for profit-oriented performance analysis applicable to Dynamic's marketing operations will be geographic sales regions.

In analyzing the revenue side of the marketing budget, there are three important measures that can be applied to each of our segment definitions:

1. *Selling price variance.* This measure reflects the difference between the planned or standard selling prices and the actual selling prices realized for the period, applied to the actual unit volume of sales achieved.
2. *Sales-volume variance.* This variance is the difference between the unit-sales volume that was forecast for the planning period and the volume that was achieved during the period with the net standard product price applied to this volume difference.

3. *Product-mix variance.* This measure applies to the variation from forecast sales revenue that is caused by changes in the proportion in which different products are sold and is independent of both price and volume variations.

To apply these measures to the appropriate feedback data, we will need an additional set of measurements for both reporting and analyzing market performance. We will define these additional measures as follows:

Forecast budget revenue. This is the forecast product-line sales in units at the standard unit prices.

Control budget revenue. This is the actual product-line sales in units for the period at the standard unit prices.

Forecast marginal-income ratio. This ratio is the percentage obtained from dividing the forecast marginal income based on standard variable costs of production and marketing by the forecast budget revenue.

Control marginal-income ratio. This ratio is the percentage obtained from dividing the control marginal income based on standard variable costs of production and marketing by the control budget revenue.

Forecast marginal income. This income measure is the forecast product sales in units at standard prices (forecast budget revenue) less all standard variable costs of production and marketing.

Control marginal income. This measure is the actual sales in units at standard prices (control budget revenue) less standard variable costs of marketing and production.

Actual marginal income (per books). This income measure is the actual product sales in units at actual prices realized less actual variable costs of production and marketing.

We can begin to see that the use of standards for beginning-of-period planning and budgeting and for end-of-period appraisal of operating performance is vital on the revenue side. It enables us to bring together the appraisal of cost and expense levels as they apply to on-going marketing activities (as in analyzing the performance of production activities) and the appraisal of the income components. This combination will be a valuable aid to marketing management in providing a framework for explaining differences between planned and actual marginal income in terms of these variance measures. Let us see how we can develop such measures for the Dynamic Power Tool Corporation.

First we will prepare a worksheet for each geographic region and develop marginal-income figures. We will assume Dynamic has three sales regions: Eastern, Central, and Western. The first figures we will need are the forecast budget revenue that was prepared at the beginning of the planning period and the control budget revenue that must be prepared at the end of the operating period. We will designate the operating period as "Year 1." You will recall that the forecast budget net revenue was $3,385,180 (cf. table 5-5) and that Dynamic made allocations to the sales regions on the basis of the relative revenue shares for the previous period (table 5-6).

At the end of Year 1, the standard prices for each product line are applied to the unit volume of actual sales to obtain the control budget revenue, and the prime standard unit cost of production is applied to actual unit sales to obtain the prime or direct variable cost of goods sold (table 5-7). The marketing costs and expenses by regions for Year 1 have also been provided so that summary worksheets can be prepared showing the marginal income and marginal-income-ratio results (table 5-8). With the foregoing working information, we can now compute the ratios for the marginal-income figures based on forecast budget, control budget, and actual results of operations for the year (table 5-9).

The three variance measures that apply to the revenue side of Dynamic's profit plan and results of operations for Year 1 can now be calculated. In each of the three, the impact of the variance measure on both revenue and marginal income can be determined. The formulas are as follows:

Selling price variance:

Actual sales in units at actual selling prices (actual revenue for the period)—actual sales in units at standard selling prices (control budget revenue)

Adjusted for any marketing costs at actual sales volume that relate to price only.

Sales-volume variance:

Actual sales in units at standard prices (control budget revenue)—forecast sales in units at standard prices (forecast budget revenue)

Results of the preceding X forecast marginal-income ratio

Table 5-6
Forecast Budget Revenue by Regions

Region	Forecast Budget Revenue
Eastern	$1,354,070
Central	1,184,815
Western	846,295
Total	$3,385,180

Table 5-7
Control Budget Revenue and Cost of Goods Sold by Regions

Region	Control Budget Revenue	Prime (Variable) Cost of Goods Sold
Eastern	$1,464,070	$439,200
Central	1,684,815	405,400
Western	671,295	191,400
Totals	$3,820,180	$1,036,000

Product (sales) mix variance:

Actual sales at standard prices (control budget revenue) X (control marginal-income ratio—forecast marginal-income ratio)

The preceding measures reflect the impact on both revenues and marginal income that selling prices of products and unit-sales volume during the period made on planned levels of revenue and profits. The mix variance, however, is properly stated only in terms of its impact on marginal income. We can now apply these measures to the worksheet data for each region.

The mix variance is negative because the control marginal-income ratio (at standard prices) was less than the forecast marginal-income ratio (at standard prices). The combined volume/mix variance for Year 1 would be (table 5-10):

$$\$67,627 - \$21,623 = \$46,004$$

The selling price variance is negative (table 5-11) because actual unit sales at actual prices was less than actual unit sales at standard prices. The average selling prices for the three product lines in the Central Region were less than standard or budgeted prices. The impact on revenue and marginal income was negative or unfavorable by $100,000 and $65,937, respectively (table 5-11). In the Western territory all three revenue variance measures are negative or below the planned levels for the year (table 5-12).

In this chapter we have focused on the revenue side of marketing operations, the development of segmentation for profit control and performance measures for the components of sales revenue. The subject of the cost side of the marketing function was discussed only in a descriptive context. Chapter 9 in part II will continue the presentation here. We will examine the preparation of budgets for marketing costs and expenses and the development of formal profit-performance reports for management review and appraisal. We will also discuss the analyses and interpretation of measures for both revenue and marketing cost variances from budgeted or standard levels.

Table 5-8
Dynamic Corporation Worksheet, Sales Region Segments, Year 1

Eastern Region	Forecast Budget Revenue	Control Budget Revenue	Actual Revenue
Sales	$1,354,070	$1,464,070	$1,464,070
Direct variable costs:			
Of goods sold	386,200	439,200	439,200
Of marketing	135,400	146,400	146,400
Totals	$ 521,600	$ 585,600	$ 585,600
Marginal income	$ 832,470	$ 878,470	$ 878,470

Central Region	Forecast Budget Revenue	Control Budget Revenue	Actual Revenue
Sales	$1,184,815	$1,684,815	$1,584,815
Direct variable costs			
Of goods sold	355,000	405,400	405,400
Of marketing	118,500	168,500	158,500
Totals	$ 473,500	$ 573,900	$ 563,900
Marginal income	$ 711,315	$1,110,915	$1,020,915

Western Region	Forecast Budget Revenue	Control Budget Revenue	Actual Revenue
Sales	$846,295	$671,295	$651,000
Direct variable costs			
Of goods sold	223,900	191,400	201,400
Of marketing	84,600	67,100	65,100
Totals	$308,500	$258,500	$266,500
Marginal income	$537,795	$412,795	$384,500

Table 5-9
Marginal-Income Ratios by Sales Region

Eastern Region

Forecast budget: $\dfrac{\$832{,}470}{\$1{,}354{,}070} = \$0.61479$

Control budget: $\dfrac{\$878{,}470}{\$1{,}464{,}070} = \$0.60002$

Actual budget: $\dfrac{\$878{,}470}{\$1{,}464{,}070} = \$0.60002$

Central Region

Forecast budget: $\dfrac{\$711{,}315}{\$1{,}184{,}815} = \$0.60036$

Control budget: $\dfrac{\$1{,}110{,}915}{\$1{,}684{,}815} = \$0.65937$

Actual: $\dfrac{\$1{,}020{,}915}{\$1{,}584{,}815} = 0.64419$

Western Region

Forecast budget: $\dfrac{\$537{,}795}{\$846{,}295} = \$0.63547$

Control budget: $\dfrac{\$412{,}795}{\$671{,}295} = \$0.61492$

Actual: $\dfrac{\$384{,}500}{\$651{,}000} = \$0.59063$

Table 5-10
Sales Revenue Variances, Year 1, Eastern Sales Region

Selling price variance

$$\$1,464,070 - \$1,464,070 = 0$$

Sales-volume variance

$$\$1,464,070 - \$1,354,070 = \$110,000$$

$$\$110,000 \times 0.61479 = \$67,627$$

Product (sales) mix variance

$$\$1,464,070 \times (0.60002 - 0.61479) = \$1,464,070 \times 0.01477$$

$$= \$21,623U$$

Table 5-11
Sales Revenue Variances, Year 1, Central Sales Region

Selling price variance

$$\$1,584,815 - \$1,684,815 = \$100,000U$$

Sales-volume variance

$$\$1,684,815 - \$1,184,815 = \$500,000$$

and

$$\$500,000 \times 0.60036 = \$300,180$$

Product (sales) mix variance

$$\$1,684,815 \times (0.65937 - 0.60036) = \$1,684,815 \times 0.05901$$

$$= \$99,421$$

Table 5-12
Sales Revenue Variances, Year 1, Western Sales Region

Selling price variance

$$\$651,000 - \$671,295 = \$21,295U$$

Sales-volume variance

$$\$671,295 - \$845,295 = \$175,000U$$

and

$$\$175,000 \times 0.63546 = \$111,205U$$

Product (sales) mix variance

$$\$671,295 \times (0.61492 - 0.63547) = \$671,295 \times 0.02055$$

$$= \$13,795U$$

6

Some Important Aspects of Control Measures

An effective company-wide management control system will ultimately involve every functional unit and managerial level in the organization from the shop foreman to the president. The use of quantitative standards serves the dual purpose of providing a framework for the periodic planning and budgeting process and as a set of guidelines for measuring performance achievement. Responsibility for establishing standards will necessarily be shared by several technical and professional line and staff specialists in each functional area.

In production, establishing labor time standards requires the expertise of industrial engineers who are familiar with the human skills required for each production activity that comes under the shop foreman's supervision. Time standards rely on careful study and experience with respect to human learning capability and past performance time achievement for skilled workers in different occupational classifications. Standards for labor pay rates, on the other hand, are based on a combination of total time and level of formal training required for a specialized skill, the degree of difficulty in performing the task or operation, and a measure of the value that the skill contributes to technical conversion in production. While pay-rate scales for different occupational classes of skilled workers fundamentally rely on expertise in personnel management, the actual hourly rate standards are established through contract involving negotiation between the company and labor-union officials. Setting standards for quantities of raw materials or component parts used in conversion also combines the knowledge of product engineering, the experience of shop foremen and supervisors as to usage rates for each type of material that is requisitioned, and allowances for normal scrap and spoilage levels per batch or per thousand units of product. Materials-price standards invariably depend on current market-price levels for each type of material or part and responsibility for maintaining records of prices bid by competing suppliers rests with the plant procurement department. Thus it is the plant purchasing officer who will be responsible for evaluating both the range of market prices offered by suppliers and the materials quality and technical performance specifications developed by the engineering department. Once it is determined that the engineering specifications can be met by one or more suppliers, the purchasing officer simply contracts with the competing supplier who offers the lowest unit price, which becomes the materials-price standard as part of the prime cost of conversion of finished goods for a particular product line.

Setting overhead standards in production relies on the plant accounting department coordinating closely with the plant manager who is responsible for developing production schedules over time. Under a product-absorption accounting system, we have seen that the purchase cost of all production machinery and facilities whose economic lives will ordinarily extend over several years of operation is allocated to time periods and then added to the prime costs of production in valuing finished goods. The fixed costs of plant facilities are known at any point in time and can easily be projected over several future operating periods. The standard overhead rate that is developed and applied to units of product in conversion depends more on the forecast of product output volume levels over a series of future periods than it does on the valuation of the classes or types of plant and equipment. The exact value of fixed assets is easily obtained from acquisition records, but the product volume forecast, sometimes called "normal capacity utilization" is at best a "good estimate" that relies considerably on past production volume levels achieved and is never precise. Once the absorption rates are established they will be applied without alteration to the manufactured value of product lines over the period of future years that the volume levels of output have been estimated. Although the plant accounting staff may get involved in very comprehensive and at times quite complicated methods for setting absorption rates, the main responsibility for their accuracy and appropriateness rests with the plant manager rather than the plant accountants and financial staff. Setting product and performance standards for the use of services by the line departments is also a shared responsibility. Service-unit supervisors and engineers who are most familiar with requirements and specifications in the line departments confer with production supervisors who have the authority to requisition maintenance, repair, engineering, or other service assistance during an operating cycle. Setting technical standards per se is properly the responsibility of service-area management, while establishing usage standards will originate with the line supervisors and be subject to review and approval by the plant manager's office.

In the marketing function, as we saw in chapter 5, standards relate either to revenue or to costs and expenses incurred to support activities such as advertising and promotion, field sales-force operations, and marketing administration. Unit-price and sales volume standards for each of the various product lines will combine to make up the revenue portion of the marketing budget and will also serve as guides for measuring and evaluating prices realized and sales volume achievement at the end of an operating period. The responsibility for setting price and sales volume standards may be shared by several members of the marketing organization. Ultimately, responsibility for unit selling prices, volume, and cost and expense standards rests with the marketing manager who approves the operating budget or some specific portion of it.

The organization chart for the Gadget Corporation in chapter 1 showed three marketing divisions organized by geographic areas, each headed by a marketing director. In turn, the marketing directors report to the company vice president, marketing. Let us assume it is company policy for the vice president, marketing, to review and approve price standards for each product line as well as volume forecasts and sales quotas for each of the divisions at the beginning of a quarter. We will further assume that the director of each marketing division has the authority to review and approve all major cost and expense standards that make up the monthly budget for the four departments in a division. The vice president, marketing, is responsible then for the specific guideline prices at which the product lines will be sold in a marketing division and for the sales forecasts and divisional volume quotas. Similarly, the division directors are responsible for cost and expense classifications for the field sales force, advertising and promotion, marketing research, and physical distribution in their respective divisions.

Both the vice president, marketing, and the division directors will rely extensively on the expertise of specialists in preparing and justifying standards that these officers approve and for which they are responsible. The vice president, marketing, must depend on the recommendations of the marketing-research department or a team of market-price analysts and product-line volume forecasters for development of specific quantitative standards that make up revenue projections for the company and that are used in turn for performance evaluation and control at the end of an operating period. The division directors likewise will depend on their department managers and the marketing budget specialists to prepare cost and expense standards for each of the departmental activity classifications.

The development, approval, and maintenance of operating standards, upon which both budget preparation and performance evaluation depend, represent a combined effort involving managers at each organization level up to the highest officer who approves and is responsible for the specific standards in question and technical specialists who are most familiar with the methods and analyses required in setting the standards. This is generally true for each of the major functional areas in the company. It is a fact of life in most organizations that a manager who has the authority for approving standards, activity plans, budget estimates, or any other aspect of functional planning and who is therefore responsible for their validity and effectiveness cannot be familiar with all the specialized technical methods and procedures that are involved. He must rely on the expertise and advice of subordinate managers and professional staff members who "build" the standards, plans, and budgets. It is the executive's talent for astute judgment gained through operating experience over time and for assimilating several different but vitally interrelated skills and types of information for making decisions within his span of authority that transcends the capability of any specialist.

An important consideration in setting quantitative standards and one that will be relevant to most functional operations is whether or not the standard is reasonable and realistic in terms of attainability. For performance evaluation and control, it does not make sense to set standards at optimum levels if either past experience or objective judgment tell us that they cannot be met by a manager and his staff who are responsible for any resulting variance. Target standards have been used by companies as incentives to line supervisors and personnel to achieve better performance levels by means of waving the proverbial carrot in front of the donkey's nose. Even when an organizational unit has been unjustifiably deficient over a number of operating periods, using an unattainable standard as a motivating device may very well produce a psychologically negative incentive and attitude on the part of subordinates, thereby defeating its own purpose.

For control, any optimum standard that cannot be met will also be an unacceptable basis for evaluating performance. The variance generated will always be unfavorable since we can expect achievement levels to fall short of the standard in every period. Then evaluation will not yield competent indicators to investigate causes for possible corrective action. They certainly cannot serve as guides to performance rewards or promotions for managers and staff personnel when such merit may be due them. Setting output volume standards in production at capacity levels when no fewer than three shifts in the plant would be required and when normal production scheduling even at peak or seasonal periods during the year has never required more than two shifts is a case in point. Such a standard will never be met under these circumstances and inventories cannot be planned on the basis of fictitious production scheduling. Unattainable standards for volume, materials, labor, or other direct production costs have no valid use other than as worker-performance incentives, and even for this purpose there are other alternatives that will yield better results.

The same considerations apply to the marketing function in setting realistically attainable standards, and this is particularly true in the case of product-line sales volume quotas. If a company uses the market-forecast approach to developing quantitative guidelines for setting quotas in sales regions and districts, a careful appraisal may be necessary to ensure that individual geographic market strengths and weaknesses are accounted for in establishing volume quotas that can be met by the sales force. General customer acceptance for generic product lines may be increasing in some areas while declining in others. Market-share differences according to geographic location will certainly affect sales volume ceilings that can be achieved. Market forecasts are very effective guides for setting sales quotas, but if they are used as the only consideration in establishing quotas or if an arbitrary policy is maintained whereby quotas are always set equal to the market forecast without adjustment based on geographic differences in market behavior, the quota may be ineffective for control of the field sales effort.

The reverse situation in setting practical standards for control and performance evaluation makes even less sense. A standard that is to be a gainful tool represents a performance level that is deemed to reflect the competence of managerial, worker, and other resources that the company has at its disposal.

Any standard, whether it be sales quota, raw-materials price, labor time to perform an operation in the shop, or the operating specifications of a machine, we assume in every case is a measure of acceptable efficiency. A standard that is so easily met that it will always be exceeded even with inefficient performance will defeat its very purpose before the fact and should find little justification for its existence.

Many standards that are used in production and marketing operations will require periodic updating if they are to be valid indicators of current performance conditions, whether internal or external to the company. The proper timing and circumstances for updating standards depends on the particular activity for which a standard is used in budgeting and performance evaluation. In production, materials-price and quantity standards are affected by different operating considerations that influence their behavior, respectively. For materials quantities, any change in product specifications for manufacture may very likely alter the number of units of a particular raw material or part that a department uses in conversion, or the type specification may be changed to eliminate that material input altogether. Decisions that alter specifications of manufacture are based on the planning decisions of production management and engineers. Materials quantity and type standards would be revised to coincide with the production period in which the new product specifications become effective. The prices of materials and component parts will also be updated if a change in type is accompanied by a cheaper or more expensive supply price structure. However, since prices are influenced almost entirely by the actions of suppliers in procurement markets outside the company, revision of price standards may be necessary whenever a purchase contract at new price levels is negotiated for materials or parts that have been in use for some time.

Thus every revision in product specifications that modifies either the type or quantity of conversion inputs will have to be examined to determine whether or not a new use standard is warranted. Similarly, either a change in suppliers or a contract renewal with the same supplier at revised unit prices will require a new price standard, with one notable exception. In any case, where management determines that new contract rates are not in accord with the most favorable market prices available under the same specifications, then the latter rates become the prevailing standard when they are known to the company and the new contract prices will yield unfavorable variances.

Updating labor time and rate standards will also involve a special set of considerations. Any line-assembly or processing operation in the shop will have a standard for labor grade, number of workers at that grade, or grade mix if two or more classes of labor perform the operation. Labor-efficiency studies that use learning-rate and completion-time measures are often relied upon for setting labor time standards in production. There are really no specific guidelines per se for determining the frequency of updating time standards. Since time standards are entirely a function of efficiency, that is, an acceptable level for the number of operations that a classification of labor will complete in a fixed time period, the standard may be adequate for several years. A change in production methods, however, usually requires the application of time studies and experimentation with worker learning rates to determine an acceptable time standard for the new method. The hourly wage rates paid for each labor grade are standards per se and are established by contract. Whenever a labor union renegotiates its contract and new hourly wage rates are specified, then the new rates become the revised standards.

Chapter 5 addressed the subject of revenue standards, cost and expense standards, and control measures for the marketing function. You will recall that revenue includes product, price, and volume elements. Since product price is the element in revenue that is influenced most by management decisions within the company, the unit market price for a product line is automatically the standard for both revenue budgeting and performance evaluation, regardless of the procedures a company uses in establishing its market prices. At any time management revises the market-price structure for a product line, it will replace the previous price structure as the new standard. Market volume standards are always estimates, particularly in budgeting, and can never be considered as firm from the standpoint of commitment to achieve the volume levels established. They are derived from market-forecasting procedures and factors relating to the behavior of competitors in different geographic locations. They are always subject to errors in human judgment and technical procedure. Market volume estimates for product lines are a vital aspect of quarterly planning for marketing operations and will also affect production scheduling and planning for inventory levels. Thus market volume estimates may be prepared annually with revisions made at quarterly intervals, or they may be prepared anew every quarter, depending on the particular policy a company adopts. Further, any alteration in the composition of a company's product lines such as the removal of any products experiencing a declining market or the addition of items in a line will most likely require a revision of volume estimates.

The standards for costs and expenses in marketing are based on a combination of program planning for activities such as sales-force operations or advertising and promotion and the behavior of specific cost classifications per se. Since most of the marketing activities are programmed for the purpose of achieving forecast or budgeted sales levels, the standards will depend on the level or size of the program and will usually be fixed for a short-term operating period. The exceptions are those classifications of marketing costs that vary in proportion to sales volume and for which standard rates can be set, similar to standard rates for the prime costs of production. For marketing programs, we assume initially that financial resources, sales-force personnel, media, and other activity requirements are available to support the size or scale of the marketing program. The budget for the program "package" containing lump-sum fixed costs is in fact the standard and would be updated or revised whenever the size of the program package or the activities themselves are modified from one period to the next. In those situations in which the size of the marketing programs require a total budget that exceeds the appropriated funds available, it is necessary to reduce the scale of planned programs or set priorities whereby some activities may be eliminated to meet the appropriations ceiling.

For control, activity performance in each functional area will yield measurable results that are compared with the activity standards and their standard costs and quantitatively presented as variances. Some standards can be used as firm commitments in budget preparation and performance evaluation, although many of the standards we use are only estimates subject to the errors of technical procedure or human judgment. The latter type of standards will be used as guides to performance achievement. The budget figures on which they are based serve as targets that management makes every effort to reach, but the figures are not absolute goals. This is usually the case for volume estimates in production scheduling and is particularly true for market sales and revenue planning. It is for this reason that our performance analysis in control makes a distinction between variations from standard and budget based on resulting product volume levels at the end of a period. Cost standards for labor and materials in production, prices, and known variable costs in marketing can be determined with a high degree of accuracy provided that they are current and are therefore treated as commitments for which managers and subordinates are held accountable.

Two very important aspects of all performance variance measures are the extent to which they are controllable or uncontrollable and the causes of variation. Chapter 3 discussed control under an absorption-accounting system and demonstrated that while allocation of overhead for fixed assets to units of product in manufacturing conversion is a very important consideration in determining the unit cost of finished goods and valuing inventories, the same measures are not valid for control. The reason is simply that all fixed overhead in the plant cannot be influenced or changed in any way by actions of the plant manager or his shop foremen. Overhead is a cost burden of capital-asset planning and investment. Although fixed overhead may be one of the largest increments in an operating budget, it is also one of the best known illustrations of a budgeted item that is uncontrollable. In general, control of an activity and its financial cost will always depend on the extent to which a manager at any level in the organization has the authority or practical capability to take action that will alter the activity and its consumption of the company's financial resources.

In production the plant manager and his supervisors have the authority and ability to change the rate of use of direct and variable resources in conversion plus related plant services and therefore are responsible for controlling their quantities based on standard cost rates. Refinements in pinpointing managerial accountability for controlling operating resources involves two factors: the extent of a manager's authority and the nature of the organization structure.

Plant services provide an excellent example of joint authority and control between organizational units. Technical expertise for repair services on machinery is the responsibility of the manager of the repair and maintenance department. The technical quality and efficiency of repair services are therefore under his control, and he is responsible for them. The frequency with which repair and maintenance are requested by a line department, however, is the responsibility of the line manager, and therefore he is in control of (and accountable for) the rate of use or quantity of services provided to his shop during the production month or quarter.

Variances in marketing are generally less subject to direct influence by managers' actions than is true for production. Virtually all production activities, including product-line volume levels, are subject to managerial control by some organizational unit in the company. Marketing operations take place in a much broader environment and often one that is more uncertain than is the case for production. A company can study customer and competitor behavior that affect changes in sales volume and use their knowledge obtained by feedback from the marketplace through the field sales organization or the marketing research staff for planning and decision making. What marketing managers cannot do is directly control the actions of customers and competitors that have their most significant impact on the sales revenue that the company will be able to achieve in an operating year or quarter. On the other hand, the costs and expenses for most programmed marketing activities are controllable by management, including maintaining the sales force and advertising and promotion, which usually comprise the largest financial expenditures.

Activity and cost variances from standard serve as a warning system to managers. They indicate in financial as well as nonfinancial terms when specific areas of activity and their cost or revenue elements are performing better than planned or less favorably and by how much. They do not tell the manager what caused the particular results indicated by the variances. The underlying causes for variances can be determined and appraised only by investigating the operations in the organizational unit to which the variance applies at the end of the period to see what happened. For example, the control system may tell us that there was an excessive number of parts used in the assembly department at a particular plant location based on standard for the second quarter of the current year, which resulted in an unfavorable cost variance of so many dollars. What the variance does not tell us is whether this result was due to defective parts coming into the department from supply inventories (which would be beyond the control of the assembly department foreman) or whether the workers were not using correct procedures in assembly thereby causing an excessive number of damaged parts. The important issue here is that corrective action cannot be taken to compensate for the unfavorable results and prevent their recurrence until the cause is investigated and known. Correcting a deficiency that can really be attributed to the purchasing department and traced back to the supplier is a far different type of action than one involving retraining of workers.

Most of the variance measures in a control system that reflect favorable or unfavorable results for specific functional operations will have more than one possible cause, and until the operation in question is investigated and the cause determined, the control system itself cannot be implemented properly to achieve acceptable levels of efficiency or any other performance criterion. We have stated that product market price is the one component of revenue that is most subject to managerial control. In chapter 9 we will see that price variances are presented in the performance reports by product lines and by various classifications of market segments. A favorable or unfavorable price variance in any marketing report will tell a manager for which product and at what particular location in the territorial marketing organization the variance from established price occurred. It will not tell him what price adjustment was made, by whom, and for what reason. It will enable him to investigate local market conditions and make an evaluation of price behavior for competitive product lines, salesmen's practices, volume movement, and the components of revenue that interact with price for the purpose of weighing alternatives and making recommendations on price standards.

In production, overhead volume variance is an aspect of control that arises when a company maintains an absorption-accounting system for plant operations. You will recall from chapter 3 that the main purpose of absorption accounting is to allocate all fixed costs of production as represented primarily by annual depreciation of plant facilities and equipment to product lines and to units of product within each line. When this same accounting system is used for management control, we face the task of measuring and evaluating the degree of utilization of plant capacity each quarter. Plant facilities, their investment base and annual amount of depreciation, as well as optimum plant capacity in units of product output per month do not change from one period to the next. Volume levels of scheduled output are most likely to change at intervals throughout the year in response to changes in product lines per se, customer demand, maintenance of inventory levels, and seasonal-sales considerations. These two conditions will usually result in overhead volume variance each quarter in the performance reports for plant operations.

What the volume variance measures is the difference between the actual use of plant facilities, which fixed overhead represents from a financial standpoint, and some long-term standard or average production output measure stated in hours of operation, units of completed products, or other volume measure of manufacture. You will recall that normal expected use of plant capacity over a fairly predictable number of operating periods is perhaps the most realistic basis for defining "capacity." We will assume the information as provided in table 6-1 for the Gadget Corporation in 198-.

This table tells us that plant activities required to complete a gadget for final inventory is one half hour per gadget and that the standard number of hours to complete 6,000 units is 3,000 direct labor hours. At an absorption rate of $8.80 per hour and standard hours for normal use of capacity of 3,740 DLH, we would

Table 6-1
Gadget Corporation Production Standards and Output, Plant 1,
Second Quarter, 198-

Standard hours for planned volume or normal capacity	3,740 DLH
Actual hours worked	3,500 DLH
Actual production volume	6,000 gadgets
Standard hours for actual production volume	3,000 DLH
Fixed overhead-absorption rate	$8.80 per DLH

then expect our average annual depreciation for facilities in plant 1 to be $131,648. The volume variance can now be determined in this way:

Standard hours for normal capacity — standard hours allowed for production volume achieved = excess capacity

and

Excess capacity × overhead-absorption rate = volume variance

Thus

$$3,740 - 3,000 = 740 \text{ DLH}$$

and

$$740 \times \$8.80 = \$6,512$$

The volume variance of $6,512 contains two elements, one being a measure of unused capacity per se and the other being a measure of how efficiently plant facilities were used during the period for the production volume achieved. Thus

a. The volume variance element representing excess capacity:

3,740   —   3,500 DLH

Planned or normal   Actual labor
labor hours   hours worked

= 240 DLH times $8.80 = $2,112

b. The volume variance element representing efficient use of capacity:

3,500 DLH   —   3,000 DLH

Actual labor   Standard hours for
hours worked   actual production
                            volume

= 500 DLH times $8.80 = $4,400

Allocation of investment in plant facilities is one of the largest increments of total production resources from a financial standpoint, without which the production function could not exist. However, when this investment is viewed in terms of the efficiency with which resources are used for control of plant operations from one period to the next, its value is quite limited. There is no course of action that a plant manager and his shop foremen can take to alter the level of investment for all major plant facilities, regardless of the particular overhead cost allocation measures employed by a company. It is for this reason that volume variances are of little use in the planning and control of on-going production activities. What the volume variance does tell us is by what percent of expected (normal) capacity actual operations either exceeded the norm or fell short of it during the year of quarter.

Both the use of standard costs and the treatment of fixed plant overhead are quite important in valuing inventories of finished products. Management frequently needs to know, "What are our current production costs to turn out gadgets, per unit?" There are two reasons why many manufacturers have continued to use overhead-absorption accounting in the production function without modification. One reason is that accepted financial accounting practice in preparing annual reports has adhered to the principle that all production costs be carried in inventory of finished products and reported as cost of sales on the company income statement as the flow of products moves from inventory to customer markets. The other reason is the view held by many managers that the "correct" cost of a gadget is the total cost of production to include fixed overhead converted to a cost-per-unit basis. There is some justification for this view if we are considering long-term operating results. One of the main uses of per-unit production cost information is for establishing product market prices. Over the total economic life of production facilities that may extend to 30 or 40 years, the sum of the market prices of a company's products must exceed total costs including the cost of fixed assets per product unit plus a margin for the company to be profitable.

There are serious practical limitations to this argument, however. A company is rarely able to price products based on long-term cost recovery of investment in plant and equipment plus a profit margin. Current competitive-pricing practices in the marketplace can severely restrict management's choice of price based on long-term projections and margins that will recover all costs, no matter how we define "all costs." The unit-margin requirement for current market pricing based on long-term cost-recovery considerations may be so large that a company prices its products "out of the market" thereby causing it to lose competitive strength in the marketplace. Further, over the period of 30 or 40 years of productive life of plant facilities, revenue will have to be sufficient to cover all internal fixed and variable costs of the company, production and nonproduction, simply to break even. For this length of time, other considerations such as product development, expansion of geographic markets, and diversification of company operations through acquisition or investment in other lines of business become significant to cost recovery of investment in existing fixed assets.

Traditional "full unit production cost" of products for market-pricing decisions under absorption accounting has little justification when these decisions are an aspect of short-term planning for operations from a practical standpoint. Management can change market prices in response to changes that occur for internal variable costs and in response to changes in the market-price structure of competitors. Again these are short-term decision considerations. Management cannot change the fixed-cost structure of its existing investment base in facilities unless it is planning to partially liquidate the business. Further, it is the profit-contribution margin that is most relevant to short-term market-pricing decisions and profit planning.

In view of these considerations, it may be wise to follow a practice of reporting inventories of finished products by increments of production value in each month or quarter of operations to include at least the following:

1. Prime or direct variable cost of manufacture
   a. at standard
   b. at actual
2. Variable overhead
   a. at standard
   b. at actual
3. Share of allocated fixed overhead for the period.

This practice would provide the main elements of inventory value that would serve the separate requirements for cost information in operating control, in short-term management decisions, and in financial reporting.

Part II
Budget Preparation and Analysis of Operating Performance

7 Budgets and Management

Chapter 1 discussed the definitions and uses of organizational cost data "for different purposes" and the behavior of operating costs as they are used in functional-area activities. Chapter 1 also discussed the two main uses of financial data within the organization, which are:

1. Determining allocations to products in the production function for the ultimate purpose of valuing inventories of finished goods and to provide a basis for establishing product-line market prices
2. The control of financial inputs to functional operations, the three activity areas common to most product-oriented firms being production, marketing, and administration

Chapter 1 also set forth that management control of operations and their attendant financial inputs are vitally related to the quantitative planning for functional-area operations and particularly for performance evaluation. In turn, budgeting represents the financial component of fiscal planning for operations for any given time segment within the year. In this regard, two main aspects of budgeting warrant our attention as a prelude to taking up management control and performance evaluation for production, marketing, and administration. They are (a) kinds of budgets and budget development and (b) managerial responsibilities as they relate to the preparation, review, and approval of budgets within the organization.

There are several kinds of functional budgets that may be used in the planning of operations for manufacturing firms and for service-type operations or nonprofit organizations. We may broadly define them characteristically as quantitative budgets or programmed budgets. Quantitative budgets are prepared in accordance with planned or prescribed levels of output such as the aggregate of the number of units in each product line to be completed in production or the volume of product-line sales to be achieved for the operating period. Our discussion in chapter 1 and in the appendix on cost behavior is applicable to the preparation of quantitative budgets and has been used most frequently in production by manufacturers. The programmed budget, on the other hand, is applicable to nonproduction service operations and to those nonprofit organizations for which the managerial function is not oriented to repetitive assembly-line activities that yield physical quantities of output. For such organizations, the functional operations themselves are planned on the basis of programming a group of interdependent activities to achieve a task-type of objective.

123

This is in contrast to the quantitative budget that is developed according to planned schedules of physical output (that is, units completed in production or sales volume achieved). These planned or "targeted" product quantity levels may be derived from estimates based on previous sales or production volume trends, or they may result from forecasts using technical models. Whatever the basis for obtaining these projections may be, the important point is that the activities are defined in terms of fixed or variable (behavior again) estimates of costs that will be required to yield the product quantity level that was forecast or scheduled. The financial level of the budget then is directly dependent on the product quantity level that is forecast. We will discuss the role of forecasting for quantitative planning and budgeting in greater detail in chapter 9. To meet product quantity level specifications, however, it is the corresponding activity and its components (that is, machining and assembling in production and the equipment, labor, and materials that attach to each of these activities) for which the operating budget must be prepared.

We may also state our case in this way. The various kinds of quantitative operating budgets that may be used in production or in other functional areas where applicable will differ according to definitions of types of costs based on cost behavior rather than according to the grouping of activities on which the budget package or proposal is based. However, it must be remembered that these cost items in a budget proposal arise because of the activity and its planned operating level and must always be identified accordingly. Common sense would tell us that this is a "truism" indeed and that without such identification by a specific activity and its planned level, the budget would serve no purpose!

At the risk of some repetition with reference to part I, we may say that management accounting translates quantitative plans (that is, product market volume forecast) into financial plans through the process of budgeting. It also may appropriately employ standards for functional operating activities as the benchmark or yardstick against which operating results at the end of a period are measured for the purpose of appraising performance. The evaluation or appraisal of performance will then have a twofold application in terms of decision making. One is the need for corrective action while the other is the use of quantitative operating results as guides to the future planning of functional activities.

We may also view management accounting as an extension of financial accounting, and when it is used as a conceptual and practical vehicle for management control, it helps us accomplish two important goals: (1) to present management's plans in the same terms and forms that are used in reporting and evaluating results, and (2) to present both plans and results by segments—for production planning and control by product line and operating-unit organizational segments; for market planning and control by product line and by functional segments such as geographic territories or customer classifications.

Although the quantitative and program type of functional or operating budgets comprise the two most commonly encountered classifications for manufacturers, we may also identify functional budgets in terms of cost behavior or in terms of organization structure. In terms of behavior, we can identify five main types:

1. Appropriation budgets
2. Fixed-forecast budgets
3. Fixed-cost (or fixed-flexible) budgets
4. Flexible budgets
5. Step budgets

The appropriations budget is most commonly used by nonprofit organizations and government agencies. It resembled the programmed budget more closely than any other budget type or form used by profit-oriented firms. Both are essentially a fund that sets an upper limit to financial expenditures allowed a specific activity or group of interrelated activities during the fiscal or calendar year. Any difference between amounts spent and the annual appropriation due to overestimates or incomplete task assignments can be treated as carryovers to the next planning period. Appropriations then represent a "bundle" of expenditures that cannot be exceeded for a specified time period. They do not involve allocations for major capital plant and equipment for which expenditures were made in prior years. Further, they are used in connection with service, research, or other program types of activity rather than for physical-product-related activities.

The fixed-forecast, fixed-cost, and step budgets are all based on the behavior of operating costs and expenses. The fixed-forecast budget is used primarily as a planning tool although it can be used with certain specific applications for control and performance evaluation, as we shall see in chapter 8. Preparation of the fixed-forecast budget primarily involves applying standard or estimated unit-cost factors to specific activity levels. And these activity levels are planned according to a forecast of the volume of products in each line that is "expected to be" produced or sold for the forecast time period. In this way, the budget is a profit plan or the "contribution" to profit that the proposed budget intends to make for that group of activities. Thus the amounts are fixed insofar as the component such as production labor and materials receive a constant or single budgeted amount in accordance with a single planned volume. Capital-allocation components for plant and equipment are included in the fixed-forecast budget and are usually constant regardless of what the planned level of activity happens to be. Table 7-1 illustrates the forecast budget for production with the activity level stated in hours of direct labor per month. Table 7-1 assumes that activities for finishing work require one grade of labor for sanding and a second grade of labor for polishing, requiring 30 minutes and 15 minutes per product unit respectively.

The reader can easily see that the amounts for all the items in the table are

Table 7-1
Supreme Furniture Company Fixed-Forecast Budget

Department: Finishing	Fiscal period: 198-
Supervisor: Mr. A. Jones	Base: Hours of direct labor
	Forecast production: 7,200 Units
	Labor rates:
	Sanding: $4.50 per hour
	Polishing: $5.00 per hour

| | Quarters | | | | |
	First	Second	Third	Fourth	Year
Forecast units	1,600	2,400	2,200	1,000	7,200
Forecast hours:					
Sanding	800	1,200	1,100	500	3,600
Polishing	400	600	550	250	1,800
Expenses:					
Supervision	$ 1,500	$ 1,800	$ 1,800	$ 1,300	$ 6,400
Direct labor:					
Sanding	3,600	5,400	4,950	2,250	16,200
Polishing	2,000	3,000	2,750	1,000	8,750
Other indirect labor	780	1,440	1,440	700	4,360
Supplies	420	510	510	415	1,855
Repair and rework	180	240	240	170	830
Set up and makeready	360	540	540	330	1,770
Maintenance	1,200	1,500	1,500	1,150	5,350
Inspection	300	390	390	225	1,305
Power and light	690	810	810	660	2,970
Depreciation	1,800	1,800	1,800	1,800	7,200
Property taxes	600	600	600	600	2,400
Insurance	240	240	240	240	960
Totals	$13,670	$18,270	$17,570	$10,840	$60,350

lump-sum or fixed-dollar figures for the planning year as well as by quarters and are based on a projection (or target level) of the product volume that is anticipated for the period. Any change in the actual volume achieved relative to the projected quantity for a given quarter will alter the fixed budget amount but only as a result of volume differences and not as a result of changes in the activity input costs themselves. This is a very important distinction both from the standpoint of planning and budgeting procedures and for control of operations.

The fixed-cost or fixed-flexible budget is a component or subset of flexible budgeting and can be used for both planning and control of operations. It may be prepared on a separate schedule to be incorporated in the overall budget of an organizational unit or group of activities for which constant costs are known and are independent of volume planning and control from the standpoint of cost behavior (table 7-2).

Table 7-2
Supreme Furniture Company Fixed-Cost Budget

Department: Finishing   Fiscal period: 198-
Supervisor: Mr. A. Jones

No variable costs
standard and applied
at all volume levels

| Expense | Quarters | | | | Year |
	First	Second	Third	Fourth	
Supervision	$1,200	$1,200	$1,200	$1,200	$4,800
Supplies	300	300	300	300	1,200
Maintenance	2,000	2,000	2,000	2,000	8,000
Inspection	250	250	250	250	1,000
Depreciation	1,700	1,700	1,700	1,700	6,800
Property taxes	450	450	450	450	1,800
Insurance	250	250	250	250	1,000
	$6,150	$6,150	$6,150	$6,150	$24,600

The fixed-cost budget will not vary in amounts as a part of professional planning and budgeting. For planning purposes, however, a distinction has to be made with regard to those items that are allocations of capital expenditures made in prior years (depreciation) and items that require the use of current working capital. Most of the account classification in a fixed-cost budget will require expenditures in the planned period, and although they are constant amounts, they are still a part of cash-flow or working-capital forecasting and budgeting. Again no variable-cost items are included in a fixed-cost budget format.

The flexible budget is of primary concern to us and is the foundation on which most of our treatment of functional management control and performance evaluation is based. The main premise of a flexible budgeting system is that a quantitative distinction exists in the activities of most functional and organizational segments of a manufacturing firm in terms of the behavior of the various recorded cost classifications that underlie a group of related activities (cf. chapter 1 and the appendix). Some of these classifications will remain constant, as we have just seen in reference to the fixed-cost budget format, while others will be variable. Variable behavior cost classifications may change as a result of changes in volume levels of activity (which is the assumption underlying most of our illustrations), or they may change as a result of the passing of time. In either case, the fact that variable-cost classifications can be expressed as rates (or coefficients) applied to a quantity of some defined activity (units of product, hours of direct labor, units of direct materials) while fixed classifications are expressed in dollar amounts is the basic distinction that makes this kind of budget system "flexible."

The flexible budget has been commonly referred to as a "rate and amount" budget and is really a synthesis of a variable-cost and a fixed-cost approach combining all activities and their account classifications for a group of activities that are functionally or organizationally interdependent. The rate is simply a cost coefficient expressing variability in terms of some quantitative measure of activity input (direct labor or materials) or output (unit production or sales volume), and the amount is the fixed-cost dollar levels for the appropriate classifications. A mathematical formula that expresses the flexible-budget relationship would be:

$$B = cX + \Sigma Y$$

This is a two-variable linear equation where

B = total budget for a group of account classifications

X = the quantity of an activity measure underlying the account classifications that most closely parallels or expresses the behavior of variable costs in the account classification group

Y = a given fixed-cost classification in the group

c = the variable-rate coefficient applied to the budgeted quantity of X

If the foregoing equation represents a planned annual flexible budget for a group of activities, then quarterly budget estimates may be presented as follows:

$$B_1 = c_1 X_1 + (Y_{1a} + \cdots + Y_{1k})$$

$$
\begin{matrix}
\cdot & \cdot & \cdot & \cdot \\
\cdot & \cdot & \cdot & \cdot \\
\cdot & \cdot & \cdot & \cdot
\end{matrix}
$$

$$B_4 = c_4 X_4 + (Y_{4a} + \cdots + Y_{1k})$$

where

$B_1, \cdots, B_4$ = total quarterly budget estimates

$X_1, \cdots, X_4$ = the quantity for each quarter of an activity measure underlying the account classifications that most closely parallel or express the behavior of variable costs in the account classification group

$Y_1, \cdots, Y_4$ = quarterly estimates for a given fixed-cost classification in the group (subscripts $a, \ldots, k$ representing the different fixed-amount cost classifications)

$c_1, \cdots, c_4$ = the variable-rate coefficient applied to the budgeted quantity of X in each of the four quarters. These coefficients will be constant except for specific quarters in which the cost components themselves change (cf. chapters 3 and 4)

Table 7-3 is a nonmathematical format to an activity budget for both variable and fixed or constant classifications using the flexible-budgeting or rate and amount approach.

Note that the only change in the cost classifications themselves for quarters II through IV is indirect labor. The variable coefficients can be applied to projected or planned volume and activity levels in preparing a forecast budget just as they can be applied to actual production or sales at the close of an operating period for performance evaluation.

The flexible-budget approach has sometimes been considered primarily a means of controlling financial performance rather than a tool for planning operations for a specific period of time. When used for performance evaluation, the variable-cost classification rates or coefficients are applied to the actual volume of activity that was experienced for the period. This approach carries a very important assumption in that the organizational unit responsible for the cost incurrence and thus for financial results of a group of activities has no managerial control over the output volume or the activity levels based on forecast volume for the period but only for the actual activity inputs (that is, production labor and materials) and their corresponding costs.

This assumption may be true for some groups of activities or organizational units and not for others depending on the particular "managerial rung" in the organizational hierarchy that is charged with setting planned output volume and upon which planned activity levels and their cost estimates are budgeted. In any case, it is certainly not inappropriate to use flexible budgeting as a forecast-budgeting tool by applying activity standards and the variable rates to projected product output volumes. The really important issue in both forecast budgeting and in performance appraisal is the operational knowledge and ability to separate the cost components and activity standard quantities by planned volume and by actual volume of output, to know what the differences mean, and to use them properly both in planning and budgeting and in decision making for financial control of operations. The importance of this point cannot be overemphasized, it is therefore stressed in the chapters on production and marketing that follow.

The fifth type of budgeting approach listed earlier is the step budget. This is really a series of fixed budgets that are applicable to different volume ranges of activity or output. The main difference between a fixed or constant budget and a step budget is that the fixed budget contains account classifications, each of which will carry the same dollar figure for every volume of output or level of activity that could be feasibly planned or forecast within the annual or short-term planning period. A step budget for a group of interrelated activities,

Table 7-3
Supreme Furniture Company Flexible-Forecast Budget

Department: Finishing	Fiscal period: 198-
Supervisor: Mr. A. Jones	Base: Hours of direct labor
	Forecast production: 7,200 units
	Labor rates:
	Sanding: $4.50 per hour
	Polishing: $5.00 per hour

Quarterly volume forecast: I: 1,600;   II: 2,400
                             III: 2,200; IV: 1,000

Quarterly forecast labor hours:

Sanding:	I: 800	II: 1,200	III: 1,100	IV: 500
Polishing:	I: 400	II: 600	III: 550	IV: 250
Total DLH	1,200	1,800	1,650	750

First Quarter

Expenses:	Rate Per DLH	Amount Per Month	Total Quarterly Budget
Supervision	–	$500	$1,500
Direct labor:			
Sanding	$4.50	–	3,600
Polishing	5.00	–	2,000
Totals	$9.50	$500	$7,100

Expenses:	Rate Per DLH (Based on Total DLH)	Amount Per Month	Total Quarterly Budget
Other indirect labor	$0.40	$ 100	$ 780
Supplies	0.15	80	420
Repair and rework	0.10	20	180
Setup and makeready	0.30	–	360
Maintenance	0.50	200	1,200
Inspection	0.15	40	300
Power and light	0.20	150	690
Depreciation	–	600	1,800
Property taxes	–	200	600
Insurance	–	80	240
Totals	$1.80	$1,470	$6,570

Second Quarter

Expenses:	Rate Per DLH	Amount Per Month	Total Quarterly Budget
Supervision	–	$600	$ 1,800
Direct labor:			
Sanding	$4.50	–	5,400
Polishing	5.00	–	3,000
Total	$9.50	$600	$10,200

Table 7-3 continued

	Rate Per DLH (Based on Total DLH)	Amount Per Month	Total Quarterly Budget
Other indirect labor	$0.60	$ 120	$1,440
Supplies	0.15	80	510
Repair and rework	0.10	20	240
Setup and makeready	0.30	–	540
Maintenance	0.50	200	1,500
Inspection	0.15	40	390
Power and light	0.20	150	810
Depreciation	–	600	1,800
Property taxes	–	200	600
Insurance	–	80	240
Totals	$2.00	$1,490	$8,070

however, will have some account classifications in which the budgeted figure will be fixed within a certain range of planned volume and then "jump" or "drop" to a different dollar amount at a higher or lower volume range but again remain constant between the upper and lower limits of the new range. In this way, the step budget would be a series of fixed budgets at different volume ranges. Table 7-4 illustrates a step budget.

The reader can easily see that the step budget is a modified form of the fixed budget. No variable costs are involved. Volume ranges are increments of output stated as percent of capacity utilization, and most of the classifications are incremental or step dollar amounts that change only from one range to another but remain fixed for any volume level within a range. It is possible to combine the flexible budget and the step budget approaches in cases where a group of activities experience a mixed pattern of operating behavior with respect to financial inputs and where classifications will combine variable, fixed, and semifixed or step patterns of cost behavior. In such instances, it is best to use the flexible-budget rate and amount formats as we have done and a separate format for step-type or incremental account classifications.

In the financial planning of operations as it relates to management control for profit-oriented firms, our focus is on functional operating budgets, which we defined as being basically of two types: quantitative budgets for production and other product volume-related functional activities and programmed budgets. We may mention briefly some other types of financial budgets that are vital to either fiscal or long-term planning but are not directly related to functional management control. Perhaps the most significant nonfunctional budgets are the capital-expenditures budget and the funds-flow or working-capital budget. The former type involves major sums of financial funding for plant and equipment acquisition and replacement or provision to meet leasehold contract obligations. Capital-expenditures budgets have long-term implications involving the provision and commitment of funds for several years through the retention of earnings

Table 7-4
Supreme Furniture Company Step-Forecast Budget

Department: Finishing
Supervisor: Mr. A. Jones

Fiscal period: 198-
Base: Hours of direct labor

Forecast production:
Five activity levels
expressed in hours of total
department direct labor

Percent of Standard Capacity Dept. DLH Range	45-60 1,000-1,300	60-73 1,300-1,600	73-86 1,600-1,900	86-100 1,900-2,200	100-114 2,200-2,500
		(Amounts per Quarter)			
Accounts:					
Supervision	$1,300	$1,300	$1,300	$ 1,300	$ 1,300
Other indirect labor	700	980	1,400	1,550	1,900
Supplies	415	450	550	700	800
Repair and rework	170	230	300	380	470
Setup and makeready	330	400	550	680	810
Maintenance	1,150	1,300	1,600	2,000	2,350
Inspection	225	300	390	500	610
Power and light	660	700	810	900	1,050
Depreciation	1,800	1,800	1,800	1,800	1,800
Property taxes	600	600	600	600	600
Insurance	240	240	240	240	240
Totals	$7,590	$8,300	$9,540	$10,650	$11,930

from operations over a series of fiscal periods, the sale of corporate bonds or other means of long-term borrowing. The working-capital budget, on the other hand, is a tool of fiscal planning, hence a component of short-term financial planning. The working-capital budget analyzes the cash flow that is expected to be provided to the firm for a period of one year from all sources such as the sale of goods or services during the planned year, receivables due from sales in prior years, short-term borrowings from banks and other lending institutions, or income from investments. A comparison is made between these anticipated sources of cash or "funds" and the expenditures of cash that will be necessary for functional operations, payroll, repayment of short-term bank loans, in fact all the firm's cash-outflow requirements other than those that relate to long-term capital expenditures and lease-funding arrangements.

We set forth the role and purpose of standards in the management control and performance evaluation of the firm's operations in chapter 1 and traced the historical setting of engineering standards as being an outgrowth of scientific management. We also stated that the use of standards was confined to the functional area of production for several decades following the contributions made by the scientific management movement. This has been the case as well for the use of quantitative standards combined with management accounting techniques for both budgeting and management control. Many firms today have not as yet "made the transition" by developing approaches comparable to those used in production for nonproduction areas of operation and organizational segments of the company. One of our important objectives in this book then is to present guidelines for the adoption of such approaches in nonproduction areas of the firm's operations for performance evaluation and control.

If we were asked, "What would you say is the overall perspective of the discussions and presentations in this book?" we would say that it is a technical and managerial function and application of the principle of "management by exception." How so? The principle quite simply stated is that any set of interdependent activities in an organization, the purpose of which is to yield a product or service output, is in itself a "system" and that it may continue to operate without interference until it is out of control. "Out of control" is the exception. Any group of activities will be operationally "out of control" under certain conditions. These conditions are when specific results deviate materially from those standards that have been set up as guidelines or when targeted objectives are not met.

The budget is a targeted objective and so are the sales forecasts and production schedules upon which budgets and operating plans are based. The data-reporting measures developed in part I and the analyses and interpretations that are the subject of part II provide the feedback to the planning process necessary to implement control. A word of caution is advisable at this time, however. Any standards for activities and any forecasts, schedules or managerial objectives that are translated and documented quantitatively are *only* guidelines. Thus results of operations may be in error either in terms of the functional activities themselves or in terms of the planning standards and goals. Any astute manager must determine realistically and objectively to which of these aspects the deviating results apply. This will be vital not only to the effective appraisal of results but also to the validity of subsequent planning for company operations.

Reporting information systems and documents or formats for performance appraisal must of necessity give consideration to the organization structure and managerial levels of reporting in the hierarchy (cf. chapter 1). Thus the kinds of information and formating required will be tailored appropriately to the types of functional activities and their relationships in each "block" on the organization chart. Similarly, the extent of detail in any planning or feedback document will depend on the number of levels in the hierarchy for a given functional area and the specific decision-making responsibilities with which each level is charged. As a rule of thumb, only such detail in the feedback process need be submitted to a managerial level that pertains to actionable authority at that level or action directed to a lower level to take.

Thus, referring to our example of the Gadget Corporation in chapter 1, the assembling-department superintendent, plant 1, would be the appropriate manager to prepare budgets and receive performance reports on materials and on labor requirements, grade composition, and manning utilization for his unit in complete detail. He is the one who has the authority and is charged with the responsibility to take corrective action when any of these activity items are out of line. The director, plant 1, need only receive summary data for these activities for planning and budgeting purposes. For performance evaluation, he will need a full report on volume achievement levels by product lines to compare with planned operating schedules that required his approval at the beginning of the period together with cost summaries only. Any deviations from plans in these summaries he will discuss with his superintendent in a review session. Similarly, at the next higher level, the vice president, production, may approve summaries of volume schedules by major product groups submitted by each plant director together with the plant budget figures in summary for the individual activity departments. In turn, he would receive operating results on volume and cost dollars according to the same summary classifications.

Before going on to formal treatment of performance reporting and appraisal based on the information system and measures set forth in part I, we will mention a few considerations on the relative roles of management and budget groups in the organization.

"Management by objectives" is by no means a new concept although it is only in recent years that it has been adopted to any significant extent by many industrial firms and most recently by government agencies and nonprofit organizations. A main tenet of this concept is that without a stated set of goals that set forth the general purpose and specific "subpurposes" that justify the existence of an organization in the first place, functional planning, staffing, and financing efforts for the organization can easily be misguided in terms of any realistic foundation or direction. Under this concept then functional planning or "strategizing" becomes meaningful or even justifiable only after conditions and guidelines of purpose for the organization have been established.

If we accept the premise that planning, coordinating, and controlling of operations in any organization, be it product or service oriented, profit or nonprofit seeking, represent the primary functional responsibilities with which a management group is charged, then what might be the respective roles of management and budgeting personnel? The budgeting teams, under the guidance of a budget director, are technically qualified personnel who draft the budget formats, develop budget standards and prepare the performance analyses for each level of management and disseminate the appropriate reports to each level. In doing so, they would confer closely with professional and technical staff members of the other departments. For example, they would have to coordinate with the personnel department for labor grades or skills and rates. They would also have to rely on the plant engineers for technical aspects including materials quantity and use standards, labor and manning utilization standards, and output capacity rates and charts. Service departments would supply the budget teams with maintenance and repair standards and schedules. Budget personnel would also need to confer with the general accounting officers for all other financial information necessary to complete preparation such as depreciation tables for organizational units and any spending or out-of-pocket financial classifications that are direct to the functional units. In this way, they can effectively carry out their main responsibility for preparing the master budget and performance evaluation plans for each of these levels for submission to the chief financial officer. Formal preparation of both budgeting and performance schedules would be within their area of responsibility, together with analysis of cost behavior, documentation of historical financial data, and development of procedures for review of budgets and performance appraisal at each organizational level.

It is the chief financial officer or the controller who would have the authority to approve information requirements for each operating level below him in the hierarchy in accordance with decision-making resonsibilities at each level. However, the divisional and plant officers would likely confer with the budget director, and jointly they would arrive at a set of budgeting and performance evaluation plans for each of these levels for submission to the chief financial officer.

Budgeting itself is an integral part of and concurrent with beginning-of-period managerial review and approval of operating plans at every organizational level. And in view of what we have said here, participative management is an implied characteristic of planning and budgeting. Thus at both divisional and plant levels, a budget committee may work best to alleviate conflicts in budget decision. However, lower levels of management would have a psychological inclination to want "more money" in budget proposals for their operating units while higher levels charged with the authority to approve or disapprove proposals may tend to resist. The committee approach to arriving at planning and budgeting decisions may provide a sufficiently democratic atmosphere so as to remove such barriers.

8

Flexible Budgeting and Performance Evaluation for Production

Management control procedures and analyses in production can be considered most appropriately in relation to production planning. There are two readily apparent reasons for this view. First, performance evaluation is undertaken through the use of measurements of the plant activities for specific past periods of time, and the results are in turn outputs of quantitative operating plans adopted at the beginning of the period. Second, the approach to production planning itself will be different depending on whether a manufacturer mass produces a product line or produces according to specific customer orders. The latter may well involve tailor-made engineering specifications, and levels of preplanned inventory cannot be determined practically in each operating period. When products are mass produced, on the other hand, the importance of the economics of working-capital management in relation to inventory volume of finished goods becomes prominent.

For mass-produced products, production volume levels can be scheduled by time periods such as quarterly or monthly. For customer-order-based production, schedules for volume and operating budgets are in fact based on specific order batches for each product line, and the concept of volume flow by time periods may not really apply. Since production volume scheduling and budgeting for mass-produced product lines depends on planned inventory levels by time periods, the latter can be determined appropriately through projections of sales for each product line and for the same time periods. On the other hand, projections of production volume for specific order placements may not be feasible when a company experiences considerable irregularity in the timing of such orders.

Control and performance appraisal in production would involve the same considerations for the development of operating standards and measurements in either case. For customer-order production, however, the unit of orientation in applying control measurements may be the individual job order rather than the plant department. Mass-production planning and scheduling for inventories could mean that the sales department in many companies must work from "available" stocks of finished-goods inventories for any particular month or quarter. In fact, volume planning by product lines really centers on the planning of inventories since they represent the critical link between sales forecasting and planning for marketing operations on the one hand and production scheduling on the other. Any volume "cushion" that may be necessary when expected sales exceed production levels must be sold from period inventory carryovers. Conversely, an unexpected sales slump would yield carryover of excess inventory to future periods, thus leading to downward adjustments in future planned production schedules.

If a company can accurately predict seasonal sales volumes based on past experience and if nonseasonal sales do not vary greatly, then an average monthly inventory level can be set that should satisfy both sales volume planning and production scheduling with a minimum risk of experiencing excess inventories or stock out.

Let us take an example. Table 8-1 gives monthly sales and production history of the Dynamic Corporation for product MT2 during the past five years. The five-year history generally reflects an upward trend in production, sales, and inventory carryovers (monthly and annually). The exception is sales volume for the fourth year although this was anticipated by the forecast of 57,000 units. Sales reflect two seasonal peaks during each year: May-June and September-November.

Volume planning procedures used by Dynamic bases production scheduling on a consideration of two factors. One is an allocation of the annual forecast of sales in each year to monthly estimates based on the month-to-month percentage changes in actual sales experienced during the year ended. The other is a targeted monthly inventory carryover sufficient to meet a planned year-end inventory level. You will notice that Dynamic has planned to achieve levels of between 22 and 27 thousand units by the end of the second and third years. Midway through Year 3, management decided that carryovers were excessive and should be reduced to between 14 and 16 thousand units. They felt that an inventory level for MT2 that would meet customer demand for four to six months in the event of plant shutdowns was "playing it a little too safe" and that an inventory stock of approximately three months would be sufficient. They also felt that equipment and manpower resources could be shifted to production of the other product lines with greater overall economy, despite a rapid growth in the marketability of MT2. Further, Dynamic had not experienced a labor strike in a dozen years, and a temporary shortage in procurement markets caused a one-month gap in production of MT2 three years prior to the present series.

In planning production for Year 4, the allocation of forecast annual sales (57,000 units) by months was made in the previous period. However, monthly production volume was scheduled so that inventory balances would decline at an average of 1,100 to 1,200 units for each of the twelve periods. In Year 5, management believed that the same inventory balance could be achieved with projected sales of 71,000 units of MT2 by setting annual production at 71,300 units (which reflects considerable confidence in the sales forecast). A constant monthly production level of 5,800 units was planned. The exceptions were the peak months of May and June when volume was set at 6,200 and September through November when the monthly schedule was 6,100 to meet the annual production target.

Table 8-1
Product MT2 Monthly Sales, Inventory, and Production Volume,
Five-Year Trend

	Production Schedule (Unit Volume)	Sales Volume (in Units)	Monthly Ending Inventory
Year 1			
		12/31/0	4,400
January	3,300	2,600	5,100
February	3,300	2,400	6,000
March	3,500	2,800	6,700
April	3,900	3,000	7,600
May	4,500	3,800	8,300
June	5,100	4,200	9,200
July	3,000	2,300	9,900
August	3,700	2,800	10,800
September	3,800	3,300	11,300
October	5,400	4,500	12,200
November	5,000	4,300	12,900
December	4,200	3,300	13,800
Totals (Y1)	48,700	39,300	
		(40,000 forecast)	
Year 2			
		12/31/1	13,800
January	3,350	2,700	14,300
February	3,500	2,650	15,300
March	3,500	2,850	15,950
April	4,050	3,200	16,800
May	4,750	4,100	17,450
June	5,450	4,600	18,300
July	3,950	3,300	18,950
August	4,300	3,400	19,850
September	5,400	4,750	20,500
October	5,950	5,150	21,300
November	5,650	5,000	21,950
December	4,150	3,300	22,800
Totals (Y2)	54,000	45,000	
		(45,000 forecast)	
Year 3			
		12/1/2	22,800
January	4,600	4,200	23,200
February	4,400	4,150	23,450
March	4,750	4,350	23,850
April	4,950	4,700	24,100
May	6,400	6,000	24,500
June	6,950	6,700	24,750
July	5,900	5,500	25,150
August	4,300	4,050	25,400

Table 8-1 continued

	Production Schedule (Unit Volume)	Sales Volume (in Units)	Monthly Ending Inventory
September	7,150	6,750	25,800
October	7,450	7,200	26,050
November	7,300	6,900	26,450
December	5,250	5,000	26,700
Totals (Y3)	69,400	65,500	
		(65,000 forecast)	

Year 4

		12/31/3	26,700
January	2,350	3,500	25,550
February	2,400	3,350	24,600
March	2,500	3,650	23,450
April	2,950	3,900	22,500
May	4,250	5,300	21,450
June	4,950	5,900	20,500
July	3,650	4,800	19,350
August	2,400	3,350	18,400
September	4,700	5,950	17,150
October	5,550	6,500	16,200
November	5,050	6,100	15,150
December	3,150	4,300	14,000
Totals (Y4)	43,900	56,600	
		(57,000 forecast)	

Year 5

		12/31/4	14,000
January	5,800	4,950	14,850
February	5,800	4,550	16,100
March	5,800	4,850	17,050
April	5,800	5,100	17,750
May	6,200	6,500	17,450
June	6,200	7,100	16,550
July	5,800	5,600	16,750
August	5,800	4,550	18,000
September	6,100	7,150	16,950
October	6,100	7,700	15,350
November	6,100	7,300	14,150
December	5,800	5,750	14,200
Totals (Y5)	71,300	71,100	
		(71,000 forecast)	

In our approach here, quantitative budgeting for plant operations is the financial application of cost standards to scheduled production volume and provides the basis for appraising the results of operations at the end of the period. A flexible-budgeting system is in fact a financial plan for both direct variable and fixed-overhead costs of a group of activities within a department. It is a budget-planning system that can be applied to any level of scheduled volume for product lines. In doing so, budgeting for direct variable inputs is easier to accomplish for purposes of management control than for overhead both in concept and in application. This is true simply because variable inputs and their costs will parallel changes in unit volume of a product line both in direction and magnitude. It is for this reason that once standard cost rates have been set for each of the variable inputs, either on the basis of product-line units or an alternate measure, these same rates can be applied to any planned volume in preparing the budget. This is what makes the budget system "flexible."

Setting standard production costs for product-line costing and inventory valuation and for control of production activities was a key topic covered in chapters 3 and 4. We will take a moment to review some of the important points. Chapter 3 dealt with the technical aspects and problems of setting cost standards under an absorption-cost system in production, while chapter 4 discussed the same considerations as they would apply under a direct costing system. In both cost-accounting systems, the cost classifications and procedures for setting standards and standard-cost coefficients or rates were essentially the same for direct variable costs. And in this regard, such variable classifications were direct to both product lines and to organizational departments.

The operating input standards themselves are obtained through engineering studies as we discussed in part I and are expressed in terms of units or batches of physical product. Standard costs are then developed through operating experience for all cost classifications except prime costs. For the latter, labor contracts specify hourly rates for each grade, and for materials, the unit prices recorded in the purchasing department become the standard-cost coefficients. These cost rates are then applied to the standards for operating inputs in preparing a budget for the production department and for any planned volume of activity.

Fixed overhead is the one area that does present a problem since it does not vary with production activity and it is a constant, although often a substantial, amount of financial allocation to a department. In chapter 3, we saw that when a company uses an absorption cost-accounting system, cost assignment of fixed overhead to product is usually a cumbersome task, particularly since distortions in product costing for valuation of inventories or for product pricing must be avoided. However, when a company uses a direct cost system (chapter 4), fixed-overhead allocation to units of product output is no longer a part of the system—for product valuation. The concept that justifies the "avoidance" of including fixed production overhead as part of the value of finished goods under direct costing is that since fixed overhead represents capital expenditure for plant and equipment at some point in time in the past, it is an essential requirement for "being in business" and the allocation of such expenditures is a function of time more properly than it is a function of production activity for any specific operating period. Such costs would exist regardless of what level of operating volume the plant produced, even if it yielded zero volume. Under direct costing then, fixed overhead is a constant charge for determining income for the period and is not included in the value of inventories.

Management control shifts the emphasis of the financial aspects of a company's production operations from the product itself to the organization and plant departments. Essentially, all variable costs are direct to the activities of an organizational unit in the plant (and this includes variable overhead) and are controllable. Why? Controllability means that the manager or supervisor who is responsible for the conduct of operations and activities in his unit can make decisions that will determine the level of activity but more particularly the amounts of the operating inputs required by the activity (labor, materials, supplies, and maintenance) and hence the financial cost of these inputs.

You will recall that in chapter 7, we set forth procedures for developing flexible budgets as a foundation not only for planning operations in accordance with production schedules for product-line volume but also as a viable approach to management control and performance appraisal. Also, in part I we developed variance measures for prime costs and for variable overhead to include spending and efficiency variation from standard or budgeted operations. The flexible-budgeting approach takes into consideration the fact that most major fixed costs are allocations to a department that may or may not be direct to the organizational unit. They cannot be influenced by managerial decisions within the department and thus from the standpoint of short-term production planning and operations, cannot be controlled at that level. A flexible-budgeting system facilitates both the financial planning for operations and the analysis and appraisal of operating results against plans in terms of these decisions.

Our task now is to prepare the formal departmental budget in production and to set forth the purpose and use of a unique feature called the "control budget." The preparation of budgets as well as drafting performance reports are based on the concepts and measurement of flexible budgeting.

Returning to our illustration of the Dynamic Corporation, we will assume that our task is to prepare the budget for the third quarter of annual production operations in the year 198-. You will recall in our discussions in chapters 3 and 4 that we had three products, MT1, MT2, and MT3, and the two producing departments were machining and assembling in plant 1. We will expand this illustration somewhat in terms of its organization by assuming the following seven departments:

Department 1: Processing and machining, works on product MT1 only

Department 2: Processing and machining, works on product MT2 only

Department 3: Processing and machining, works on product MT3 only

Department 4: Assembling, works on all three products

Department 5: Service and maintenance

Department 6: Power plant

Department 7: Plant administration

For purposes of simplification, we will assume that each of the operating departments has a single grade of labor and that the standard contract rates are as shown in table 8-2. Similarly, variable overhead is shown in table 8-3. The standard production time per product unit in minutes is shown in table 8-4. Further, the department product standards are as shown in table 8-5. Scheduled production volume, based on quarterly sales projections, are:

Product MT1	12,000 units
Product MT2	10,500 units
Product MT3	5,500 units

Budgeted fixed overhead for the third quarter in each department is shown in table 8-6. We can now prepare a preliminary operating plan to include the producing departments (departments 1-4) for plant 1, third quarter, 198- (table 8-7).

Department 5, service and maintenance, provides auxiliary services to each of the producing departments. The procedure used is to set a constant number of hours at 700 per month that is programmed for this department. In addition, there are portions of monthly fixed maintenance expenses that represent basic service requirements to each of the producing departments. They are shown in table 8-8. In addition, service for machinery repairs, cleaning, and lubrication are direct to each of the producing departments, as shown in table 8-9. Variable-rate and fixed-amount standards for planning and budgeting purposes in department 5 are shown in table 8-10. The variable rate of $7.00 is used for maintenance service in excess of 700 hours per month (or 2,100 hours per quarter). The budget for department 5 for the third quarter can now be developed as shown in figure 8-1.

Table 8-2
Standard Direct Labor Hourly Rates

	Department			
	1	2	3	4
Grade No.	4	17	8	5
Rate	$3.60	$3.00	$4.50	$6.00

Table 8-3
Variable Overhead Rates per Labor Hour

	Department			
	1	*2*	*3*	*4*
Variable overhead per DLH	$2.20	$2.40	$2.90	$9.00

In developing the preceding data, it was necessary to apply the appropriate time-conversion factors for determining allocations or transfers to the operating departments at the variable maintenance rates given and to prorate the fixed monthly budget figures to a quarterly basis. We are now ready to develop the complete budget plan for the quarter (tables 8-11 and 8-12).

The foregoing quarterly budget we developed is in fact a statement in financial terms of the production volume and activity schedule by product lines and by departments for plant 1. It is now our task to monitor actual production activity for the quarter and develop formal presentations for performance evaluation. All standards needed for this purpose were set forth earlier in connection with preparing the plant budget.

In doing so, no problems will arise in determining allocation rates to each product line for fixed overhead as we had in chapter 3 under an absorption-cost system. We are concerned only with control of production activities and their resource inputs. Further, for purposes of management control we need always focus our attention on those financial inputs for activities that are direct to the organizational unit in question and over which there can be managerial decision-making influence within the unit.

The product and activity standards remain the same as they were at the beginning of the third quarter for each department. It is now our task to develop worksheets for all departments and to prepare and evaluate the performance reports for departments 1, 2, and 3. Actual expenses for the period are known, and the production output for the period was as shown in table 8-13.

Performance results relating to direct labor and variable overhead are presented in table 8-14 for each department.

Table 8-4
Standard Production Time per Product Unit
(minutes)

	Department			
	1	*2*	*3*	*4*
MT1	30			30
MT2		60		20
MT3			120	60

Table 8-5
Department Product Variable Cost Standards

	Dept. 1 (MT1)	Dept. 2 (MT2)	Dept. 3 (MT3)
Processing and Machining			
Materials	$4.80	$2.40	$6.60
Direct labor	1.80	3.00	9.00
Variable overhead	1.10	2.40	5.80
		Dept. 4	
	MT1	MT2	MT3
Assembling			
Materials	$ 0	$3.00	$4.00
Direct labor	3.00	2.00	6.00
Variable overhead	4.50	3.00	9.00
Total variable	$15.20	$15.80	$40.40

Materials prices per unit actually paid for production in the third quarter are:

Department 1	(MT1)	$4.80
Department 2	(MT2)	3.00
Department 3	(MT3)	6.00
Department 4	(MT1)	0
	(MT2)	3.50
	(MT3)	4.80

Materials-price variances are assigned to the plant purchasing unit, which organizationally is department 7. Quantity variances for purposes of management control are a function of actual usage and thus are assigned to each of the producing departments. Standard product specifications for materials and actual quantities consumed in production for the quarter are as shown in table 8-15. The materials-usage or quantity variances, on the other hand, are charged to each

Table 8-6
Budgeted Fixed Overhead, Plant 1, Third Quarter, 198-

Dept.	Title	Amount
1	Processing and machining	$ 34,200
2	Processing and machining	24,900
3	Processing and machining	52,340
4	Assembly	25,100
5	Service and maintenance	8,460
6	Power plant	28,850
7	Administration	86,150
Total		$260,000

Table 8-7
Dynamic Corporation, Plant 1, Production Schedule and Budget,
Departments 1 through 4, Third Quarter, 198-

	Scheduled Production		Variable Costs			Fixed	
Dept.	Units	DLH	Materials	Labor	Overhead	Overhead	Total
1	12,000	6,000	$ 57,600	$ 21,600	$ 13,200	$ 34,200	$126,600
2	10,500	10,500	25,200	31,500	25,200	24,900	106,800
3	5,500	11,000	36,300	49,500	31,900	52,340	170,040
4		15,000[a]	53,500[b]	90,000	135,000	25,100	303,600
Totals			$172,600	$192,600	$205,300	$136,540	$707,040

[a]		DLH		[b]		Rate	
	Units	× Per Unit	DLH		Units	× Per Unit	
MT1	12,000	1/2	6,000	MT1	12,000	$0	$0
MT2	10,500	1/3	3,500	MT2	10,500	$3	31,500
MT3	5,500	1	5,500	MT3	5,500	$4	22,000
Totals			15,000				$53,500

of the producing departments since decisions affecting usage and therefore control of quantities consumed is within these departments (table 8-16).

Summaries of departmental performance data with variances from budget are presented for fixed overhead in table 8-17. Table 8-18 summarizes the performance variances from budget for all variable and fixed expense categories by department. Service and maintenance (department 5) budget and performance data with transfers to operating departments are presented in table 8-19.

The variable expenses for service and maintenance then show the following variances from budget:

	Budget	Efficiency Variance	Spending Variance	Percent Achieved
Efficiency	$27,783	$(210)	$ —	0.992
Spending	27,993	—	(406)	0.985

For control purposes, the spending variance is the only increment that applies to fixed expenses and for service and maintenance, as shown in table 8-20.

Tables 8-21 and 8-22 are examples of performance reports for individual operating departments and are included to assist the reader in interpreting performance. You will note that performance data and percent of achievement against budget are presented for both the current quarter and cumulative operations for the year (year-to-date). Table 8-22 presents account classification detail for overhead in department 1. Performance results for service and maintenance (department 5) are presented in tables 8-23 through 8-25.

Table 8-8
Monthly Fixed Maintenance Expenses Allocated to
Operating Departments

Dept.	Basic Monthly Fixed Charges to Departments
1	$1,150
2	900
3	1,650
4	1,380
Total	$5,080

The foregoing technical aspects of quantitative planning and budgeting for production and the formating and analyses of the results of operations serve in combination to provide all the information that is necessary to interpret performance for management control. The interpretation and use of the data we have analyzed is the task now ahead of us.

At the moment it seems that we face a large volume of refined data analyses and formats for interpretation. In fact, the task is not as formidable as it appears initially, and it is perhaps best to segregate the information according to the types of activity and their account classifications. In production, the main categories of resources with controllable financial classifications are direct materials, direct labor, and variable overhead. The budget plan for departments 1, 2, and 3 has been presented in table 8-7. You will recall from part I that we had defined and developed measures for the controllable variances for all prime costs and for variable overhead as follows:

Direct materials:	Price variance
	Use or quantity variance
Direct labor:	Rate variance
	Use or efficiency variance
Variable overhead:	Efficiency variance
	Spending variance

Table 8-9
Labor Hour Ratios for Allocation of Service and Maintenance to
Operating Departments

Dept.	Direct Labor Hours	Direct Maintenance Dept. Labor Hours
1	16	1
2	10	1
3	8	1
4	20	1

Table 8-10
Variable-Rate and Fixed-Amount Standards, Department 5

	Rate Per Direct Maintenance Hour	Fixed Amount Per Month
Supervision	$ 0	$2,000
Maintenance labor	4.00	2,200
Maintenance supplies	1.80	800
Heat, light, and power	1.20	1,400
Depreciation on equipment	0	1,500
Totals	$7.00	$7,900

We also mentioned the control budget as being a unique feature of our performance system. It is simply a translation of the forecast budget to a unit-volume basis that takes actual production at the end of the period for performance evaluation. Thus the forecast budget is the application of department standards to planned or scheduled volume while the control budget is the application of these same standards to the volume achieved. The assumption here is that the organizational department does not control production volume as such. Ordinarily, each operating unit in the plant will meet the volume that has been scheduled if it is within operating capacity limits. Reasons for not meeting scheduled volume would be changes in schedule due to period changes in sales forecasts or orders, sudden shortages in materials or parts supplies or in the required labor force. Such factors are generally beyond the direct control of operating management at the plant department level. These product volume

Supervisor: V. Small		Total Maintenance Hours: 5,650	
		Direct Maintenance Hours to Departments 1-4: 3,550	
	Variable	Fixed	Total
Supervision	$ 0	$ 6,000	$ 6,000
Maintenance labor	14,200	6,600	20,800
Maintenance supplies	6,390	2,400	8,790
Heat, light, and power	4,260	4,200	8,460
Depreciation on equipment	0	4,500	4,500
Gross maintenance budget	$24,850	$23,700	$48,550
Less transfer to operating departments	24,850	15,240	40,090
Net maintenance budget	$ 0	$ 8,460	$ 8,460

Figure 8-1. Plant 1, Department 5, Service and Maintenance Budget, Third Quarter, 198-

Table 8-11
Dynamic Corporation, Plant 1, Production Schedule and Budget,
Third Quarter, 198-

Dept.	Units	DLH	Materials	Labor	Overhead	Fixed Overhead	Total
				Variable Costs			
1	12,000	6,000	$ 57,600	$ 21,600	$ 13,200	$ 34,200	$126,600
2	10,500	10,500	25,200	31,500	25,200	24,900	106,800
3	5,500	11,000	36,300	49,500	31,900	52,340	170,040
4		15,000	53,500	90,000	135,000	25,100	303,600
5					0	8,460	8,460
6					0	28,850	28,850
7					0	86,150	86,150
			$172,600	$192,600	$205,300	$260,000	$830,500

variations from scheduled production would of course be investigated to determine the specific cause for deviation and the extent to which responsibility does or does not apply to the plant department in question.

Labor variances based on control budget are drawn from table 8-14 and are shown in table 8-26.

All the financial data in parentheses indicate that performance was below standard or unfavorable based on the control budget while the other data not in parentheses reflect above-standard or favorable performance. The interpretation of operating results for labor is straightforward. The efficiency variance tells us that excess hours were used in departments 1 and 2 while there was an above-standard utilization of labor hours in department 3. Causes for unfavorable utilization of labor time may be that too few people at the standard grade (based on manning charts) were assigned to production in these departments for the level of output achieved, that retraining may be indicated if efficiency variances are unfavorable in successive periods, that the wrong labor grades were assigned to an operation, or that methods of supervision are inadequate.

The labor-rate variances in departments 1 and 2 are similarly unfavorable meaning that they were higher than standard. If the labor contracts were renegotiated at any time during the period resulting in higher rates, this cause for

Table 8-12
Schedule A, Department 5 Transfers to Operating Departments

Dept.	Budgeted DLH	Maintenance Conversion	Maintenance DLH	Variable Rate	Transfer Budget
1	6,000	16	375	$7.00	$ 2,625
2	10,500	10	1,050	7.00	7,350
3	11,000	8	1,375	7.00	9,625
4	15,000	20	750	7.00	5,250
Total					$24,850

Table 8-13
Production Volume, Plant 1, Third Quarter

Month	MT1	MT2	MT3
July	2,500	2,000	2,500
August	3,000	3,500	1,200
September	5,500	6,500	2,800
Total units	11,000	12,000	6,500

unfavorable rate variances would require a revision of the rate standard and would not therefore be a reflection on performance as such. However, a higher-than-standard labor grade used for an operation would have to be interpreted as a deficiency in performance for the rate portion of the labor variance. Causes for favorable or above-standard performance in department 3 as to efficiency may simply be the result of on-the-job improvement over time based on experience or it may be caused by an increase in the competence of supervision. Only persistently favorable labor-efficiency variances in several successive production periods, however, would warrant a revision in labor time standards. Otherwise, the interpretation would be that the superior performance achieved on a continuing basis will justify the awarding of merit compensation or promotion.

As to rate variances, a favorable result may be caused by the use of a grade less than standard, although such a cause we would expect will be accompanied by below-standard performance as to efficiency or use of labor time. Favorable performance for both components of direct labor such as we have here would logically occur only in rare instances and errors in the data per se may be indicated.

Table 8-27 provides variable overhead variances taken from table 8-14.

Chapters 3 and 4 developed performance measures for variable overhead and defined the two components as being the efficiency variance and the spending variance. Those chapters also developed overhead-classification schedules and observed that variable overhead items were entirely variable or contained a variable rate as well as a fixed amount. The rates were based on some variable measure of activity input such as hours of direct labor. The efficiency variance always applies to the variable item (or variable component) of overhead expenses. Since our rate is based on the variable behavior of direct labor hours, we would expect that the performance pattern for overhead should correspond to that of direct labor. This is exactly what we find. Variable overhead is below standard based on control budget in department 1 and department 2 and exceeds standard in department 3. Ordinarily, this means that for control purposes, variable overhead cannot be varied independently. In determining causes for variation in direct labor and taking any indicated corrective action from one period to another, the efficiency component of overhead should be self-adjusting. It is primarily for this reason that the underlying account

Table 8-14
Dynamic Corporation Variance Worksheet, Direct Labor and Variable Overhead, Third Quarter, 198-

Direct Labor

Dept.	Direct Labor Hours — Standard[a]	Direct Labor Hours — Actual	Standard Labor Rate	Standard Hours at Standard Rate (Control Budget)	Actual Hours at Standard Rate	Actual Hours at Actual Rate (Actual Expense)	Variance — Efficiency	Variance — Rate
1	5,500	5,700	$3.60	$19,800	$20,520	$20,730	$ (720)	$(210)
2	12,000	12,450	3.00	36,000	37,350	37,775	(1,350)	(425)
3	13,000	12,850	4.50	58,500	57,825	57,400	675	425
4	16,000	15,820	6.00	96,000	94,920	94,920	1,080	0

Variable Overhead

Dept.	Direct Labor Hours — Standard[a]	Direct Labor Hours — Actual	Standard Variable Overhead Rate	Standard Hours at Standard Rate (Control Budget)	Actual Hours at Standard Rate	Actual Variable Overhead Expense	Variance — Efficiency	Variance — Spending
1	5,500	5,700	$2.20	$ 12,100	$ 12,540	$ 13,040	$ (440)	$(500)
2	12,000	12,450	2.40	28,800	29,880	29,600	(1,080)	280
3	13,000	12,850	2.90	37,700	37,265	37,265	435	0
4	16,000	15,820	9.00	144,000	142,380	142,600	1,620	(220)
5				0[b]	300[b]	560	(300)	(260)
6				0[b]	0[b]	450	0	(450)

[a]These are standard hours allowed at actual production volume achieved. ( ) Unfavorable variance.
[b]Variable overhead of service departments included in budgets of operating departments at standard rates.

Table 8-15
Schedule B, Department 7, Materials-Price Variances

Dept.	Product	Standard Price	Actual Price	Actual Unit Production	Price Variance
1	MT1	$4.80	$4.80	11,000	$ 0
2	MT2	2.40	3.00	12,000	(7,200)
3	MT3	6.60	6.00	6,500	3,900
4	MT1	0	0	11,000	0
	MT2	3.00	3.50	12,000	(6,000)
	MT3	4.00	4.80	6,500	(5,200)
					($14,500)

classifications are not presented in the performance report for plant 1. This fact does not diminish the importance of appraising the efficiency of variable overhead for each reporting period and the relationship of its achievement to that of other direct variable activity inputs.

The spending variance is a more important issue for financial control of overhead. It applies to all overhead items that are fixed and to the fixed component of overhead items that are semivariable. These amounts based on budget and the spending variances for department 1 are shown in table 8-22. The spending variance will always represent the difference between the control budget amount for each overhead item and the out-of-pocket (or working-capital) expenditures for the item during the period. It is for this reason that the individual classifications must be examined when conducting the performance review. Causes for actual expenditures being less than the control budget figures or overrunning the control budget can properly be determined in reference to

Table 8-16
Schedule C, Operating Departments, Materials-Usage Variances

Dept.	Product	Standard Units Per Product	Actual Production	Standard Materials Allowed
1	MT1	4	11,000	44,000
2	MT2	3	12,000	36,000
3	MT3	3	6,500	19,500
4	MT1	0	11,000	0
	MT2	2	12,000	24,000
	MT3	1	6,500	6,500

Actual Quantities Used	Difference	×	Standard Price	=	Materials-use Variance
44,000	0		$4.80		$ 0
36,000	0		2.40		0
20,000	(500)		6.60		(3,300)
0	0		0		0
24,200	(200)		3.00		(600)
6,900	(400)		4.00		(1,600)

Table 8-17
Dynamic Corporation, Plant 1, Fixed-Overhead Variance Summary,
Third Quarter, 198-

| Dept. | Standard Direct Labor Hours | | Standard Amounts per Step Budget | | | Variance | |
	Forecast Volume	Actual Volume	Forecast Volume	Actual Volume (Control)	Actual Expense	Volume	Spending
1	5,500	5,700	$ 34,200	$ 34,450	$ 34,650	$(250)	$(200)
2	12,000	12,450	24,900	25,400	25,200	(500)	200
3	13,000	12,850	52,340	52,340	52,340	0	0
4	16,000	15,820	25,100	24,950	24,950	150	0
5			8,460	8,460	8,670	0	(210)
6			28,850	28,850	29,050	0	(200)
7			86,150	86,150	85,970	0	180
Totals			$260,000	$260,600	$260,830	$(600)	$(230)

each classification. Totals are only a summary reflection that expenditures exceeded or fell short of the control budget.

Key items appearing in table 8-22 are supervision, indirect labor, maintenance, and utilities. Supervision, as we discussed in part I, is rarely a variable item of overhead. It is fixed for specific ranges of production since the number of supervisors remain constant within a volume range and the "cost of supervision" is based on salary scales rather than hourly rates by grade level. However, as a specific output range is exceeded or as production volume falls to a lower level, the number of supervisors required by a department for a given period will increase or decrease accordingly. This will cause the fixed-cost pattern to change in jumps or steps upward or downward. For department 1, the budgeted supervision was the actual amount incurred for the volume of production achieved. This was also the experience of the department for the year to date. Had supervision resulted in an unfavorable spending variance, it would clearly reflect inefficiency in terms of established standards. Adding more supervisors than the requirement for the volume range is unwarranted. A favorable variation from budgeted standards for supervision, while resulting in a smaller number of supervisors for the department based on standard, may very well result in below-standard performance and higher offsetting inefficiency for other inputs, particularly direct labor. Thus any favorable variance reflected in the performance reports will warrant investigation to determine causes and the impacts on other labor inputs. Favorable variances for supervision in successive operating periods, with no offsetting-cost performance deficiencies in other areas of a department's labor force may very well warrant merit awards or promotion. If favorable variances contine to persist, however, management would then be wise to consider the advisability of upgrading the performance standards themselves.

Table 8-18
Dynamic Corporation, Plant 1, Summary of Production Variances from Standard Costs, Third Quarter, 198-

Dept.	Materials		Labor			Variable Overhead		Fixed Overhead	
	Price	Usage	Efficiency	Rate	Efficiency	Spending	Spending	Total
1	$ 0	$ 0	$ (720)	$(210)	$ (440)	$ 500)	$(200)	($ 2,070)
2	(7,200)	0	(1,350)	(425)	(1,080)	280	200	(9,575)
3	3,900	(3,300)	675	425	435	0	0	2,135
4	(11,200)	(2,200)	1,080	0	1,620	(220)	0	(10,920)
5	–	–	–	–	(300)	(260)[a]	(210)	770
6	–	–	–	–	0	(450)[a]	(200)	650
7	(500)	–	–	–	0	0	180	(320)
	($15,000)	$(5,500)	$(315)	$(210)	$235	($1,150)	($230)	($22,170)

( ) Unfavorable.

[a]Excess of variable costs incurred over charges to operating departments at standard charging rates. Labor and supplies cost variances for these two departments are included in the variable-spending variance but reported in detail on the departmental-performance reports.

Table 8-19
Dynamic Corporation, Plant 1, Variable Maintenance, Department 5,
Third Quarter, 198-

Classification	Rate per Direct Maintenance Hour	Budget for Standard Hours Allowed (Control)	Budget for Actual Direct Labor Hours	Actual Variable Maintenance Exp.
Supervision	$ 0	$ 0	$ 0	$ 0
Maintenance labor	4.00	15,876	15,996	16,300
Maintenance supplies	1.80	7,144	7,198	7,250
Heat, light, and power	1.20	4,763	4,799	4,849
Totals	$7.00	$27,783	$27,993	$28,399

	Standard DLH Allowed (Actual Volume)	Maintenance Hours Per DLH	Maintenance Hours (Control)	Actual DLH	Maintenance Hours Per DLH	Maintenance Hours (Actual)
Dept. 1	5,500	16	344	5,700	16	357
Dept. 2	12,000	10	1,200	12,450	10	1,245
Dept. 3	13,000	8	1,625	12,850	8	1,606
Dept. 4	16,000	20	800	15,820	20	791
			3,969			3,999

Table 8-20

Plant 1, Fixed Maintenance, Department 5, Third Quarter, 198-

	Fixed-expense Budget	Actual Fixed Expense	Spending Variance
Supervision	$ 6,000	$ 6,400	$ (400)
Maintenance labor	6,600	6,450	150
Maintenance supplies	2,400	2,650	(250)
Heat, light, and power	4,200	4,700	(500)
Depreciation on equipment	4,500	4,500	0
Totals	$23,700	$24,700	$(1,000)

Indirect labor would include administrative and clerical personnel required in nonproduction phases of the department's activities. This classification may include both a variable rate and a fixed amount under flexible budgeting. Any deviation from the budgeted standard for indirect labor will be reflected as part of the variance for variable overhead. The spending variance would again pertain to out-of-pocket expenditures and may relate to both variable and fixed components of indirect labor. The results in table 8-22 show that this classification is inefficient or unfavorable both in the third quarter and year to date and by a very comparable achievement percent of budget in each case. Causes for variation in spending variances for indirect labor may range from misassignment of personnel with particular qualifications or skill specifications that are not in accordance with the work requirements in the department to excess hours worked over budgeted hours. Underutilization of time (hours) resulting in a favorable spending variance would also be investigated and may be the result of either excess efficiency or inadequate manning for the control budget volume level. Again repeated favorable spending variances for labor may justify adjusting the standards to make them tighter.

Maintenance and utilities may be expected to reflect significant portions of efficiency variation from plant department budgets for manufacturers engaged in "flow-through" production of standardized products. In table 8-22 of our illustrations, we note that the maintenance budget is unfavorable as to spending efficiency for the third quarter, which is atypical for the year as a whole. The maintenance and service functions are performed by department 5 and then are allocated by fixed and variable amounts to the producing departments. Causes for spending variances in maintenance and for production rework as well may range from negligence to unforeseeable breakdowns in tools and machinery. Only investigation of specific causes in either category will enable a plant manager or his foremen to determine what action will be required to bring substandard performance back in line. We have treated maintenance in our illustrations here as a part of general plant-service operations and as a separate organizational unit. Direct services to the producing departments are properly the responsibility of those departments as to both spending and efficiency

Table 8-21
Dynamic Corporation, Plant 1, Performance Report, Department 2, Third Quarter, 198-

	Third Quarter			Year-to-date		
	Budget	Variance	Percent Achieved	Budget	Variance	Percent Achieved
Direct Materials						
Materials-usage variance	$211,200	$ 0	100	$645,600	$(7,400)	98.8
Direct Labor						
Labor-efficiency variance	19,800	(720)	96.5	58,600	(3,300)	94.6
Labor-rate variance	20,520	(210)	99	59,400	1,700	103
Overhead Expense						
Variable-efficiency variance	12,100	(440)	96.5	36,300	(2,000)	94.6
Variable-spending variance	12,540	(500)	96.1	37,550	(3,000)	92.6

Table 8-22
Dynamic Corporation, Plant 1, Performance Report, Department 1, Overhead-Spending Variance

Classification	Third Quarter			Year-to-date		
	Budget	Variance	Percent Achieved	Budget	Variance	Percent Achieved
Supervision	$ 7,347	$ 0	100	$ 22,300	$ 0	100
Indirect labor	8,834	(698)	92.6	26,600	(2,200)	92.3
Supplies	1,114	204	122	3,200	650	125.5
Repair and rework	4,549	(551)	89.2	13,700	(1,800)	88.4
Setup and makeready	2,457	269	112.3	7,200	(810)	90
Maintenance	6,075	(275)	95.6	20,100	1,870	110.2
Heat, light, and power	6,890	351	105	28,800	850	103
Depreciation	2,791	0	100	8,373	0	100
Taxes	53	0	100	159	0	100
Insurance	165	0	100	495	0	100
Totals	$40,275	$(700)		$130,927	$(1,440)	

Table 8-23
Dynamic Corporation, Plant 1, Performance Summary, Department 5, Third Quarter, 198-

	Standard Hours	Actual Hours
Service and programmed maintenance	2,100	2,100
Hours charged to operating departments	3,550	3,590
Total hours	5,650	5,690

	Budget	Variance	Percent Achieved
Maintenance-efficiency variance	48,550	(280)	99.4
Maintenance-spending variance	48,830	(300)	99.4

deviations from control budget. It is most important for the reader to understand this point.

While maintenance or other plant services and utilities should as a rule be readily controllable within each using department as to efficiency and financial expenditure, this is not the case for other allocated classifications of overhead. Of particular importance in this regard are depreciation, property taxes, and insurance. These classifications of overhead for any period of operations are either based on capital expenditures or prepayments made in prior periods. Thus they are entirely "fixed" in terms of both operating efficiency and spending. It is for this reason that they have no practical performance implications at the plant department level even though they may comprise a substantial portion of a plant department's overhead budget. As we have mentioned previously, the real "control" of such overhead classifications remains at higher organizational levels

Table 8-24
Maintenance Expense Spending Variances

	Budget[a]	Actual Expense	Variance	Percent Achieved
Supervision	$ 6,000	$ 6,000	$ 0	100
Maintenance labor	20,960	21,200	(240)	98.8
Maintenance supplies	8,862	8,830	32	100.3
Heat, light, and power	8,508	8,600	(92)	98.9
Depreciation	4,500	4,500	0	100
	$48,830	$49,130	(300)	

[a]Budget allowances for control purposes based on 5,690 maintenance hours less transfer of 2,100 to operating departments equals 3,590 actual hours. The above data represent variable-rate and fixed-amount dollars combined.

Table 8-25
Efficiency and Spending Variance Calculations

	Efficiency	Spending
Standard hours @ standard rate	$48,550	$ 0
Actual hours @ standard rate	48,830	48,830
Actual maintenance expense	0	49,130
	$ (280)	$ (300)

of management where capital investment and operating decisions to incur such expenditures are made.

We saw in chapters 3 and 4 that direct materials or component parts represent a primary classification in determining a product's unit cost of production. They also represent a primary classification of variable financial input for management control within producing or assembling departments. The two control measures we developed were the price variance and the quantity or usage variance. The performance results for plant 1 pertaining to direct materials by product lines are contained in Schedule B and Schedule C (tables 8-15 and 8-16). Price variances relate organizationally to the purchasing operation rather than to the producing departments since it is procurement and not line production that has the responsibility for supply market-price evaluation and the awarding of purchase contracts. For our hypothetical company, the Dynamic Power Tool Corporation, purchasing has been designated as department 7.

Price variances recorded in Schedule B are calculated in accordance with materials used by each of the four producing departments. This means that price variances are determined on the basis of production volume, whereas for many companies it may be more logical and more practically feasible to base price variances on acquisition volume and bypass their assignment to the producing departments. Deviations from standard performance for both materials prices and quantities should be among the easiest of all classifications to pinpoint regarding causes. Favorable price variance would ordinarily be the result of obtaining supply contracts at unit-price rates that are more favorable than those experienced by the company in previous periods and upon which price standards have been based. However, price standards would have to follow the primary consideration of type and quality specifications for materials or component

Table 8-26
Direct Labor Variances

Department	Efficiency Variance	Rate Variance
1	(720)	(210)
2	(1,350)	(425)
3	675	425

Table 8-27
Variable Overhead Variances

Department	Efficiency Variance	Spending Variance
1	(440)	(500)
2	(1,080)	280
3	435	0

parts. This means that favorable price variances may be a reflection of superior performance on behalf of procurement management but only when there have been no sacrifices made in terms of type and quality standards. Conversely, an unfavorable price variance may be a reflection on inadequate performance in cases where supply markets were not investigated thoroughly and impartially to obtain a lower price in accordance with the standard. It may also indicate that market-price levels have increased among all available suppliers, which is of course an economic circumstance that is beyond the reach of management's responsibility in making purchasing decisions. In the latter circumstance, price standards themselves would have to be revised to reflect the current market. Any proper investigation as to the causes of unfavorable supply price variances ought to reveal which of these circumstances did in fact exist since the interpretation as to performance deficiency would be quite different in either case.

Unlike prices, variation from standard for quantities of materials or component parts are the responsibility of the producing departments and are properly assigned to the particular department that actually uses each type or grade in its operations. Unfavorable performance in usage may clearly reflect negligence or waste or may be the result of unforeseen and thus temporarily uncontrollable defects in tools or machinery. Pinpointing either of these causes will always be necessary before determination can be made as to whether handling and labor have been deficient or whether special service and maintenance are required. These considerations are made over and above tolerances for normal or expected maintenance.

The overall performance profile for department 2 for the third quarter is presented in table 8-21. Similar profiles can be prepared for the other operating departments in plant 1 and likewise in other producing plants in the company. The achievement percents are a ready means of initially comparing the performance of one set of activities or cost inputs with another for a given department or one department with another department where operations or activities are deemed comparable and thus valid for this purpose.

A common approach to measuring, analyzing, and evaluating past performance is to compare financial results of operations based on control budget with the expense level actually experienced during the previous period. Thus current period performance can be evaluated against year to date as we have set forth in the presentations in this chapter. This approach can be extended to include the same quarter for the previous year. To make interyear comparisons more accurate, we would first adjust the data for certain classifications so as to reflect the economic conditions prevailing in the current year. For example, we can make direct comparisons in the volume levels against forecast for the same quarter in two successive years. However, variable costs of production, particularly labor and materials, may very well have experienced rate or price changes within the twelve-month interim. The important point regarding any such adjustments is that they should be clearly explained to management and preferably developed on separate schedules. Adjustments can properly be made when the actual incremental changes in labor rates or procurement prices are known and can be made readily available. Otherwise, unadjusted data comparisons can still be valid for performance appraisal, even though imprecise.

We saw in chapter 1 how the evolution of scientific management provided the framework for the development of modern management control and financial evaluation of operating performance. The combination of industrial engineering research, which gave rise to the establishing of activity standards, and managerial accounting and budgeting techniques were first applied in production, and for many companies over the years, the practical application of these methods was not extended beyond production. In the two chapters that follow, we will explore the application of these same concepts and comparable measurement techniques for performance appraisal in marketing and in administration.

9

Flexible Budgeting and Performance Evaluation for Marketing

We may view the primary objective of marketing activities for profit-seeking companies dealing in either physical products or services as being the attainment of revenue from the sale of such goods or services. To any knowledgeable accountant, financial manager, or marketing executive, the first monetary item to appear on the company's periodic income statement is sales revenue. This item represents the total financial returns from all functional marketing operations that were undertaken for a specific period of time in the past.

A fundamental economic fact that applies to all profit-seeking business organizations is that without generating sales through integrated marketing effort as represented by such activities as personal selling or advertising and sales promotion, the company simply could not remain in business. In the language of the financial profession, it could not sustain its operations as a "going concern." To the marketing executive, the attainment of sales revenue is his foremost concern as a planner and as a manager.

An ultimate financial goal of the business is to optimize the profits achieved through coordinated functional operations of production, marketing and administration, and in relation to a particular level of invested capital and rank or position within the industry. In order to achieve this goal, the corporate organization of necessity must generate revenues through a careful planning and coordinated implementation of its marketing activities. Financially, the sales revenue resulting from marketing operations must also support the other functional activities of the company (production, research and development, company administration, and other staff functions) even before a targeted profit goal can be reached.

When we use the very important but also very generalized word "planning" for business operations, we may examine or reflect upon what it is we really mean. There are several different kinds of business planning with respect to both the goals and purposes for which plans are developed and the time period involved. In our introduction to chapter 5, we discussed two very specific categories of planning, namely, project planning and period planning. In the discussion, we made an essential distinction between the two types. "Project planning" refers to a specific and clearly stated set of task or work-completion objectives, but with respect to an independent professional or single-purpose venture. A marketing-research effort to examine consumer preferences for use of leisure time to provide a basis for development of new product or service markets involving leisure-time needs and activities, a research and development assignment to determine the uses of transistor chips in the home or office, or an industrial-engineering study to devise methods for improving the efficiency of assembly operations in a manufacturing plant are all examples of projects. These projects are "self-contained," hence independent of other projects and of functional activities of the company that are essential to creating, building, or processing the product or service and to providing and maintaining sales flow in external markets. Since these activities are expected to continue throughout the business life of the organization, the operational and budgetary planning for these activities must be undertaken for specific periods of time such as a month, a quarter, or a year.

We may also define an operating plan more broadly than we have done here and in chapter 5. We may say that it is a comprehensive guide for many independent and interrelated operations of the business organization over *any* designated period of time in the future. We are now shifting our emphasis away from specific types of plans, and in the discussion that follows, we will distinguish between two time frames that we will call short term and long term. We will consider short-term planning to include a period of one year or less and long-term planning to include a time frame of five to ten years or more.

There are two important justifications for this distinction. First, management objectives themselves will differ depending on whether we are referring to short-term or long-term time periods. Second, the nature and types of business activities themselves will differ depending on whether the period is one year or greater than a year. Project planning, for example, may incorporate only three to six months or may range up to several years. Task-oriented advertising research projects are usually short-term, whereas technical research-and-development projects considered to be exploratory assignments to develop new products for which market potential is still unknown may require an indefinite period of several years. We have said that the functional activities in production, marketing, and administration are expected to continue throughout the life of the organization. While this is true, the periods for which functional-activity plans and budgets are prepared are usually short term, encompassing the "planning year" for ongoing product or service operations or a month or quarter within the planning year.

Long-term (also called long-range) planning will include major financial plans for fixed capital commitments to the busines enterprise such as the acquisition of plant and equipment facilities that will have useful service lives and will yield profitable returns to the company for many years ahead. New business planning involving merger with other corporate enterprises in the same industry, acquisition of companies in unrelated industries through purchase, as well as plans for expansion of product lines or services already being produced and marketed are familiar kinds of ventures for which long-term plans are drawn up for top-management approval and implementation. Corporate growth is perhaps the primary goal of long-term planning for profit-seeking product and service companies.

A major objective of short-term functional-activity planning and budgeting is to optimize profits resulting from operations by the end of the planning year. It is an objective that is perhaps most familiar to functional line managers. It means that management wishes to formulate functional plans and conduct operations so as to achieve the greatest difference between revenues derived from sales on the one hand and all costs and expenses incurred for the year as a result of the combined marketing, production, and administrative effort. Further—and this will be of great importance in our presentations and analyses in this chapter—each functional-activity area or organizational unit (responsibility center) will make its own direct contribution to total company profits for a given planning and operating year. This contribution is reflected in the achievement levels experienced as shown in performance reports and based on planned volume schedules, operating standards, and budgets developed at the beginning of the year.

Long-term and short-term planning for the business enterprise are not always independent arenas, and there are times when they will conflict and will require reconciliation or a determination of priorities related to conflicting objectives by top management. Pricing decisions are a common case in point, particularly when they involve new products or services entering the marketplace. In such instances, management's objective from a short-term standpoint may very well be to achieve the highest possible volume of sales in units or a high target share of the market in relation to anticipated sales volume within the industry for competitive products or to provide a strong sales incentive when there are no close competitors.

Management may then set a price for the first year or two that is quite low, perhaps just covering the cost of direct functional activities or even below cost. This has sometimes been called "market-penetration pricing," and such a policy might be followed by companies entering established product or service markets for the first time or undertaking ventures in markets that are new altogether.

Such a pricing policy would hardly be consistent with any short-term planning and budgeting objective to optimize profits. However, attaining an optimum level of production and sales in units or service contracts for the coming year will more than reflect a management goal for achieving a high level of profitability over the longer term, say five or ten years hence. The fixed and variable costs of production and marketing may be nearly equal to or above short-term revenues. However, management anticipates that total company growth by way of expanding current operations will eventually result in a reduction of total fixed and variable costs in relation to sales revenue over the next five to ten years. These results would provide economies from a larger scale of overall operations and achieve optimum profits over the long-term period.

Our purpose in the foregoing statements is to give the reader some important perspectives on the role of company planning and to point out a few of the important differences between long-term and short-term goals as they relate to functional planning. However, we will also remind the reader at this point that the entire system of budget preparation and performance evaluation as it is presented in this book is intended to be a model for short-term functional planning, appraisal, and decision-making purposes with the most prominent objective being the attainment of optimum profitability.

In the functional area of marketing, most operating activities are short term from the standpoint that they are planned and evaluated for an operating period of one year or for an interim period such as the quarter. Perhaps the most important activities that are undertaken for the purpose of providing a company with sales volume is product units or in service contracts and consequently with revenue are personal selling or sales-force management activities and what is called "mass-media selling" or advertising and sales-promotion activities. Operating plans and budgets will include the number of geographic sales offices and sales-force personnel requirements to achieve total anticipated sales for the next year or quarter. Planning and budgeting for advertising and sales-promotion programs will involve specifications and dollar-expenditure levels for selected media according to geographic sales regions or territories and in support of personal selling or sales-force operations.

Other marketing activities that are included in the operating plan and budget are conducted as auxiliary phases to the main task of selling for the marketing function. They are primarily related to the storing of finished products prior to sale and their distribution after sales have been transacted. Thus marketing budgets will provide annual and quarterly cost estimates of warehouse facilities for inventories and warehouse handling in accordance with planned sales volume and by geographic locations. Estimates of shipping charges by various routes and transportation methods to deliver products to customers will be incorporated in the marketing-activity plan and budget at the beginning of the year, together with cost estimates for marketing administration.

We emphasize at this point that one of our most important tenets is that the anticipated sales volume is the necessary basis for preparing short-term quantitative operating plans and their supporting cost estimates for both marketing and production. Another important tenet is that the financial goal of short-term functional operations is to achieve an optimum level of bottom-line performance or profitability for each functional unit within the organization.

Since the anticipated sales volume provides the basis for annual activity planning and budgeting in marketing and production, then the first and most essential step in arriving at annual sales estimates is the sales forecast. This forecast is a projection of the actual quantity of manufactured product in units or the number of service contracts that the company expects to sell in the year ahead. These estimates are then used to prepare planned or forecast revenue by applying the projected or standard prices for the year per unit of product or per service contract to the physical volume of sales that have been forecast. Similarly, the sales forecast will in turn provide the basis for developing product-line production schedules and plans for inventory levels for the year.

A wide variety of procedures or methods for estimating sales have been used by manufacturing companies. Among the oldest and more commonly used forecasting methods is the sales build-up or "ground-floor" approach. This type of estimate is prepared according to products or product lines and according to geographic markets or sales regions. Members of the field sales force provide the basic data for the forecast because they are the members of the marketing organization who are in a position to directly observe the selling behavior of their own company's products as well as sales patterns of competitors' products and in terms of both physical volume and pricing. The estimates prepared by salesmen and sales managers are based on observations of sales trends in the recent past. They are most readily prepared by geographic areas or regions and according to customer classifications. Then these separate estimates are combined to obtain a total company forecast from which the activity plans and budgets are prepared.

Alternatively, the professional marketing and economic research staff within the company or outside consultants who specialize in forecasting can develop projections by product lines and geographic markets. Among the technical procedures used by forecasters are statistical correlation and regression analyses, time-series forecasting methods, and econometric models. These approaches to preparing market-demand and product-line sales forecasts will often trace the quantitative relationship between historical changes in general economic factors such as national consumer purchasing power, total industrial production or investment in plant and equipment, and total industry sales for the company's products. In this way, the market potential for products on an industry-wide basis can first be projected. Then a forecast of total company sales by product line is obtained by applying the company's percentage share of the market to this market potential that is forecast for the industry.

Theoretical and applied techniques of quantitative market and economic forecasting have expanded rapidly in recent years. Today forecasting has become a highly specialized though complex profession in itself. Our purpose here is to present a brief overview of forecasting and to pinpoint its role in planning and budgeting for the marketing function. The use of a combination of forecasting methods rather than a single procedure may prove an effective means of obtaining an accurate forecast. However, it is important to note that the application of different methods will invariably produce different quantitative predictions of unit sales volume and revenue. This means that a reconciliation of projections to obtain a single sales forecast is a vital responsibility to company operations as a whole in the year ahead. It is for this reason that the chief marketing executive will ordinarily have the responsibility for any necessary reconciliations and for deciding the final forecast sales figures to be used in developing activity plans and budgets.

The planning of short-term operating activities combined with the forecast of sales volume then comprise the starting points for formulating plans and preparing budgets. The comprehensive annual budget is actually a formalized set of standards developed by way of projecting sales revenue and the costs and expenses that will be necessary to sustain all functional marketing activities undertaken to generate planned levels of sales volume transactions.

Planned sales revenue is obtained by applying the company's planned price structure for each product line to the projected unit sales for a line and obtaining an aggregate for total revenue. Thus the marketing budget will appropriately set forth the sales objectives in unit volume, target prices, and the revenue for each product line. In turn, these figures will serve as the bases or standards for evaluating marketing performance for the revenue side of the budget at the end of the year or interim period within the operating year.

The marketing budget will include next a comprehensive statement of planned dollar levels for costs and expenses involving each of the activities within the total marketing function. They are usually set on the basis of recent operating experience with sales volume levels achieved, any current changes in activity-cost rates, facilities acquisitions, salary scales, and so on, and in consideration of the marketing effort required to achieve the planned sales volume.

Chapter 5 stated that all costs and expenses incurred to support the marketing function can be viewed either in terms of their relation to the transacting of market sales or in terms of cost behavior for the activity classifications themselves (cf. chapter 5, p. 96 ff.). Certain marketing activities will precede sales transactions during the period, and they are undertaken for the specific purpose of influencing sales volume behavior in customer markets. Budget categories for these activities will ordinarily include personal selling and sales-force management by geographic designation, salesmen's salaries and incentives, advertising-media and sales-promotion programs, market research and development, and travel and personal expense accounts.

Most marketing expenses that are incurred for the purpose of generating sales volume during the operating year will not be suited to a flexible-budgeting approach. The reason is that by their very nature they precede sales and hence do not respond to changes in sales volume behavior. Very few of these budget categories will experience a variable or semivariable cost pattern, with the exception of travel, which may be semivariable. The activities themselves are planned on the basis of programming, and the budget contains primarily fixed and semifixed "doses" of expenditures that will change only with broad-range shifts in anticipated sales from one year to the next.

It is possible, however, that program plans for any of these categories and their corresponding budget levels may be changed (for example, increased or cut back) for one or more quarters within the year if the sales forecasts are revised for any reason such as changes in planned price levels, product-line composition, or similar actions undertaken by competitors or because of an unexpected increase or decrease in customer buying activity. Quarterly revisions in programmed costs for any of these reasons would mean that they will be semifixed for the year as a whole.

A major expense item that normally can be expected to vary directly with sales volume fluctuations will be salesmen's commissions and bonuses if these items are included in the marketing budget. Nonprogram fixed costs, which we will refer to as "committed costs," will include period charges for depreciable assets relating to the marketing function such as depreciation on building, equipment, and office facilities at headquarters (home office) or depreciable facilities at regional and branch sales offices to include company-owned automobiles for the sales force.

The other major group of activities included in the annual marketing plan and budget we described in chapter 5 as being those that follow sales transactions in time and thus are undertaken as a result of the realization of sales volume. Most of these items relate to the physical-distribution and inventory-carrying aspects of the company's operations. Included in this group for budgeting purposes are transportation (freight and related shipping charges) to customer locations; the period costs of warehousing facilities and warehouse handling; inventory management; and customer-order processing, billing, and collection activities. For most of these classifications, it is advisable to study cost behavior over time for each major classification since they will tend to be variable or semivariable throughout the operating year in relation to experienced levels of sales volume. These items then will be quite suited to a flexible budget or standard rate and amount schedule in preparing the marketing budget. An obvious exception will be warehouse buildings and facilities to which the committed fixed-cost budget approach will be applicable. Further, most cost items related to inventory management other than warehouse handling charges may experience semifixed cost behavior by months or quarters within the year.

Costs and expenses for marketing administration will include managerial salaries and related compensation, the salaries of staff and clerical personnel, office supplies, depreciation on administrative facilities, and insurance and property taxes traceable to the marketing function. These items may be broken down further in the budget by responsibility centers or in consideration of the degree of functional and organizational decentralization of total marketing operations.

The behavior of expenses incurred for marketing administration is not directly influenced by sales volume levels experienced during the year, nor do these items cause changes in sales volume per se. They will usually be constant with respect to short-term fluctuations in sales. Hence program planning and budgeting will be more suitable than rate and amount schedules for marketing-administration costs and expenses.

Before we move on to the formal preparation of a marketing budget, a word of caution is in order with respect to fixed-cost items and interim-period budget revisions. What we have called "programmed" and "committed" costs are not really fixed in an identical sense for purposes of budget planning and revision. Committed costs such as depreciation on buildings and facilities are fixed for the total length of their economic lives, and budget levels will be pretty much the same from one operating year to the next. This is not true of program costs for advertising, promotion, or maintaining the sales force. With regard to these classifications, any significant changes that may be experienced in the forecast of sales volume from one year to another or even within a planning year will usually warrant revisions in program plans in the same direction (increase or decrease) and by the same relative amounts as revenue impact resulting from the new sales volume level that has been forecast.

In developing the functional budget and profit plan for marketing activities, we will resume discussion of our model example of the Dynamic Power Tool Corporation. You will recall from chapter 8 that our treatment of the production budget and end-of-period performance appraisal involved the third quarter of Year 1 in a general operating plan covering five years (cf. chapter 8, p. 142 ff.). At that time Dynamic had acquired several years of operating experience with formalized standard-cost and flexible-budgeting procedures in its plant operations. Although plans were under way to employ a comparable system in nonproduction functional areas, it was not until the beginning of Year 3 that the system was fully developed and ready for implementation in the operating areas of marketing and administration. As for production, plans and budgets for these areas are prepared annually and for each quarter within the year. The new system was first used for both budgeting and performance evaluation purposes at the beginning of Year 3. Our illustrations in this chapter and in chapter 10 will be taken for the fourth quarter of that year.

In preparing the marketing budget for the fourth quarter, we will approach the task functionally on a "build-up" basis using Dynamic's geographic-market organization structure. The company initially prepares a sales forecast by each product line for the planning year and for each quarter. This forecast is then broken down for budgeting purposes by sales districts, a district being the smallest territorial segment in Dynamic's sales organization. The district operating budget and profit plans are then drawn up and combined to develop a similar plan for each region. The company has three sales regions, namely, Eastern, Central, and Western. The regional plans are in turn combined to prepare the total marketing budget and profit plan for the period. The final step is approval of the company sales forecast and total marketing budget and profit plan by the vice president, marketing, the vice president, finance, and the senior vice president, operations.

We will develop two formal master-budget and profit-plan presentations in accordance with the foregoing procedures. The first will be for Central Region marketing operations, which combines the sales plans and budgets for products MT1, MT2, and MT3 in the three districts of Cleveland, Minneapolis, and St. Louis. The second master budget and profit plan will be for all three regions, which will be used in turn to prepare the overall marketing profit-contribution summary for the fourth quarter.

The underlying schedules required to accomplish our task need provide us only with the information that is relevant to prepare the formal marketing budget by segments and to ultimately arrive at an estimate of the direct contribution to total company profits that is expected from marketing activities at the end of the period. On the revenue side, we will need the planned or standard unit selling prices both list and net for each product line and the forecast sales volume for each geographic segment (districts and regions). On the cost side, we will require the direct variable (prime) production cost per unit for each product line and all variable, programmed, and committed costs and expenses in the budget that are *direct* to the segment and hence relevant to its operations and its expected contribution to company profitability.

For the three districts in the Central Region and for the three marketing regions, the relevant data are presented in table 9-1. Forecast sales volume by Central Region sales districts are shown in table 9-2. Direct programmed and committed fixed costs by districts for the Central Region are shown in table 9-3. Forecast sales volume by sales regions are shown in table 9-4. Direct programmed and committed fixed costs by sales regions are shown in table 9-5. Budgeted home-office costs are shown in table 9-6.

In preparing the budget for the Central Region, we will use the information provided for the district designated Cleveland. The reader may wish to follow this example in preparing similar budget detail for either of the other Central Region districts and compare results with the final budget and profit-contribution plan (table 9-9).

The net sales revenue is a projection of the net or standard selling price for each product line applied to the forecast sales volume for the period. Ordinarily, the net price is the company's published or list price less any cash or quantity discount adjustments (cf. chapter 5). The budgeted revenue for Cleveland is shown in table 9-7. From budgeted net revenue, we deduct the direct variable production cost of forecast volume to obtain what we call the "sales margin." The sales margin is the basic contribution to be made by marketing operations in Cleveland to cover all other operating costs in the district (table 9-8).

Marginal income for the district is the next dollar figure presented in our budget. The marginal income for any marketing segment in our system is always the production margin less all variable costs that are direct or traceable to the segment. It is also called "variable marginal income." Variable marketing expenses that are direct to the Cleveland sales district are:

Sales commissions:	3% of net revenue	
	= 3% of $309,000 =	$ 9,270
Freight and shipping:	4% of net revenue	
	= 4% of $309,000 =	12,360
Sales travel and expenses:	3% of net revenue	
	= 3% of $309,000 =	9,270
Total		$30,900

Table 9-1
Dynamic Corporation Planning Information, Marketing Budget, Fourth Quarter, 198-

Standard selling prices and production costs

1. *Selling prices per unit*

	MT1	MT2	MT3
List price	$35.00	$32.00	$56.00
Cash discount	1.00	2.00	3.00
Net standard selling price	34.00	30.00	53.00

2. *Production costs per unit[a]*

	MT1	MT2	MT3
Direct variable (prime) cost	$15.30	$9.00	$26.50
Percent of standard net selling price	45%	30%	50%

[a]Product-line margins above variable production cost based on forecast (standard) net selling prices.

	Net Standard Selling Price	−	Unit Prime Cost of Production	=	Unit Margin above Production
MT1	$34.00		$15.30		$18.70
MT2	30.00		9.00		21.00
MT3	53.00		26.50		26.50

Standard Variable Marketing Costs
Sales commissions: 3% of net revenue
Freight and shipping charges: 4% of net revenue
Salesmen's travel and expenses: 3% of net revenue

The final figure in our budget for the fourth quarter is the district-contribution margin. This is the difference between the variable marginal income for a functional segment or organizational unit and all direct fixed costs. In our example here, fixed costs that are direct to the district are salesmen's salaries and office administration. The district-contribution margin then is the planned profit at the forecast sales level that we expect the Cleveland district to *contribute* to total company profit to be achieved in the fourth quarter. The complete operating budget and profit plan for the Central Region is presented in table 9-9.

We now move from the smaller operating units within the marketing function to the larger regional segments in preparing our fourth-quarter budget.

Table 9-2
Forecast Sales Volume by Central Region Sales Districts

	Cleveland	Minneapolis	St. Louis	Total
MT1	4,000	5,000	6,000	15,000
MT2	4,000	2,500	1,500	8,000
MT3	1,000	1,000	1,300	3,300

Each regional budget is a combination of the district projections of revenue, costs, and expenses with the addition of those fixed-cost classifications (both programmed and committed) that are common to the individual districts but are direct to each region in that they are necessarily incurred to support marketing activities and *only* those activities undertaken by the region. As in table 9-9, the key budget figures will be product-line net revenue and variable production costs, marginal income, and total profit contribution from marketing activities for each region. Thus we will develop budget detail for the Eastern Region as in table 9-10. Direct variable production costs are shown in table 9-11. And for variable marketing expenses:

Sales commissions:	3% of net revenue	
	= 3% of $960,100 =	$28,803
Freight and shipping:	4% of net revenue	
	= 4% of $960,100 =	38,404
Sales travel and expenses:	3% of net revenue	
	= 3% of $960,100 =	28,803
Total		$96,010

The marginal income for the Eastern Region is the difference between the sales margin of $529,410 and the variable marketing expenses of $96,010. All fixed costs that are direct to the region are deducted next from marginal income in arriving at the sales region-contribution margin. Regional fixed-cost information may be found in table 9-5. The completed budget and profit-contribution plan for the three regions is presented in table 9-12.

The budget plans that we have presented here necessarily require a direct cost-accounting system. The outstanding advantage of a direct cost system for planning and budgeting phases of normal short-term operations is that it enables a company to develop budget presentations for each functional operating segment or organizational unit that will show both the total marginal-income contribution (above the required variable costs) and the total contribution that the segment or unit is expected to make toward company earnings for the year or quarter. It is a target projection of profitability at the beginning of the operating period. No similar system can be validly implemented by operating

Table 9-3
Direct Programmed and Committed Fixed Costs by Districts
for the Central Region

Classification	Cleveland	Minneapolis	St. Louis	Total
Sales salaries	$11,000	$12,727	$14,456	$38,183
Office administration	3,000	4,000	4,000	11,000
Total				$49,183

Table 9-4
Forecast Sales Volume by Sales Regions

	Eastern Region	Central Region	Western Region	Total
MT1	12,800	15,000	9,000	36,800
MT2	4,600	8,000	6,500	19,100
MT3	7,300	3,300	4,900	15,500

segments or responsibility centers within the company where costs that are common to two or more segments (or organizational units) are allocated.

In illustrating our point here, we have developed in table 9-13 the fourth-quarter profit-contribution plan for the company by product lines. As for geographic budgets in the marketing system, you will see the marginal-income and contribution margin figures presented for total company operations and by product lines. Of significance in this budget format is the final category, "common fixed costs." These are the budgeted programmed and committed fixed costs for the functional areas in the fourth quarter that are indirect with respect to segments or units within functional areas or organization structure and are not traceable to product lines. They are included in the budget format by primary function only in projecting net profit before income taxes for the period. A summary schedule of the fourth-quarter budget and profit contribution projected for total marketing activities appears in table 9-14.

For many years the main emphasis given to financial performance by the marketing managements of industrial companies was sales revenue. Cost effectiveness was considered important but only in terms of the impact of costs on sales volume. The important goal was to incur whatever level of costs would generate the highest attainable volume of sales and industry share of the market. However, in recent years the perspective of marketing management in many companies has focused more on profit impact both in the planning phases of marketing and in evaluating the results of marketing operations. Considerably more emphasis is now being given to profit-contribution reporting and minimization of marketing costs at specific levels of planned sales volume.

Table 9-5
Direct Programmed and Committed Fixed Costs by Sales Regions

Classification	Eastern Region	Central Region	Western Region	Total
Sales salaries	$30,167	$38,183	$27,083	$ 95,433
Advertising and promotion	20,806	24,000	20,238	65,044
Warehouse storage	10,474	13,497	16,852	40,823
District offices	11,700	11,000	18,000	40,700
Managerial salaries	7,000	8,500	8,000	23,500
Totals	$80,147	$95,180	$90,173	$265,500

Table 9-6
Budgeted Home-Office Costs

Advertising and promotion	$ 60,650
Marketing administration	56,400
Marketing research	18,400
Warehousing and storage	16,150
Total	$151,600

For purposes of optimizing this contribution to profit that is made by the marketing effort, companies are now more inclined to evaluate marginal income through the use of direct costing for marketing activities according to functional segments, including not only product lines and geographic areas but also salesmen and even customer classifications. By using a direct-cost approach in the accounting system, behavior of costs can be analyzed at different sales levels over time, and planned profit-contribution margins at the beginning of the operating period can be prepared. It also provides a basis for end-of-period performance evaluation by market segments and in terms of the contribution margin achieved.

Two general points must be emphasized in our discussion of marketing performance. The first is that sales volume is more volatile in terms of both its behavior and the underlying causes of this behavior than is production volume in successive operating and performance appraisal periods. The reason for this is that sales volume levels for either product lines or services depend on two sets of factors or influences, one internal to the company and the other external.

Internal influences that may restrict sales volume achievement (scale of marketing operations) would primarily relate to the financial resources or funds that will be available to support marketing activities in the short term and the production facilities or plant capacity that exists as a result of capital investment made in prior years. These influences are much more subject to management's decision making and control over time, however, than is true for certain factors that impact on sales volume and revenue but are external to the company and thus independent of management's decision making and control. Changes in consumer demand for generic classifications of products or services reflect an

Table 9-7
Budgeted Revenue, Cleveland

	Net Price Per Unit	X	Forecast Sales	=	Budgeted Revenue
MT1	$34.00		4,000		$136,000
MT2	30.00		4,000		120,000
MT3	53.00		1,000		53,000
Total					$309,000

Table 9-8
Budgeted Cost of Sales, Cleveland

	Prime Cost Per Unit	X	Forecast Sales	=	Cost of Goods Sold
MT1	$15.30		4,000		$ 61,200
MT2	9.00		4,000		36,000
MT3	26.50		1,000		26,500
Total					$123,700

economic condition that is usually beyond direct managerial influence. Changes in consumer demand may have a vital impact on the level of company sales and revenue in successive operating periods and will also tend to yield a comparable impact (increase or decrease) on industry-wide sales.

Table 9-9
Dynamic Corporation Budget and Profit-Contribution Plan,
Central Region, Fourth Quarter, 198-

	Cleveland	Minneapolis	St. Louis	Total
Revenue				
Forecast sales	$324,000	$311,000	$330,800	$1,965,800
Cash discounts	15,000	13,000	12,900	40,900
Forecast net sales	$309,000	$298,000	$317,900	$ 924,900
Direct Variable Costs				
Cost of goods sold	$123,700	$125,500	$139,750	$ 388,950
Sales margin	185,300	172,500	178,150	535,950
Sales-margin ratio	0.599676	0.578859	0.560396	0.579468
Marketing				
Sales commissions	$ 9,270	$ 8,940	$ 9,537	$ 27,747
Freight and shipping	12,360	11,920	12,716	36,996
Sales travel and expenses	9,270	8,940	9,537	27,747
Totals	$ 30,900	$ 29,800	$ 31,790	$ 92,490
District marginal income	$154,400	$142,700	$146,360	$ 443,460
District marginal-income ratio	0.499676	0.478859	0.460396	0.479468
Direct Fixed Costs				
Sales salaries	$ 11,000	$ 12,727	$ 14,456	$ 38,183
Office administration	3,000	4,000	4,000	11,000
Totals	$ 14,000	$ 16,727	$ 18,456	$ 49,183
Sales District contribution margin	$140,400	$125,973	$127,904	$ 394,277

Table 9-10
Budgeted Revenue, Eastern Region

	Net Price Per Unit	X	Forecast Sales	=	Budgeted Revenue
MT1	$34.00		12,800		$435,200
MT2	30.00		4,600		138,000
MT3	53.00		7,300		386,900
Total					$960,100

Competitive behavior of other companies marketing similar products or services is also beyond direct control of management but can significantly affect sales and revenue achievement for an individual company. For example, any action undertaken by a major competitor to improve the quality of a product or service, lower the unit price, or increase the volume of advertising in support of the selling effort could severely reduce company sales volume and market share. Selling price is the one component of revenue that is entirely controllable.

The second point is that for all of our analyses and interpretations regarding performance appraisal, there are two financial bases that are important to us: sales revenue and the bottom-line-based contribution margin. The contribution margin enables us to pinpoint achievement by product lines or services and by segments within the overall marketing operations of the company. The contribution-margin measurements themselves account for the interacting effects of revenue and direct costs and expenses (variable and programmed fixed) that are specifically relevant to the product line or functional segment being evaluated.

In performance evaluation for marketing, the two profit-based measurements that we develop and analyze in the segment-performance formats correspond to those already set forth in the presentations for budget and profit planning. They are the variable marginal income and total segment-contribution margin. Marginal income contains four separate components:

1. Sales volume
2. Sales mix of products
3. Selling prices of products
4. Variable marketing and production costs

Table 9-11
Budgeted Cost of Sales, Eastern Region

	Prime Cost Per Unit	X	Forecast Sales	=	Cost of Goods Sold
MT1	$15.30		12,800		$195,840
MT2	9.00		4,600		41,400
MT3	26.50		7,300		193,450
Total					$430,690

Table 9-12
Dynamic Corporation Budget and Profit-Contribution Plan,
U.S. Regions, Fourth Quarter, 198-

	Eastern	Central	Western	Total
Revenue				
Forecast sales	$1,004,000	$965,800	$797,400	$2,767,200
Cash discounts	43,900	40,900	36,700	121,500
Forecast net sales	$ 960,100	$924,900	$760,700	$2,645,700
Direct Variable Costs				
Cost of goods sold	$430,690	$388,950	$326,050	$1,145,690
Sales margin	529,410	535,950	434,650	1,500,010
Sales-margin ratio	0.551411	0.579468	0.571382	0.566962
Marketing				
Sales commissions	$ 28,803	$ 27,747	$ 22,821	$ 79,371
Freight and shipping	38,404	36,996	30,428	105,828
Sales travel and expenses	28,803	27,747	22,821	79,371
Totals	$ 96,010	$ 92,490	$ 76,070	$ 264,570
Regional marginal income	$ 433,400	$443,460	$358,580	$1,235,440
Region marginal-income ratio	0.451411	0.479468	0.471381	0.466961
Direct Fixed Costs				
Sales salaries	$ 30,167	$ 38,183	$ 27,083	$ 95,433
Advertising and promotion	20,806	24,000	20,238	65,044
Warehouse and storage	10,474	13,497	16,852	40,823
District offices	11,700	11,000	18,000	40,700
Managerial salaries	7,000	8,500	8,000	23,500
Totals	$ 80,147	$ 95,180	$ 90,173	$ 265,500
Sales Region-contribution Margin	$ 353,253	$348,280	$268,407	$ 969,940

The four components of marginal income and related formulas for performance analysis have been discussed in chapter 5, and the reader may find it helpful to review them (cf. chapter 5, p. 100 ff.). The first three of these components pertain to sales revenue, and the marginal-income figure is the difference between revenue and variable costs of marketing and production. The following is an explanation of these components in terms of their effect on variations in marginal income.

The combined volume and product-mix variances account for the difference between the actual marginal income and the standard marginal income that is

Table 9-13
Dynamic Corporation Product-Line Budget Summary, Fourth Quarter, 198-

| | Total Company | | Product Lines | | | | | |
| | | | MT1 | | MT2 | | MT3 | |
	Amount	Percent	Amount	Percent	Amount	Percent	Amount	Percent
Net Sales Revenue	$2,645,700	100.0	$1,251,200	100.0	$573,000	100.0	$821,500	100.0
Standard Variable Costs								
Cost of goods sold	$1,145,690	43.3	$ 563,040	45.0	$171,900	30.0	$410,750	50.0
Cost of marketing	264,570	10.0	125,120	10.0	57,300	10.0	82,150	10.0
Totals	$1,410,260	53.3	$ 688,160	55.0	$229,200	40.0	$492,900	60.0
Marginal income	$1,235,440	46.7	$ 563,040	45.0	$343,800	60.0	$328,600	40.0
Direct Fixed Costs								
Production	$ 298,964	11.3	$ 152,472	12.2	$ 80,720	14.1	$ 65,772	8.0
Marketing[a]	265,500	10.0	119,475	9.6	61,065	10.7	84,960	10.3
Totals	$ 564,464	21.3	$ 271,947	21.8	$141,785	24.8	$150,732	18.3
Product-line contribution	$ 670,976	25.3	$ 291,093	23.2	$202,015	35.2	$177,868	21.7
Common Fixed Costs								
Production	$ 280,440	10.6						
Marketing	151,600	5.7						
Administration	93,182	3.5						
Research and development	26,400	1.0						
Totals	$ 551,622	20.8						
Net Profit Before Income Taxes	$ 119,354	4.5						

[a]For simplification, we have treated direct fixed costs of marketing as being the same for product lines as they are for regions in classification and in amount. This may not be the case in practice. For example, warehouse and storage may be traceable to each region but common to product lines within a region.

Table 9-14
Dynamic Corporation Marketing Profit-Plan Summary,
Fourth Quarter, 198-

Forecast Sales Revenue (Net)		$2,645,700
Region variable costs:		
Cost of goods sold	$1,145,690	
Marketing	264,570	1,410,260
Forecast Marginal Income		$1,235,440
Fixed marketing costs:		
Direct to regions	$ 265,500	265,500
Region Contribution Margin Planned		$ 969,940
Common marketing costs:		
Budget for home office	$ 151,600	151,600
Marketing Profit Contribution Planned		$ 818,340

the result of the difference between forecast sales at standard prices and end-of-period actual sales volume at standard prices. The selling price variance accounts for the difference between the actual marginal income and the standard marginal income that is the result of the difference between sales volume at actual prices (actual revenue) and actual sales volume at standard prices (control budget revenue). In sum, revenue-related differences between forecast or planned marginal or variable income and actual marginal income experienced by the end of an operating period are caused by differences in unit-sales volume, in the proportions in which sales by product lines have occurred for the period, and by unit prices for a given line being different from standard or planned prices. One of our main goals in performance analysis within the marketing function is to appraise the effects of each component on the marginal income achieved for a particular marketing segment.

The reader will find a complete formal presentation for operating results in the fourth quarter in tables 9-15 through 9-20. Market segmentation corresponds to the three geographic regions used in illustrating budget and profit planning. For each region, a performance variance analysis is illustrated, which then serves as working data for preparing the segment-performance report. The unit-sales volume achieved for each region that is necessary to complete the "control budget" and "actual" columns appears in table 9-21.

Taking the Eastern Region as our working example for analysis (table 9-15), you will notice that marginal income for the segment is developed in two steps. The first we have called the "sales margin," which is net sales less direct variable costs of production. It is the sales margin that enables us to analyze the effects of sales volume, product-mix, and selling price variations on income. Thus

Table 9-15
Dynamic Corporation Variance Analysis, Eastern Region, Fourth Quarter, 198-

	Forecast Budget	Control Budget	Actual Revenue/Cost	Variances	
				Volume/Mix	Price/Cost
Revenue					
Sales	$1,004,000	$1,168,540	$1,161,190	$164,540	($ 7,350)
Cash discounts	43,900	50,210	48,730	(6,310)	1,480
Net sales	$ 960,100	$1,118,330	$1,112,460	$158,230	($ 5,870)
Direct Variable Costs					
Cost of goods sold	$ 430,690	$ 496,155	$ 496,155	($65,465)	$ 0
Sales margin	529,410	622,175	616,305	92,765	($ 5,870)
Ratio to net sales	0.551411	0.556343			
Marketing					
Sales commissions	$ 28,803	$ 33,550	$ 33,400	($ 4,747)	$ 150
Freight and shipping	38,404	44,733	44,603	(6,329)	130
Sales travel and expenses	28,803	33,550	33,650	(4,747)	(100)
Totals	$ 96,010	$ 111,833	$ 111,653	($ 15,823)	$ 180
Regional marginal income	$ 433,400	$ 510,342	$ 504,652	$ 76,942	($ 5,690)
Direct Fixed Costs					
Sales salaries	$ 30,167	$ 31,067	$ 32,380	($ 900)	($ 1,313)
Advertising and promotion	20,806	20,900	22,890	(94)	(1,990)
Warehouse and storage	10,474	11,100	11,500	(626)	(400)
District offices	11,700	11,850	12,170	(150)	(320)
Managerial salaries	7,000	7,400	7,850	(400)	(450)
Totals	$ 80,147	$ 82,317	$ 86,790	($ 2,170)	($ 4,473)
Region-contribution Margin	$ 353,253	$ 428,025	$ 417,862	$ 74,772	($10,163)

Sales Volume Variance

Actual sales at standard prices (control budget revenue, net)	$1,118,330
Less: forecast sales at standard prices (forecast budget revenue, net)	960,100
Difference	$ 158,230
Multiply by forecast marginal-income ratio	0.551411
Favorable sales volume variance	$ 87,250

Product-mix Variance

Actual sales at standard prices (control budget revenue, net)	$1,118,330
Multiply by difference between control marginal-income ratio at actual sales and marginal-income ratio at forecast sales (0.556343 -0.551411)	0.004932
Favorable product sales-mix variance	$ 5,515
Sales volume and produce-mix variance	$ 92,765

Selling Price Variance

Actual sales revenue, net	$1,112,460
Less actual sales at standard prices (control budget revenue, net)	1,118,330
Difference	($5,870)
Less variable marketing costs relating to net prices only	0
Unfavorable net selling price variance	($5,870)

Variable marketing costs are then presented. For Dynamic's regional sales operations, the classifications for variable costs are developed for planning purposes by percentage rates, and the "actual" column simply carries the costs incurred for the period. The sales margin less variable marketing costs for the region will be the variable marginal income. The final section includes programmed and committed fixed costs that are direct to the region.

The performance reports for each region present a complete record of all product sales variances and of all variances in marketing costs and expenses in terms of their favorable or unfavorable financial impact on planned operating

Table 9-16
Dynamic Corporation Performance Report, Eastern Region,
Fourth Quarter, 198-

Forecast Contribution Margin			$353,253
Sales Volume Variance			
Increase in marginal income from additional $158,230 revenue above forecast ($158,230 × 0.551411)		$87,250	
Less resulting additional cost allowances:			
Variable costs: Sales commissions	($4,747)		
Freight and shipping	(6,329)		
Sales travel and expenses	(4,747)	(15,823)	
Fixed costs: Sales salaries	(900)		
Advertising and promotion	(94)		
Warehouse and storage	(626)		
District offices	(150)		
Managerial salaries	(400)	(2,170)	
Net sales volume variance			$ 69,257
Product-mix Variance			
Increase in marginal income resulting from increase in marginal-income ratio ($1,118,330 × 0.004932)			5,515
Profit contribution for actual volume			$428,025
Selling Price Variance			
Price concessions to customers		(7,350)	
Cash discounts less than budget		1,480	
Net selling price variance			(5,870)
Variable Cost Spending Variance			
Sales commissions		150	
Freight and shipping		130	
Sales travel and expenses		(100)	180
Fixed-cost Spending Variance			
Sales salaries		(1,313)	
Advertising and promotion		(1,990)	
Warehouse and storage		(400)	
District offices		(320)	
Managerial salaries		(450)	(4,473)
Region-contribution Margin Achieved			$417,862

Table 9-17
Dynamic Corporation Variance Analysis, Central Region, Fourth Quarter, 198-

	Forecast Budget	Control Budget	Actual Revenue/Cost	Variances Volume/Mix	Variances Price/Cost
Revenue					
Sales	$965,800	$946,400	$908,900	($19,400)	($37,500)
Cash discounts	40,900	38,700	40,200	2,200	(1,500)
Net sales	$924,900	$907,700	$868,700	($17,200)	($39,000)
Direct Variable Costs					
Cost of goods sold	$388,950	$384,650	$384,650	$ 4,300	$ 0
Sales margin	535,950	523,050	484,050	(12,900)	(39,000)
Ratio to net sales	0.579468	0.576236			
Marketing					
Sales commissions	$ 27,747	$ 27,231	$ 26,061	$ 516	$ 1,170
Freight and shipping	36,996	36,308	34,748	688	1,560
Sales travel and expenses	27,747	27,231	26,061	516	1,170
Totals	$ 92,490	$ 90,770	$ 86,870	$ 1,720	$ 3,900
Regional marginal income	$443,460	$432,280	$397,180	($11,180)	($35,100)
Direct Fixed Costs					
Sales salaries	$ 38,183	$ 38,183	$ 39,053	$ 0	($ 870)
Advertising and promotion	24,000	23,500	23,500	500	0
Warehouse and storage	13,497	13,497	14,140	0	(643)
District offices	11,000	11,000	11,400	0	(400)
Managerial salaries	8,500	8,500	8,500	0	0
Totals	$ 95,180	$ 94,680	$ 96,593	$ 500	($ 1,913)
Region-contribution Margin	$348,280	$337,600	$300,587	($10,680)	($37,013)

profit contribution for the period. Table 9-16 presents performance results for the Eastern Region within the framework of five variance classifications:

Revenue variances: Sales volume variance
                          Product sale-mix variance
                          Selling price variance

Marketing cost and
expense variances: Variable cost spending variance
                          Fixed cost spending variance

What the performance report shows in effect is a complete description of marketing transactions that account for and reconcile differences between planned segment profitability and actual profit achieved. All items and their financial impact in the performance report are taken from the last two columns on the variance worksheet. As the reader will note, those variances having an unfavorable impact on profit are recorded in parentheses. The items relating to sales volume and mix components reconcile the difference between planned profit (per forecast budget) and actual profit at standard prices and costs (per control budget). The items relating to selling price and spending variances for marketing costs and expenses reconcile the difference between actual profit at standard (per control budget) and the regional profit-contribution achieved.

We will now evaluate and interpret the results of marketing operations for the three regions. In doing so, it is important to remember that the two essential areas for consideration are the impact of product-line sales activity on revenue and the impact of costs and expenses to support marketing operations on regional marginal income and profit contribution.

Table 9-22 gives comparative summaries for product-line sales revenue, which are drawn from the performance reports.

The first noticeable impact on revenue is a highly favorable sales volume above forecast for the Eastern Region in the amount of $87,250. Either the sales force is achieving volume at superior levels based on forecast and planned quotas, or regional price concessions may have been offered to customers in addition to planned or standard net product-line prices. Although there is an unfavorable price effect on the sales margin, the amount of $5,870 is relatively small. This result probably reflects a superior volume performance per se for the Eastern Region and that salesmen may be offering nonstandard price concessions only on the lower-priced product lines. A favorable product-line mix of $5,515 would support this interpretation. The decision-making implications for marketing management (assuming our interpretation is investigated and found to be valid) would involve sales volume planning for lower-priced lines and price-level standards for the top-priced lines. To optimize profit impact for the Eastern Region in future periods, a policy of supporting higher volume standards on low-priced items and providing additional advertising and promotion or in-

Table 9-18
Dynamic Corporation Performance Report, Central Region,
Fourth Quarter, 198-

Forecast Contribution Margin			$348,280
Sales Volume Variance			
Decrease in marginal income from $17,200 revenue less than forecast ($17,200 × 0.579468)		($9,967)	
Less resulting reduction in cost allowances:			
Variable costs: Sales commissions	$516		
Freight and shipping	688		
Sales travel and expenses	516	1,720	
Fixed costs: Advertising and promotion		500	
Net sales volume variance			(7,747)
Product-mix Variance			
Decrease in marginal income resulting from decrease in marginal-income ratio ($907,700 × 0.003232)			(2,933)
Profit contribution for actual volume			$337,600
Selling Price Variance:			
Price concessions to customers		(37,500)	
Cash discounts over budget		(1,500)	(39,000)
Variable Cost Spending Variance			
Sales commissions		1,170	
Freight and shipping		1,560	
Sales travel and expenses		1,170	3,900
Fixed-cost Spending Variance			
Sales salaries		(870)	
Warehouse and storage		(643)	
District offices		(400)	(1,913)
Region-contribution Margin Achieved			$300,587

creased compensation incentives for salesmen may be feasible. The more expensive items could be "holding their own" as to price and volume level achievement and sales-margin impact.

Revenue results in the Western Region indicate to us a pattern that is clearly

Table 9-19
Dynamic Corporation Variance Analysis, Western Region, Fourth Quarter, 198-

	Forecast Budget	Control Budget	Actual Revenue/Cost	Variances Volume/Mix	Variances Price/Cost
Revenue					
Sales	$797,400	$710,860	$710,860	($86,540)	$ 0
Cash discounts	36,700	32,890	32,700	3,810	190
Net sales	$760,700	$677,970	$678,160	($82,730)	$ 190
Direct Variable Costs					
Cost of goods sold	$326,050	$309,495	$309,495	$16,555	$ 0
Sales margin	434,650	368,475	368,665	(66,175)	190
Ratio to net sales	0.571381	0.543497			
Marketing					
Sales commissions	$ 22,821	$ 20,339	$ 20,339	$ 2,482	$ 0
Freight and shipping	30,428	27,119	28,000	3,309	(881)
Sales travel and expenses	22,821	20,339	20,929	2,482	(590)
Totals	$ 76,070	$ 67,797	$ 69,268	$ 8,273	($1,471)
Region marginal income	$358,580	$300,678	$299,397	($57,902)	($1,281)
Direct Fixed Costs					
Sales salaries	$ 27,083	$ 23,570	$ 24,000	$ 3,513	($ 430)
Advertising and promotion	20,238	19,225	19,000	1,013	225
Warehouse and storage	16,852	15,900	16,150	952	(250)
District offices	18,000	15,600	15,600	2,400	0
Managerial salaries	8,000	8,000	8,000	0	0
Totals	$ 90,173	$ 82,295	$ 82,750	$ 7,878	($ 455)
Region-contribution Margin	$268,407	$218,383	$216,647	($50,024)	($1,736)

Table 9-20
Dynamic Corporation Performance Report, Western Region,
Fourth Quarter, 198-

Forecast Contribution Margin			$268,407
Sales Volume Variance			
Decrease in marginal income from $82,730 revenue less than forecast ($82,730 × 0.571381)		($47,270)	
Less resulting reduction in cost allowances:			
Variable costs: Sales commissions	$2,482		
Freight and shipping	3,309		
Sales travel and expenses	2,482	8,273	
Fixed costs: Sales salaries	3,513		
Advertising and promotion	1,013		
Warehouse and storage	952		
District offices	2,400	7,878	
Net sales volume variance			(31,119)
Product-mix Variance			
Decrease in marginal income resulting from decrease in marginal-income ratio ($677,970 × 0.027884)			(18,905)
Profit contribution from actual volume			$218,383
Selling Price Variance			
Cash discounts below budget			190
Variable Cost Spending Variance			
Freight and shipping		(881)	
Sales travel and expenses		(590)	(1,471)
Fixed-cost Spending Variance			
Sales salaries		(430)	
Advertising and promotion		225	
Warehouse and storage		(250)	(455)
Region-contribution Margin Achieved			$216,647

unsatisfactory based on forecast. Sales volume is below standard by $47,270, while sales mix is unfavorable by $18,905. The impact of price levels on the sales margin is quite in line with standard pricing. Sales volume is undoubtedly underachieved, and because there are no material deviations from standard in

Table 9-21
Unit-Sales Volume Achieved by Regions

Product Line	Eastern Region	Central Region	Western Region	Total
MT1	16,100	16,000	6,900	39,000
MT2	5,940	7,000	2,960	15,900
MT3	7,410	2,900	6,690	17,000

prices realized, an unsatisfactory product sales mix warrants an investigation of sales results by product lines. It is possible that volume quotas are substantially underachieved on any two of the three product lines while one of the lines is yielding superior volume achievement accounting for the disparity in mix. If this is the case, then substandard volume products may require additional sales and promotional support or possible revisions in unit pricing, while the one favorable line may require an increase in the volume standard to optimize profit impact.

Our summary indicates that profit impact for the Central Region is "down on all counts" and may warrant revision in promotional and personal selling plans and certainly in price structure if the sum of the product lines is to maintain an adequate share of the total market. The critical indicator is the fact that below-standard price achievement has been experienced in the amount of $39,000 with no favorable offset on either volume or mix. It may have been necessary to offer substantial price concessions in one or more lines simply to sustain a volume level and market share that would be competitive. Two points are apparent in such a situation. First, a single-period experience of this sort is no signal that the Central Region is headed for disaster, and experience may soon reverse the slump. If the trend continues, however, and if total company profitability is reasonably in line with planned results, management could decide to remedy the situation by revising the price structure in the ailing line to maintain volume and market share or adopt a "wait-and-see" policy for a few operating periods without undue damage.

We will now turn to the second area of analysis of operations in relation to profit performance, namely, planned and achieved costs and expenses for marketing activities. The concepts and procedures for the control of marketing costs and expenses are not essentially different from those that apply to production. The reader will recall that in terms of behavior, there are two primary types of classifications, namely, activity costs, which are variable with changes in product line-sales volume, and programmed and committed fixed costs.

In organizing the data on the performance reports for the purpose of reconciling forecast profit contribution with the achieved contribution margin in the fourth quarter, we will consider the presentation in table 9-16. Similar to the components of revenue, the favorable and unfavorable differences between forecast or budgeted costs and expenses and actual results are taken from the

Table 9-22
Sales Revenue Variances by Regions

	Eastern Region	Central Region	Western Region
Sales revenue (per control budget)	$1,118,330	$907,700	$677,970
Sales revenue (per forecast budget)	960,100	924,900	760,700
Difference	$ 158,230	($17,200)	($ 82,730)
Multiply by forecast marginal-income ratio	0.551411	0.579468	0.571381
Sales volume variance	$ 87,250	($ 9,967)	($ 47,270)
Actual sales at standard prices (control budget)	$1,118,330	$907,700	$677,970
Multiply by difference between control MIR and forecast MIR	0.004932	0.003232	0.027884
Product sales-mix variance	$ 5,515	($ 2,933)	(18,905)
Actual sales revenue, net	$1,112,460	$868,700	$678,160
Less actual sales at standard prices (control budget revenue, net	1,118,330	907,700	677,970
Difference	($ 5,870)	($ 39,000)	$ 190
Less variable marketing costs relating to net prices only	0	0	0
Selling price variances	($ 5,870)	($ 39,000)	$ 190

last two columns on the variance-analysis worksheet. Both variable and fixed classifications are organized on the format on two bases: the components of each classification that relate specifically to sales volume and the components that are independent of sales volume. The former represent the difference between budget for planned product-line sales volume (forecast) and budget for actual sales volume (control). The latter are spending-variance components, comparable to our performance analysis in production, and represent the difference between budget for actual volume achieved and actual expenses incurred for the period. They are labeled "spending variances" on the performance reports and are taken from the last column on the analysis worksheet.

For the Eastern Region, variable-cost differences arising from sales volume variation are unfavorable for both variable and fixed classifications in the amounts of $15,823 and $2,170, respectively. This would have to be the case since achieved sales volume exceeds forecast volume. For the Central and Western Regions, this situation is the reverse (but not necessarily for the same classifications) since the control budget shows that actual sales volume for all product lines is below forecast volume. Two points are critical regarding the interpretation of volume variances for variable and fixed marketing costs and their profit impact. The first is that unfavorable cost variances will not mean that volume performance or the sales margin is "unfavorable." We would expect costs for variable and programmed activity classifications to be above the forecast budget if actual volume is above forecast. Conversely, we will expect costs for these items to be below the forecast budget if actual sales volume is below forecast. Thus in terms of revenue and profit impact on sales margins, additional "volume variance" costs are a necessary increment for superior volume and profit achievement. The second point of importance is that volume variance costs are rarely controllable as such since managerial control in terms of revenue, product-line market share, and profit contribution is exercised through the ability to influence sales volume levels per se.

Control with respect to those variable and programmed fixed-expense classifications that reflect spending variances is a very different matter. As in production, these variances are always related to actual sales volume for an operating period, and reflect overspending or underspending with respect to budget at that volume. Variable and programmed fixed expenses are always subject to control by marketing management. Table 9-16 shows that variable-cost spending variances for the Eastern Region are negligible, while programmed budget variances may be significantly unfavorable in the amount of $4,473. However, since overall profit performance is superior in this region for the fourth quarter, management may tend to view the classifications reflecting overexpenditure as not serious enough to signal investigation and implementation of cost-cutting procedures for these activities. One simple criterion that can be effective is to set a tolerance percentage for spending variances over budget based on the percentage increase in achieved profit contribution for the segment over planned profit contribution. Unfavorable spending variances above the planned "tolerance" level would be investigated. In view of what we have set forth, the reader may now wish to examine the spending variances for the other regions and render interpretation regarding their impact on planned and achieved profit contribution. The performance report by product lines and the achievement summary for total marketing operations appear in tables 9-23 and 9-24, respectively, and can be compared readily with their counterparts for fourth-quarter planning in tables 9-13 and 9-14.

In this chapter we have emphasized profit planning and budgeting and functional performance analysis and interpretation by marketing segments in a way that is quite comparable to our treatment of management control by product lines and organizational centers in production. We have defined "marketing segments" as being either product lines or functional and organizational areas of operation in which activity planning and budgeting are imple-

Table 9-23
Dynamic Corporation Product-Line Profit-Achievement Summary, Fourth Quarter, 198-

| | Total Company | | Product Lines | | | | | |
| | | | MT1 | | MT2 | | MT3 | |
	Amount	Percent	Amount	Percent	Amount	Percent	Amount	Percent
Net Sales Revenue	$2,659,320	100.0	$1,356,250	100.0	$398,920	100.0	$904,170	100.0
Standard Variable Costs								
Cost of goods sold	$1,190,300	44.7	$ 596,700	44.0	$143,100	35.9	$450,500	49.8
Cost of marketing	267,791	10.1	131,320	9.7	47,240	11.8	89,231	9.9
Totals	$1,458,091	54.8	$ 728,020	53.7	$190,340	47.7	$539,731	59.7
Marginal income	$1,201,229	45.2	$ 628,230	46.3	$208,560	52.3	$364,439	40.3
Direct Fixed Costs								
Production	$ 298,964	11.2	$ 152,472	11.2	$ 80,720	20.2	$ 65,772	7.3
Marketing[a]	267,791	10.2	136,580	10.1	40,700	10.2	90,511	10.0
Totals	$ 566,755	21.4	$ 289,052	21.3	$121,420	30.4	$156,283	17.3
Product-line profit-contribution achieved	$ 634,474	23.8	$ 339,178	25.0	$ 87,140	21.9	$208,156	23.0
Common Fixed Costs								
Production	$ 280,440	10.6						
Marketing	151,600	5.7						
Administration	95,682	3.6						
Research and development	23,000	1.0						
Totals	$ 550,722	20.7						
Net Profit Before Income Taxes	$ 83,752	3.1						

[a]For simplification, we have treated direct fixed costs of marketing as being the same for product lines as they are for regions, in classification and in amount. This may not be the case in practice. For example, warehouse and storage may be traceable to each region but common to product lines within a region.

Table 9-24
Dynamic Corporation Marketing Profit-Achievement Summary,
Fourth Quarter, 198-

Actual Sales Revenue (Net)		$2,659,320
Region variable costs:		
Cost of goods sold	$1,190,300	
Marketing	267,791	1,458,091
Actual Marginal Income		$1,201,229
Fixed marketing costs:		
Direct to regions	$ 266,133	266,133
Region contribution Margin Achieved		$ 935,096
Common marketing costs:		
Actual for home office	$ 164,890	164,890
Marketing Profit Contribution Achieved		$ 770,206
Marketing Profit-Achievement Percent		94.12

mented for all phases of marketing activity, our examples here being geographic districts and regions.

There are several important advantages to this approach to activity budgeting and performance evaluation in terms of planning and decision making and in terms of effective profit performance. Segment analysis itself enables a company to pinpoint all financial planning and results by organizational subdivisions within the overall marketing function where these units are operationally self-contained or independent of each other. Operations planning and performance appraisal in terms of profitability for the total marketing function only will tend to "bury" the separate effects of financial behavior for each subdivision and their profit impact as well. Further, cost control and maintaining equitable cost standards or performance objectives for cost effectiveness can be conducted with greater accuracy and more favorable profit achievement when market conditions for individual product lines, geographic areas, or even classifications of customers are independent, and practical operating experience may be quite different for each area. The analysis of revenue by components, which we have explored in detail, can be invaluable to market decision making by product lines in terms of volume planning and forecasting, maintaining competitive market share within an industry, and the periodic evaluation and setting of pricing policies.

10 The Administrative Budget

Production and marketing are usually regarded as being the most significant areas of total operating activity for a manufacturing company, certainly from the standpoint of annual planning and budget requirements and in terms of their combined contribution to total profit achievement. Corporate administration is the third major area of continuing activity requiring annual budget preparation and performance appraisal. Total expenditures for this function usually appear on the company annual report under the heading "general and administrative expenses." Corporate administration serves primarily in an auxiliary role to the other functions of production and marketing, with the exception of what is commonly called long-range or long-term corporate planning. Corporate planning as part of company administration is often the responsibility of the president or chief operating officer and planning committees to include the senior executive officers representing, at least, production, marketing, and finance. The composition of corporate planning committees will vary for individual manufacturers depending on structural organization, priority of functions, and titles and designated responsibilities of the senior officers. It is not unusual for the president to designate one of his senior officers as committee chairman or director of corporate planning, reporting directly to him in this role.

The other activities within the administrative function for which short-term planning and budgeting are essential will be company-wide professional or staff services to internal operations such as finance, personnel and legal services, and corporate liaison with external publics including industrial, public, and government relations. Listed below is a composite of functional activities and professional responsibilities that may typically comprise corporate administration for a manufacturing firm.

The chief executive or chief operating officer and his staff who are responsible for overall direction of functional activities, company organization, and long-range financial and operating goals.

Finance to include the duties of the treasurer for operating-funds management, controllership, and tax planning and management.

Personnel charged with responsibility for recruiting and training, payroll, and job evaluation.

Industrial relations to include wage and salary guidelines, trade-union relations, and labor-contract negotiations.

Public and government relations responsible for publicity, trade relations, and operating activities subject to government regulation.

Corporate legal staff.

Since professional services comprise the majority of activities coming under corporate administration, planning and budgeting will not be as complex as they are for production and marketing. On the other hand, professional services per se are not really subject to quantitative measurement either in terms of identifiable activity or in terms of pinpointing costs assignable to an activity. For example, we know in advance of an annual or quarterly planning period what the cost of a corporate lawyer will be if he works full time at a specific salary. What we usually don't know is his volume level of legal activity for the planning period that we can quantify in the operating plan for administration. Assuming the lawyer is a specialist in drafting and reviewing labor contracts based on management-union negotiation, the volume or amount of contract work may vary considerably annually or by quarters. For this and many other types of professional services, it is at best difficult and perhaps impossible either to plan or to control activity levels by operating time periods. Nevertheless, professional salaries must be paid for each period whether the workload is heavy or light.

Planning and budgeting for administration is conducted as part of the total operating budget. Individual budgets are prepared for organizational units or departments in accordance with specific professional, auxiliary, or advisory services performed by each department and for the same time periods for which plans and budgets are drawn up in production and marketing. The separate budgets will include detail for at least three cost items that are involved in providing any type of professional service: staff salaries and wages, materials and supplies, and depreciation on equipment and facilities assigned to a specific administrative function or service department. The department budget may also include a total projection of man-hours required for the period and a summary description of activities to be performed in so far as this detail can be accurately projected. The separate department budgets will be combined to prepare a budget summary for administration that will specify the total planned expenditure for each service area.

The most important distinction between activity planning and formal drafting of the budget for administration in comparison to either production or marketing is this: We do not have scheduled or forecast quantities of "product" flowing through each department or service area for the operating period, nor do we have the capability to establish budgeting and performance standards for most types of administrative services. In production, we have the technical means for planning production schedules by product-line volumes and for establishing product-quality specifications through engineering standards. We also have cost and quantity standards for the input of materials and parts by type, labor-rate standards per hour, and labor-time standards per product unit produced. In marketing, we are able to prepare quantitative forecasts of sales also by product lines, set sales quotas by geographic areas, and establish unit-price standards. As we have seen, these measures provide the necessary means for preparing very accurate activity plans and schedules and their corresponding target levels for financial expenditure. They also provide the means to evaluate the efficiency of operating results at the end of a period.

In administration, budgeting and performance evaluation work is simpler in that there are no comparable volume levels for professional service activities, nor are there work or product unit standards. On the other hand, the absence of such measures makes it nearly impossible to evaluate the efficiency of operating performance by the same criteria and with the use of any techniques similar to those available in production and marketing. Thus a substantially modified approach to budgeting and performance appraisal will be necessary for administrative services, using some new concepts and measurements.

In our previous discussions, we have not defined or used the phrase "task management," although it is quite appropriate for many kinds of administrative and professional services. Essentially, task management involves the setting of activity levels not by volume of physical units but by specifying an activity objective or workload to be accomplished within a certain timeframe. Then estimates of the human and physical resources required to complete the task or a portion of it within the timeframe are made, and sufficient cost information (that is, salary levels, materials and supply costs, depreciation rates) is provided to budget these resource estimates. In task planning, the activities to be performed are itemized and described in a proposal that then serves as the documentation in support of the formal budget for the activity area. For the chief executive's office, task activities for the fourth quarter might include:

Corporate planning committee: review three-year summary of product group performance, five-year plan for research and development, capital-expenditure plans for the next fiscal year, and plant-location proposals.

Year-end review meetings with heads of finance, production, and marketing.

Review of plans for proposed decentralization of structural organization and functional operations by product group delineation.

Preparation for annual stockholders' meeting.

For each of these activities, the task objectives for the fourth quarter can be defined, and estimates of time, staff personnel, supplies, facilities, and travel requirements would be prepared for each task objective. Then based on information for salary levels and cost documentation for physical requirements (for example, supplies, facilities, and travel arrangements), the budget for the chief executive's area of total administration will be formalized. Using the same approach, similar task objectives and related resource requirements can be drawn up for legal, personnel, and other service departments where activity planning by specific objectives is appropriate.

Administrative services involving task-objective assignment continue throughout the year and although they are essential to the functioning of total company operations, neither the planning nor the level of these professional activities is directly related to or dependent on the volume of normal production and marketing operations on which short-term bottom-line results depend. Some administrative task work such as corporate planning is long term and may have no direct bearing on normal annual or quarterly operations in the near future.

The second primary type of work in general administration is routine or sufficiently standardized to be accurately measurable and may very well be undertaken in support of normal short-term production and marketing operations. This work may also be dependent on and vary with changes in production and marketing volume. Measurable work involves systematic or clerical operations that can be accurately quantified and estimated in terms of hour requirements and the types and quantities of supplies needed similar to direct labor and materials in production. An example would be part-time clerical or staff assistant employees who are hired at hourly wage rates rather than on the basis of a fixed salary scale. They may be assigned to customer relations as part of general administration. Both the number of employees engaged in customer correspondence and communications work and the total man/day requirements for an operating period will vary in direct proportion to changes in estimated sales volume levels. In company personnel, employee hiring and training may also be a direct function of planned levels of production and marketing operations, although it is organizationally assigned to general administration and is included in the administrative budget. For routine or repetitive work, the specific activities and their cost amounts can be standardized and applied to changing levels of production or sales volume, depending on which of these functions they most directly support. A flexible-budget approach may be quite suitable for these activities.

With the exception of repetitive and measurable work, virtually all expenses for advisory and service functions in corporate administration are constant amounts and remain so throughout the operating period. They are not sensitive to short-term changes in either output or sales volume levels. This means that for most services and their corresponding account classifications, the budget is essentially fixed. Costs for budget preparation and performance evaluation will be either programmed or committed lump-sum amounts depending on the classification. For the legal department, the underlying documentation for the fourth quarter would provide the "task load" anticipated by specifying the professional services (for example, contract preparation and review by type, labor-union negotiation meetings, hearing dates) and the projected man-hours or man-days for each.

The time estimates are then converted into dollar amounts by assigning the professional staff members to be involved in each activity and allocating their respective salary increments for the quarter to each designated task. All supplies and materials are similarly budgeted to each task assignment by the best available estimates. In this way the programmed section of the budget is prepared. Committed costs for depreciable assets that are direct to the legal department (for example, office furniture and equipment) are usually a fixed amount that remains the same for each quarter unless there are additions to or deletions from the inventory of direct fixed assets during the year.

The budget for administrative service departments is essentially an appropriation, and the amount of the appropriation request will be based on the task-load or activity planning documentation. Thus it will be a fixed-cost budget for those departments that develop an activity program for each quarter. For some departments such as finance, the professional activities themselves remain pretty much the same in successive operating periods. For example, in the finance department responsibilities such as cash-flow management, budget summary review, controllership, and auditing will remain the same throughout the year. Task planning is less important for administrative departments where primary activity types are continuing and the fixed-cost budget may be prepared without the need for a separate activity plan in each operating period. For any activities where past experience has clearly shown a correlation between expenditure levels and substantial changes in production or sales volume, a step budget may be effective since it eliminates the need to prepare a new plan and budget for approval when these changes occur during the year.

Formal drafts of an activity plan budget for one administrative department (in this case, the legal department) and a budget summary for general administration of the Dynamic Power Tool Corporation are presented in tables 10-1 and 10-2.

Performance evaluation for the administrative function involves some important differences when compared to appraisal of operating results in production and marketing. The distinctions relate to both the measurement of performance deviations from budget per se and what these quantitative differences mean. For both production and marketing, we have seen that measures of operating results in comparison to budget comprise three significant variances. The reader will recall that for cost classifications in the performance reporting structure by activity area or department, we have the following:

1. *Volume Variance:* measures the difference between budgeted and actual cost levels that results from the difference between forecast or planned volume of output or sales and actual volume at the end of the period.
2. *Efficiency Variance:* measures the utilization of time or human and physical resources by comparing budgeted and actual marketing results at the same output level (that is, actual production output or sales volume achieved).
3. *Spending Variance:* measures the savings or overexpenditure of funds based on budget at the actual output level.

Table 10-1
Dynamic Corporation, Legal Department Budget,
Fourth Quarter, 198-

Classification	Man-days	Amount	Percent
Professional			
Contract preparation and review	58	$ 5,800	30.3
U.S. government regulation hearings	24	2,400	12.5
Court assignments	30	3,000	15.7
Unallocated	8	800	4.2
Totals	120	$12,000	62.7
Nonprofessional Salaries			
Secretarial and clerical	80	3,500	18.3
Others	40	1,200	6.3
Totals	120	$ 4,700	24.6
Fixed Assets			
Office equipment	N.A.	1,160	6.2
Office furniture	N.A.	700	3.6
Totals		$ 1,860	9.8
Supplies	N.A.	560	2.9
Totals		$ 560	2.9
Department Budget		$19,120	100.0

As we have mentioned, general administrative activities are of two types that may serve in an auxiliary role with respect to the production and marketing functions, although neither of.them involves varying levels of physical product flow per se. The task type of activity is a project plan that is drawn up for implementation at the beginning of each operating period. Continuing activities do not require replanning and new project descriptions since their purpose and content remain the same in successive periods throughout the year. For both types of services, there is only one budget-variance measure that appears in the performance reports for specific areas and in the general administration perfor- mance summary. It is commonly called a cost savings or cost overrun, and a parallel measure in production or marketing would be the spending variance. Performance reports are presented in tables 10-3 and 10-4 corresponding to the formal budget examples developed for the fourth quarter.

The fourth-quarter performance report for the legal department sets forth the data for budgeted and actual service man-days and expenditure levels by individual activities contained in the task plan. This approach enables manage-

Table 10-2
Dynamic Corporation General Administration Budget Summary,
Fourth Quarter, 198-

Classification	President's Office	Finance Department	Personnel Department	Legal Department	Total
Salaries					
Professional	$25,914	$12,760	$ 8,500	$12,000	$59,174
Other	7,990	4,375	3,590	4,700	20,655
Totals	$33,904	$17,135	$12,090	$16,700	$79,829
Fixed Assets					
Office equipment	2,100	1,775	1,050	1,160	6,085
Office furniture	1,604	592	460	700	3,356
Totals	$ 3,704	$ 2,367	$ 1,510	$ 1,860	$ 9,441
Supplies	582	2,000	770	560	3,912
Totals	$ 582	$ 2,000	$ 770	$ 560	$ 3,912
Administration Budget	$38,190	$21,502	$14,370	$19,120	$93,182

ment to pinpoint either savings or overruns based on the budget for professional time and cost levels so that variances can be investigated easily and any necessary adjustments made either in the task plan itself or in the appropriation amount. The performance summary for the total administrative function presents budgeted and actual expenditures with the corresponding savings or overruns for each major classification by service area. Only the task plan detail for a given department has been omitted in the total performance report. The primary benefit of this procedure is that senior management for administration is informed of all savings and overruns relevant to the period by each department. The underlying information relating to task planning and achievement remains with the department manager who is responsible for planning and control within his own area of operations.

In performance evaluation, the terms "efficiency" and "effectiveness" have sometimes been used interchangeably, although they have substantially different meanings and uses depending on the type of functional operation in question. We will define these terms as follows:

Efficiency: the length of time required and the level of direct expenditure incurred to perform an operation.

Effectiveness: the degree to which a goal that has been set for an operating task is attained in terms of quality and completion.

For central administrative services, we do not have efficiency measures in

Table 10-3
Dynamic Corporation, Legal Department Performance Report,
Fourth Quarter, 198-

Classifications	Man-Days Budget	Man-Days Actual	Expenditures Budget	Expenditures Actual	Expense Variance
Professional					
Contract preparation and reviews	58	62	$ 5,800	$ 6,200	($ 400)
U.S. government regulation hearings	24	30	2,400	3,000	($ 600)
Court assignments	30	30	3,000	3,000	0
Unallocated	8	8	800	800	0
Totals	120	130	$12,000	$13,000	($1,000)
Nonprofessional Salaries					
Secretarial and clerical	80	80	3,500	3,500	0
Other	40	40	1,200	1,200	0
Totals	120	120	$ 4,700	$ 4,700	0
Fixed Assets					
Office equipment	N.A.		1,160	1,160	0
Office furniture	N.A.		700	700	0
Total			$ 1,860	$ 1,860	0
Supplies			560	1,149	(589)
Totals			$ 560	$ 1,149	(589)
Total Department			$19,120	$20,709	($1,589)

performance appraisal for the very reason that we cannot develop cost standards in common units of time or resource inputs that are applicable to a single volume level of achievement such as we have used in production and marketing. However, we are able to budget activities and appraise operations in time units of man-hours or man-days and in terms of suitably accurate expenditure allocations so that overruns in operating results can be pinpointed by specific activity and investigated as to causes.

A final issue of importance to central administrative services is the quality-attainment level as it is used in the preceding definition of effectiveness. The quality level is not an aspect of performance that can be either established or objectively determined as to results through quantitative financial measures. There is simply no suitable or even valid means whereby the performance quality of a public-relations campaign undertaken to strengthen a company's corporate image in trade relations or the degree to which the legal department is successful in presenting management's position at a court hearing can be evaluated through the use of financial measures. The criteria for determining quality attainment for

Table 10-4
Dynamic Corporation General Administration Performance Summary, Fourth Quarter, 198-

Classification	President's Office			Finance			Personnel			Legal			Total		
	Budget	Actual	Expense Savings/Overrun	Budget	Actual	Expense Savings/Overrun	Budget	Actual	Expense Savings/Overrun	Budget	Actual	Expense Savings/Overrun	Budget	Actual	Expense Savings/Overrun
Salaries															
Professional	$25,914	$25,914	$ 0	$12,760	$10,400	$2,360	$ 8,500	$ 9,100	($600)	$12,000	$13,000	($1,000)	$59,174	$58,414	$ 760
Other	7,990	8,430	(440)	4,375	4,800	(425)	3,590	3,400	190	4,700	4,700	0	20,655	21,330	675
Totals	$33,904	$34,344	($440)	$17,135	$15,200	$1,935	$12,090	$12,500	($410)	$16,700	$17,700	($1,000)	$79,829	$79,744	$ 85
Fixed Assets															
Office equipment	2,100	2,250	(150)	1,775	1,775	0	1,050	1,350	($300)	1,160	1,160	0	6,085	6,535	(450)
Office furniture	1,604	1,604	0	592	900	(308)	460	460	0	700	700	0	3,356	3,664	(308)
Totals	$ 3,704	$ 3,854	($150)	$ 2,367	$ 2,675	($ 308)	$ 1,510	$ 1,810	($300)	$ 1,860	$ 1,860	$ 0	$ 9,441	$10,199	($ 758)
Supplies	582	800	(218)	2,000	2,750	(750)	770	1,040	(270)	560	1,149	(589)	3,912	5,739	(1,827)
Totals	$ 582	$ 800	($218)	$ 2,000	$ 2,750	($ 750)	$ 770	$ 1,040	($270)	$ 560	$ 1,149	($ 589)	$ 3,912	$ 5,739	($1,827)
Total Administration	$38,190	$38,998	($808)	$21,502	$20,625	$ 877	$14,370	$15,350	($980)	$19,120	$20,709	($1,589)	$93,182	$95,682	($2,500)

most professional activities has to be established through guidelines and objectives applicable to the individual profession. And the determination of the quality level achieved would rely on executive judgment and not on financial standards, inputs, and returns.

The subject of innovation and change in industrial environments is not frequently dealt with in writings on budget systems and management control. Change is nevertheless an ever-present and vital factor for corporate growth and profitability. The primary role of research and development undertaken by industrial companies is to create change through the introduction of new products or product-line extensions. The objective of this work is the expansion of production operations and customer markets and to achieve new profit levels. Through research and development, management causes change in the levels of production and sales volume for the company, its competitive position in the industry, and its profit growth. For many companies and particularly for high technology manufacturers, research and development and product-market expansion become major aspects of corporate planning.

From the standpoint of continuing functional operations, research and development is really a separate area that is not directly associated with production, marketing, and administration. The main purpose of research and development is the expansion of company production and sales operations and ultimately an increase in total profit return for the company. Thus research and development operations are long term with respect to both planning and profit contribution. Although planning and review of operations is normally conducted every year, research-and-development work is project oriented, and individual projects may vary in length of time from start to completion from one year to three or five years and even longer for highly experimental product or process development work. In any operating year, there may be several separate projects adopted in the research-and-development plan varying in length of total planned time and in degree or stage of completion.

We have stated previously that budget procedures for many types of operations, particularly in marketing and administration, are conducted by working on the separate activity areas, determining the material, manpower, equipment, and other resource requirements for an individual area or subset of related activities, assigning cost factors to each area in making up the budget estimates, and then adding them together to arrive at the total budget proposed for the department or activity group. The approach used in budgeting research and development is often the reverse. A total appropriation is designated each year as the first step in the budgeting process. The actual amount of the appropriation can be set in various ways, and the policy adopted for determining the total annual appropriation level is normally the responsibility of top management.

A policy that calls for a constant appropriation ceiling each year for several consecutive years may be adopted. This amount would be included as part of the annual funds flow or working-capital plan without anticipated change from one year to the next. Market success and profit return for research-and-development ventures can be highly unpredictable, and many projects will never result in any sales or profit "payoff" even to the extent of recovering development costs. Because of the high-risk nature of research and development, a fairly "safe" policy for determining the appropriation ceiling is to take a percentage of projected annual sales or total planned profit for the company. In this way, the appropriation will vary with changes in the level of normal operations from one year to the next and thereby avoid the risk of disproportionately high expenditures in years of low volume and profit levels for the company. Policy for setting appropriation ceilings must rely on executive judgment, past experience regarding success/failure ratios, and "calculated faith" in the prospective market payoff for projects that are close to completion.

Individual project plans will be drafted or updated each year and cost estimates made for labor, materials, and fixed assets similar to budgeting in production. Two problems arise in drafting the annual activity plan and budget for research and development. One is the varying length of time estimated for individual projects and the stage of completion that a project has reached. The other difficulty is that the sum of the budget estimates for individual projects may exceed the total appropriation for the year. Reconciling these aspects for planning purposes can be accomplished by ranking projects in order of priority, taking into consideration their relative stages of completion and each project's potential success and long-term contribution to company growth and profit expectations. When the budget estimate has been prepared for each project and they have been ranked as to priority, only the lower priority projects that exceed the annual appropriation would be postponed or abandoned.

Performance evaluation for research and development presents the same considerations that we find for professional services in administration. Since research and development involves project planning and task-oriented appraisal, the objective aspects of performance within a management control system will reflect the degree of task completion and cost savings or overruns. Technical quality levels of achievement and future likelihood of project success are beyond the reach of objective financial measurement. However, procedures for determining the relationship between task-completion attainment and expenditures at the end of a period based on budget can have a substantial impact on management decisions as to project approval or continuation in future operating periods. The important problem for management control is to present this relationship quantitatively and in such a way that it can be understood easily and properly by management.

The research-and-development budget for the fourth quarter (table 10-5) presents complete time and cost detail for each of the four projects in the shop. The reader will note that both time and cost estimates are designated for the total project as well as for the current budget period. This procedure facilitates a clear comparison of current period budget to total appropriation for each project by priority rank and by stage of completion with respect to the overall

Table 10-5
Dynamic Corporation Research-and-Development Budget, Fourth Quarter, 198-

Project Title	Date Started	Completion Date	Total Quarters	Priority Rank Current Period	Percent Task Assignment	Expenditure Ceiling	Current-period Budget
MT3 Product-line Extension	January 1977	December 1981	20	1	6.00	$145,000	$ 8,000
Air Saw Project	October 1978	June 1982	15	2	8.00	75,000	5,500
Project Zebra	July 1979	June 1982	12	3	9.00	100,000	8,500
MT1 Product-line Extension	April 1978	December 1979	7	4	10.00	40,000	4,400
Totals						$360,000	$26,400

time allocation. The performance report (table 10-6) shows project-expenditure variances from budget for the quarter and one additional measure that we have called the "task/cost effectiveness index." This index states the relationship between the degree of task completion and budget achievement in terms of percentages for the current period and for the project to date. For example, the first ranked project was 90.0 percent complete as to task assignment and at an expenditure level of 112.5 percent of the quarterly budget. The ratio of the two percentages yields a project effectiveness index of 80.0 percent for the period. Similarly, the effectiveness index for the second ranked project to date is 100.0 percent. This tells us that since the project was initiated in October 1978, its cumulative track record has been perfect with respect to both technical completion and expenditures based on the original appropriation.

While change in product-line composition and the total operating volume of a manufacturing company can be accomplished through planned technological research and development, management planning and operating levels also depend on economic changes that are external to the business enterprise. These changes may result from the general level of economic activity such as alternating periods of expansion or recession, which impact on the activity levels of many industries. They may also include shifts in customer preferences and expenditures for specific product lines or services within the market boundaries of a particular industry or the technological innovations of directly competing companies that will alter their relative market share or position. These economic changes will likely have their greatest impact on volume levels of marketing and production activity for the company. Although management may have little influence on the causes or magnitude of these economic changes, it may be necessary to revise operating budgets to adjust to the expected impact they will have on short-term marketing and production levels.

The focal point of budget revisions that are based on economic conditions external to the company is the sales forecast for product lines. Any substantial modification in forecast sales volume that affects the operating budget may require revision of the budget amounts for most variable and programmed classifications in the operating plan for marketing. Depending on company size and complexity of operations, the task involved can be extensive. For this reason, it is advisable that budget revisions be conducted only when management is confident that the volume change resulting from the new forecast is large enough to materially affect both the required level of financial expenditures and the profit contribution in the current period.

There is no "scientific approach" or objective guidelines that will assist management in deciding whether or not to overhaul the budget during an operating period. The total time and cost of budget-revision work would have to be estimated as accurately as possible and compared to the expected benefits derived from cost savings based on a more restricted budget or the expected impact on relative profit-contribution levels. Unless the comparison significantly justifies undertaking midperiod revision of the total operating budget, then it

Table 10-6
Dynamic Corporation Research-and-Development Performance Report, Fourth Quarter, 198-

Project Title	Priority Rank Current Period	Current-period Budget	Current-period Expenditures	Variance	Task/Cost Index Current Period	Task/Cost Index Total Project
MT3 Product-line Extension	1	$ 8,000	$ 9,000	($1,000)	0.900/1.125 = 0.800	0.850
Air Saw Project	2	5,500	4,125	1,375	0.850/0.750 = 1.133	1.000
Project Zebra	3	8,500	9,375	(875)	0.750/1.103 = 0.680	0.800
MT1 Product-line extension	4[a]	4,400	500	3,900	—	
Totals		$26,400	$23,000	$3,400		

[a]Project abandoned November 15, 198-.

would be best to use the revised forecast for preparing operating plans in the next period.

If the revision is undertaken, it will first affect the operating plans for the marketing function. The most logical approach to preparing the new budget is simply to replace the original forecast budget with new estimates and then to follow through with preparation of control budget amounts at the end of the period using the revised volume, assuming that there have been no midperiod product-line or unit-cost standards. Although this procedure yields the desired results, at the same time it will obscure in the reports the fact that major budget revisions were made some time after approval and implementation of the original plans. This problem can be overcome easily by retaining the original forecast budget for all classifications and presenting an additional column for all material revisions with the heading "Revised Forecast Budget." While it does add somewhat to the detail, this approach also informs management that the budget was substantially revised during the operating period and it will reflect the impact ("forecast variance") that the revision had on major revenue and expense items in the operating plan.

Revision of the production schedule and budget does not obviously follow from the change in the sales volume forecast. In view of the fact that sales volume, inventory levels, and scheduled production volume are all interdependent, a decision to change the production schedule and budget in the same period as the forecast revision would have to take into consideration the effect that the incremental change in expected sales will have on current inventory levels. For example, it may not be advisable to incur the additional expense of overhauling the production schedule and budget unless the forecast revision clearly indicates that inventory shortages are likely to prevail and market demand cannot be met in the period of the forecast revision. If there is no likelihood of inventory shortages, which would be the case for substantial reductions in forecast volume, then adjustments in inventory levels and scheduled production volume that are necessary to meet the revised forecast can be postponed until the next planning period.

11 Summary and Perspectives

Management control is a conceptual and technical subject that has considerable potential application in many types of organizations including profit-seeking industrial enterprises, social-service organizations, educational and health institutions, and government agencies. It is a subject that addresses itself to the pragmatic planning and evaluation of functional operations with the specific objective of establishing and maintaining efficient conduct of interrelated activities of an organization and cost effectiveness based on clearly established standards and guidelines. While the main focus of management control is the planning and conduct of functional activities, the professional application of management control systems must necessarily be concerned with several managerial and applied specialties of organization life that are interrelated and upon which the success of its activities depend. For industrial enterprises, they include formal organization structure and design, designated responsibilities and reporting levels, vertical communications within the organization, financial planning and funding, cost accounting, and industrial engineering.

With its emphasis on efficiency and cost effectiveness, the theoretical and conceptual development of management control and the use of control systems will undoubtedly experience greater expansion over the next several years than has been typical of the past two decades. It is the writer's view that recent economic history provides the explanation and justification for future growth and profitable rewards of applied management control. The primary cause may be traced to the impact of hyperinflation as a pervading and hazardous characteristic of economic behavior in the United States and abroad. Increasing stringency in the supply of long-term capital and short-term funds in money markets for competing industrial and nonindustrial needs, the rapid rise of product and service prices at all levels within domestic and international economies, the inability to maintain adequate ceilings on interest rates, and the recent severity of recessions combine to magnify the need for more efficient and cost-effective functional planning and control in almost any human organization, regardless of its specific size or purpose.

This book has addressed profit-seeking industrial firms that produce and market physical products. The planning and evaluation of operations for these companies must be oriented therefore to the primary functions of producing or processing product lines and the marketing of finished products with the auxiliary services of general company administration being the third main sector of operations within the company. Our approach to management control has dealt with these three functions and the component activities of each by time periods. Short-term planning and evaluation initially focuses on operations by functions and by periods of time such as the quarter or month within the operating year.

The organization and implementation of functional budget planning and performance evaluation as a two-part system, however, takes the company's formal organization structure as the basis for practical planning, budgeting, and control of activities for two reasons: The first is the more obvious fact that a product-oriented company's production, marketing, and administrative operations are conducted within a formal network of sections, departments, and divisions that represent vertical and horizontal lines of communication, authority, and responsibility. Without a skillfully designed organization structure that satisfies the activity requirements of each function, almost any complex enterprise would become hopelessly chaotic and dysfunctional.

The second reason lies in the word "responsibility." The term "responsibility center" has gained increasing popularity in writings on planning, budgeting, and financial control and with good reason. Each block on a company's organization chart, whether it be in the general area of production, marketing, or administration, is assigned a specific group of activities or duties and is charged with the responsibility for carrying them out. It is also staffed with skilled technical or professional personnel and a supervisor or manager. The preparation of budgets and the conduct of activities upon which performance evaluation is based involves human decision making throughout the operating period, and the results of operations at the end of the period reflect the impact of these decisions for which the organizational unit is responsible. Formal performance evaluation then must be conducted and control exercised in accordance with defined boundaries of groups of activities and the supervisory personnel responsible for them. The structural framework that provides these activity boundaries and levels of responsibility is necessarily the organization chart.

Within the formal organization structure, we made further reference to areas of operating activities as being segments or activity points. These segments are the primary building blocks for both budgeting and performance evaluation. They may be responsibility centers as represented by vertical and horizontal blocks on the company's organization chart, or they may be groups of activities defined on the basis of product-line delineation, types of services, geographic areas, or other basis whereby human, physical, and financial resources are self-contained and readily identifiable with each segment. Examples of the former would be the processing, assembling, finishing, and maintenance departments in the production plant; the legal and personnel departments in administration; or research and development. These are all separate functional units located on the company organization chart and thus are responsibility centers. They may also be geographic sales regions, product lines, or customer classifications as we have seen in the marketing area. The important point to keep in mind is that for any activity segment, planning and budgeting can be undertaken for a given operating period according to these individual segments, and each makes its own direct and quantifiable contribution to total company profit for the period being evaluated and for the year.

Further, if operations planning and performance evaluation are conducted only at high organizational levels in the company such as the division in large and complex companies or the "sales department" for companies having several product lines and extensive geographic markets, the separate effects of activity results and financial behavior at lower levels or subdivisions and their profit impact will be obscured. Each may experience different behavior patterns in terms of quantitative operating levels, manpower, materials, facilities and other resource inputs, operating efficiency, cost effectiveness, and profit-contribution achievement within the same time period. The segment focuses attention on those organizational units or groups of related activities where inefficient performance can be traced easily and corrective action taken. This will facilitate more effective operating results in line with planned objectives and budgets and better achievement records for staff and managerial personnel.

Budget preparation and performance appraisal are conducted by functional areas and formally in terms of responsibility centers and other identifiable segments. Performance measures are considered and prepared in terms of the contributions that operating units make toward the earning of profit for the company. In financial terms the contribution margin is a subset of company income and is the bottom-line measure that relates performance appraisal to the beginning-of-period profit plan.

In a strict sense, the contribution margin is the dollar amount by which a portion of sales revenue that can be identified with the activities of an organizational unit or segment exceed the operating costs and expenses that are direct to that subset of company activities. Responsibility centers and segments in the marketing function will be the most logical and appropriate activity points to develop budgets and appraise performance in terms of the contribution-margin measure. A portion of company revenue and costs and expenses can be directly identified with each activity point in marketing. On the other hand, we cannot reasonably imply that profit contribution is not a vital and measurable aspect of budgeting and performance appraisal for responsibility centers or segments in production and administration. This simply is not the case. The very fact that the use of standards and planned quantity and activity schedules for operations in areas other than marketing serve as the basis for budgeting and in turn as the basis for performance evaluation, and further that the financial results of operations are measured as deviations or variances from budgeted standards reflect profit contribution. The amount of the variance (favorable or unfavorable) is in fact the measure of profit improvement or shrinkage based on budget that each activity classification or resource input in a center has made to total company profit.

While revenues are directly traceable only to activity points in marketing, the costs and expenses of resource inputs to operations will be incurred by every center or segment in the company. It is for this reason that the use of direct costing and measurable quantity standards are vital to planning and budgeting but more especially to successful performance evaluation. The term "direct costing" has two meanings, one being associated with variable behavior in volume levels and the other being the traceability to or origin of cost or expense classifications for a particular responsibility center or activity point. The latter definition is the one that is important for management control, and it includes direct variable costs as we have seen.

Since controllability means the degree to which supervisors and managers charged with the responsibility for carrying out operating plans in each functional area can make decisions that affect the amount of resource inputs as well as the volume level of activity per se, they can control the costs and expenses incurred by these resources. In production, the supervisor of the finishing department in plant 1 of the Supreme Furniture Company can decide "how much" skilled labor, sanding and polishing materials or tools, and small equipment are necessary to meet his output schedule for the month or quarter. In marketing, the regional sales manager usually has discretion in periodic planning for the size of his sales force, local promotion activity, or travel allowances to meet quotas based on forecast sales for each line of furniture. These resource inputs are direct to the organizational unit or activity point as defined. Their variable cost and spending increments can also be increased or cut back at the discretion of the respective managers, and this fact defines their responsibility from the standpoint of profit contribution. Stated another way, it is the decision-making latitude that a manager or supervisor has over resources that are direct to operations for which he is responsible that sets the limits of his managerial control and the level of his performance achievement.

We have also discussed and given examples of the use of standards in budgeting and performance evaluation. The origin of quantitative standards can be traced to the early twentieth-century research by industrial engineers and the pioneers of scientific management. While many of the concepts and measurements for developing standards are still confined to manufacturing production, their application to nonproduction functions for manufacturers, to other business enterprises, or even to nonprofit organizations may very well be a future development in the practice of management control. Standards provide a definite advantage in reducing reliance on judgment and taking the guesswork out of quantitative activity planning. Further, they provide greater objectivity to performance measures and enhance the credibility of the evaluations made of operating results. The disadvantage is that only repetitive activities can be observed effectively over time for the purpose of developing reliable quantitative standards.

We have presented the subjects of planning and budgeting and performance appraisal of operating results as being mirror images of each other both in concept and in terms of technical and analytical treatment. The budget process is the translation of activity plans and their estimated manpower and physical resource requirements into a financial roadmap that is oriented to profit objectives. Planned activity levels are based on forecasts of product output that management expects to produce and sell for the month or quarter within the year.

We have dealt with the classification and construction of budgets in two essential and interrelated ways, namely, according to analyzed cost behavior based on changes in activity levels or scheduled production output and forecast sales. In the context of changing product volume levels over time within the planning year, we have stressed that the behavior of production and sales volume are necessarily related to each other for both planning and control purposes, even though they are organizationally independent. The planning of production volume over time depends on and therefore must be based on the planned quantity of product-line sales in the marketplace with inventory levels being the connecting link.

Cost behavior for budgeting purposes depends on changing levels of product manufacturing and sales, and the classifications of budgets have been made in terms of cost behavior. Thus functional-activity classifications that experience varying behavior with changes in volume of production output or sales will yield variable costs, while those classifications that are independent of and remain constant with volume changes in production or sales are fixed and so are their financial costs. The definition and application of budgets for specific groups of activities within a major function and its organization structure are based on these concepts of cost behavior. Variable, step, semifixed, and fixed-cost budgets reflect the degree of variability or constancy with which the financial requirements for resources are anticipated and therefore planned based on experience with changes in volume of physical product movement from plant operations to the customer.

The flexible-budgeting system is a viable application of direct-costing methods and resource standards for planning and budgeting at those organizational levels in the company that are responsible for line operations in production, warehousing and storage, and marketing. It is a system that uses the company's knowledge and past experience with product movement, resource requirements, and their attendant costs in each line organization unit in preparing budgets for short-term future operations. The objectivity and accuracy of flexible-budgeting systems come from careful technical examination of past operating experience and proper use of adjustments for changes in standards and resource costs based on current economic conditions in all instances where they differ from past experience. When flexible-budgeting systems are properly and carefully implemented, they can yield highly reliable results not only for the management and budgeting of a company's physical and monetary resources but also for performance evaluation.

Many professional and administrative areas of an enterprise are not directly involved with the manufacturing, servicing, or marketing of primary lines of business. Their activities are essentially auxiliary to the main functions of producing and selling, and they must be planned anew at the beginning of the year or quarter. We have discussed some prominent examples including advertising and promotion, legal services and research and development. The concepts and techniques of program planning and budgeting to include task management and financial appropriations, project planning, and priority ranking are more readily applicable to program and professional services than the methods of quantitative budgeting. Although the methods and techniques used in program planning and budgeting are often not as complex as they are for quantitative budgeting, it is also true that management planning and decision making will place greater reliance on judgment for both planning and performance appraisal than is the case for functional operations that employ quantitative budgeting procedures.

The concepts of management by objectives and management by exception are vital to our treatment of planning and budgeting and performance evaluation in the foregoing chapters. Planning and budgeting systems represent the practical application of the philosophy of management by objectives while performance reporting and appraisal with variance analyses based on plans and budgets are indeed the application of management by exception for control. Quantitative plans for volume levels of scheduled production output and sales quotas based on market projections provide the foundation for implementation of functional operations in future short-term periods. The planning for resources that will be necessary to achieve planned product volume levels are developed through the use of standards and then translated into budgets by applying cost-accounting methods. When functional and departmental budgets are approved by management, they become the quantitative objectives and financial guides to the conduct of operations during the period for each organization unit or activity group and its supervisor or manager. Performance reports at the end of the operating period are prepared and analyzed in terms of the budgeted activity levels and their cost assignment for each classification in the budget. Operating results that deviate from budgeted objectives will reflect superior or unfavorable performance, hence the exceptions, and in turn serve as guides to decision making for control and also as guides to activity planning and budgeting in future periods.

In performance evaluation for functional operations in production and marketing, both the forecast budget and the control budget are used to analyze variances for more effective appraisal of operating results in all major activity classifications. These measures apply the predetermined standards for resources and for production costs and selling prices to volume levels of product output or sales. The difference between the two measures is that scheduled production and forecast sales at the beginning of the period are reflected in the forecast budget, whereas actual factory volume output and product-line sales units achieved by the end of the operating period are used to develop the control budget. Toward what purpose? We have emphasized that performance evaluation is undertaken for managerial control of human and material resources and their cost requirements. And control toward optimum efficiency and effective use of resources and consequently optimum achievement of profit levels is exercised within specific organization units, activity groups, or segments through supervisory or managerial decision making.

For example, in production it is unlikely that the supervisor of the machining department in the plant "controls" the planned volume of product output for any month or quarter. The schedule of production is set at higher management levels, and it is a primary tenet that managerial control is exercised at that level in the organization where decision-making authority is delegated and exercised. Volume variances therefore are not ordinarily within the domain of the supervisor's authority and responsibility from the standpoint of performance achievement. What he can control are the direct labor, materials, and auxiliary service resources and their costs that are used in the machining department, and they must be analyzed as to their quantitative and financial performance at the product volume levels achieved for the operating period and based on standards for his department. Similarly, the district sales manager can control the costs of manpower, facilities, and expense items that are directly assigned to his district and that are subject to his authority for short-term planning and decision making. He is also expected to meet his quota for sales volume when it is realistically attainable. What he cannot control is the product forecast sales volume when it is the responsibility of higher managerial authority in the marketing organization. Volume variances are more likely to reflect the effectiveness of senior management planning, and it is necessary to determine for any period of time whether the variances result from errors in forecasting and scheduling for which senior management is responsible or whether they result from deviations in operating efficiency at lower middle-management levels.

We observed that general administrative activities and professional services are the program or task types that do not depend on product flow for purposes of planning and budgeting. This means that performance evaluation is undertaken by comparing the program results and financial costs incurred with the planned activities that were developed and set as objectives for the particular period being appraised. Effectiveness of results against plans can be analyzed and interpreted from performance reports on two bases. One is the cost savings or overrun and the other is the nonfinancial appraisal of the degree of task completion obtained by comparing specific task accomplishments with the corresponding goals set forth in the activity plan. For service or professional departments, devising guidelines that will measure both aspects of performance may be essential not only for financial control but for effective future program planning in administration as well.

Formal development of budgeting and performance evaluation systems will depend on the individual company's complexity and diversification according to product lines or services and the number of vertical levels of management. It will also depend on the number of divisions and plant locations and the degree of autonomy and responsibility that each has for production planning, staffing, procurement and financing, as well as the complexity of markets served. There is no single set of guidelines for constructing and maintaining an adequate budgeting and management control system that may be used for all industrial enterprises, even within a well-defined industry. Hence the system itself has to be tailored to an individual company's operations by function and after careful examination of the organization structure, managerial responsibilities and decision-making mandate by vertical levels.

Nevertheless, some general comments regarding formal system construction and use are in order. Our first observation is that the degree of complexity in the system with respect to the number of budget and performance reporting documents and the extent of detail that each contains will be based on a combination of two considerations: the number of identifiable functional activities assigned to each block on the organization chart and the number of managerial review and reporting levels from lower supervision through middle management to the top echelons in the company. The preparation and approval of operating budgets, when viewed as a periodic and recurring process (which it is, of course!) is most equitably carried out in pyramid fashion from "bottom to top" in the organization, not the other way around.

This is the case simply because the very act of delegating authority and responsibility down through the organization places the individual manager in the best position to observe and gain first-hand knowledge of the behavior of those activities assigned to him. This also means that he is in the best position to know the resource requirements of the activities. If performance feedback to his unit is adequate for these activities and for the material and manpower resources and facilities assigned to him, he is also in the best position to observe and render judgment as to cost requirements. The purpose of budget approval by higher levels and by review committees for large divisions or an entire functional area is to provide objectivity in decision making and in regard to requests made at lower levels. Managers at higher levels of authority are in the best position to weigh and compare the requests and needs of the several activity groups in the division or functional area and in view of total short-term budget ceilings set by senior management. Compromises will always be a fact of life in budget negotiations between levels of authority. Even so, the managers who are closest to day-to-day operations are usually best able to build the foundation in the periodic budget development and approval process.

Performance reports tell the reviewing officer what happened at the conclusion of an operating period on the basis of planned activities and their approved costs. We have stressed that the amount of detail for activities together with corresponding variances from budget be limited in the feedback process to those items for which a request for funds was originally made to the next higher level. It does not make much sense to burden the vice president, marketing, with expense account detail for every salesman in all of the company's field offices or districts. The district sales manager is properly the man to review performance detail for his salesmen and submit a summary report by activity classifications for the total district force to his boss at the regional level, and so on.

Performance reporting to senior management in each functional area will place greater emphasis on trend information by summary financial classifications only in each of the divisions for which a senior officer is responsible. Planning and budget decisions at senior levels involve careful examination of the relationship between long-term capital commitments and short-term appropriations to meet the operating requirements of several divisions or directorships. In production, current-year and three- to five-year financial plans for several plant locations are examined at one time (usually at annual intervals) and in relation to each other. These same considerations apply to the other functional areas. The senior officers for marketing have to consider the current-year operations and appropriations for each of the marketing divisions in relation to short-term sales forecasts and three- to five-year capital plans and requirements based on long-term projections.

Senior management has a broader perspective in regard to organizational scope and through time than is the case for middle management. On the other hand, senior officers are not concerned with the extensive detail in planning and control for manpower and physical resources on a monthly or quarterly basis with which middle management is inevitably involved. This means that senior management will require performance reports that summarize only the primary fixed and variable classifications in each division together with the variances and preferably brief descriptive explanations for deviations. In this way, the performance review will cover fewer financial classifications, but will enable senior management to examine the relationship of these classifications and financial results across several divisions so that valid and meaningful comparisons can be made for the same reporting period.

Although monthly performance data are important to middle management, senior officers are unlikely to require reports more frequently than each quarter except at their request or when significant deviations appear. However, in view of the fact that long-term capital planning and financial appropriations have to be integrated with resource requirements and funding of operations from one quarter to the next, two types of trend reports may be useful. The first will show the same classification data for each division for the current quarter, for the same quarter in the previous year, and cumulative for the current year by actual financial achievement and achievement rates (based on budget) in each of the three timeframes. The second report will trace a three- to five-year financial history or past annual trend of summary results by division and a projected or target budget for the same time intervals in the future. The first report yields an accurate reading of the short-term trend and can be used for planning the major appropriation levels for the next year and to update long-term budget projections. While it is true that both types of reports rely on past experience for planning and decision making by senior management, they still may provide the best foundation for guiding top-management decisions.

We have approached functional planning, budgeting, and management control with the philosophy that all three aspects—quantitative planning, budget preparation, and control of operating results—are interrelated through time. No single aspect of the system can be viewed as being independent of the other two in concept or in application for profit-oriented manufacturing companies. We have also presented our subject with the view that the organization structure is the proper foundation on which the system is built and maintained. Further, the essential purpose of such a system is to provide management at any organizational level with the quantitative and financial information that is most appropriate to the decision-making needs and responsibilities of each manager toward effective planning, efficient performance and improved profit achievement for the company.

This subject as it has been presented in the foregoing chapters is a general model that may serve as a guide to the development and use of budgeting and control by profit-seeking firms, recognizing that every company is unique with regard to its formal organization, size, complexity of functional operations, competitive environment, and managerial philosophy. Although the specific approach we have taken is oriented to the product-manufacturing company, several of the concepts and decision-making considerations for planning and control discussed in this book will also apply to profit-oriented organizations that provide services, even though their functional activities are quite different from those of manufacturing firms. It is for this reason that reference has been made to service-type companies on those points in the discussion where parallels are deemed to exist.

Technical systems in management control are often regarded as comprising a specialized professional area that concerns only financial managers and controllers. Systems development and implementation are essentially the responsibility of financial executives and those with technical expertise in accounting and management information systems. However, we cannot overemphasize the fact that functional executives at all levels in the business enterprise are vitally involved in budget preparation and the effective use of performance reports in managing their areas of operation. It has been our sincere intent that both managerial groups may benefit equally from our efforts here.

Appendix A: Some Technical Aspects of Cost-Behavior Analysis

For any corporate function or organizational unit, we usually think of cost behavior from the standpoint of the extent to which costs change or do not change; that is, the extent to which a given classification of costs is variable or fixed. In this regard, we think of cost behavior as being a function of time periods (month, quarter, fiscal year, long term), but more particularly as a function of changes in the level of an activity measure that generates the cost incurred. This activity may be output such as the volume of product completed in the production department or the unit volume of sales in the sales department. Or the activity measure may be an input such as labor time, parts or materials in production, or salesmen's time in the field.

The most fundamental way of determining the behavior of costs for a particular activity is judgment based on the knowledge and intuitive ability that a manager acquires through long experience working with the people and activities in his organizational unit. The superintendent of the machining department will know the exact quantity of material A that is required to complete operations on a batch of gadgets if his operations are not too complex and if the number and variety of inputs are few. At the end of a production run his records of material A use will enable him to make a fairly accurate judgment as to whether there have been overages. He knows that the quantity of material A is variable with the number of gadgets his employees work on during a week or a month. He also knows the unit cost of the material and quick calculations will enable him to determine whether actual costs for the month are more or less than they should be. Similarly, if salesmen are paid at a rate of 4 percent of dollar sales volume, the cost of salaries will always be variable based on sales, and the sales manager will have no difficulty in calculating the monthly payroll for a small sales force.

Complex departmental activities, however, make it prohibitive for a manager to keep track of cost rates and behavior for every activity input. More objective and routinized methods must be employed. Test studies have been used commonly for this purpose in production operations. By setting different volume levels for output, research engineers can determine the requirements for materials-input levels and for labor-grade combinations (often called "labor mix") and hours at each output level. The accountant then applies cost factors for units of each material and hourly rates for each grade of labor to determine the degree of variability in cost behavior with production volume.

A third means of analyzing cost behavior is through study of past periods of operation. This is a highly useful way of approaching the problem, although it assumes that the record-keeping system for an organization's activities is thorough. In production, continuing records would be maintained for each department as to output volume by time periods. For the same time periods, individual activities, all specific inputs of materials with quantities and unit purchase prices, as well as labor by individual grade, hourly rates, and hours used would be recorded. In the sales department, records would include weekly or monthly volume by product lines, items within product lines and prices received based on purchase orders. Input costs for the sales department would primarily represent salaries and commissions of salesmen, managerial salaries and those of administrative and clerical personnel, together with overhead for buildings and equipment.

Analysis of cost behavior would have to begin with an examination of existing account classifications for most organizational units. A knowledge of cost behavior by major functional account groups is in turn a refinement for setting up a flexible-budgeting system since departmental-overhead accounts would need to be segregated into fixed, variable, and semivariable classifications. Overhead items such as depreciation on plant and equipment, managerial salaries, and real-estate taxes and insurance will usually be fixed for short-term planning and budgeting periods, materials handling or maintenance supplies may be semivariable, while power and utilities may be either semivariable or variable. Initial segregation of individual accounts into these categories of variability may be accomplished by inspection and good judgment, and only rough approximations need to be made in doing so. For further refinement in analyzing cost behavior, several statistical methods can be used quite effectively for this purpose, and we will discuss the most common procedures.

It becomes quite apparent in our discussions of quantitative planning and budgeting and particularly in our treatment and presentations on control measures and analysis that we are concerned not only with the behavior of costs in successive time periods of operation but in relation to activity volume changes as well. For example, if an account group happened to be semivariable, that is, it contained both fixed and variable costs, then computations for analysis would have to show the amount of fixed expenses when unit volume of production (or sales) is zero. They would also have to show the variable-cost rate per unit over the range of activity for which that rate is valid. When an organizational unit has only one product line or one service, then the volume levels are simply based on that product or service. However, when there are several products or services, then choosing an alternative measure to volume may be necessary. Alternative measures to plant department operations may be direct labor time in hours or units of raw-materials input, and for marketing operations, commission sales hours in the field may be appropriate.

The reader should note carefully two points that are generally true of activity measures selected in lieu of unit product volume. The first point is that no assumption can be made that labor, materials, or any similar measure "causes" overhead to exist. Any one of them is merely selected as the most equitable measure for assigning overhead to product lines or to organizational units for purposes of management control. Also any measure such as direct labor is selected because it is the one that most closely varies with changes in unit volume of production, based on the experience of the particular organizational unit that adopts the measure.

Comparability of the data over time is essential, however, if a meaningful analysis of cost behavior patterns is to be developed through past experience. For example, if we want to know the relationship between the variability of the cost of material A in the machining department and volume of production output, the price of material A would have to be adjusted for each of the past periods used in the analysis to reflect current prices paid to outside suppliers by the purchasing department. The reason for this adjustment is that the price trends in outside supply markets will affect the cost of material A but not in terms of the level of production activity in the machining department. Similarly, the cost of a particular grade of labor will vary with the volume level of product output in the machining department. However, labor cost is a combination of the hourly rate paid to workers and the labor time used to complete a production run. The hourly rate will vary through time, but as a result of negotiated labor contracts which are independent of production schedules and operations of the machining department. For this reason, it is best to adjust hourly rates for those past periods used in the analysis so they will reflect current contract rates.

Figure A-1 presents a graphic illustration of the four major types of cost-behavior patterns that may describe a cost classification for an organizational unit's activities. In the machining department of the Gadget Corporation, the following classifications are used to present each of the cost-behavior patterns:

1. Materials, direct labor: Variable cost
2. Machinery and equipment: Fixed cost
3. Utilities and maintenance: Semivariable cost
4. Indirect labor: Semifixed cost

In figure A-1, both direct inputs to production (materials and direct labor) vary in proportion to changes in the volume of production output. Any classification of input whose cost can be expressed as a *rate* per quantity of output will be completely variable with changes in the level of output. For direct labor, the current rate for Grade 1 we will say is $2.80 per hour. If analysis of past production runs shows that the average time for Grade 1 labor is 15 minutes to complete the assigned operation on one unit of product, then the rate per gadget is $0.70. In increments of 1,000 product units, variable cost of Grade 1 labor would be as shown in table A-1.

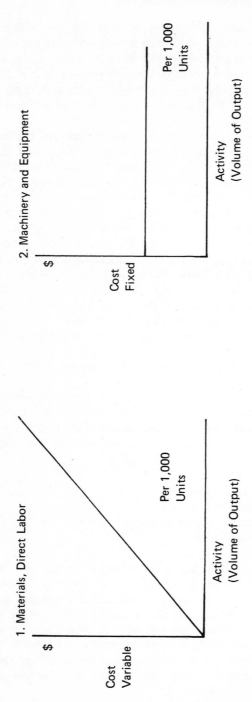

Figure A-1. Plant 1, Machining Department, Cost Classification and Behavior

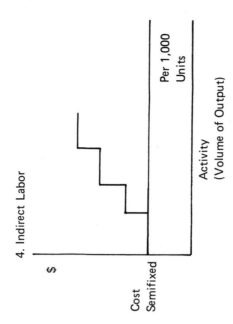

4. Indirect Labor

$

Cost Semifixed

Per 1,000 Units

Activity (Volume of Output)

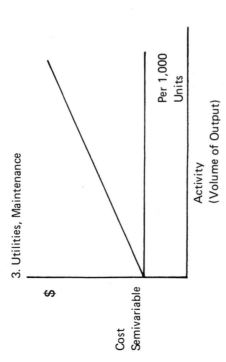

3. Utilities, Maintenance

$

Cost Semivariable

Per 1,000 Units

Activity (Volume of Output)

The second classification, machinery and equipment, reflects the opposite pattern of behavior to direct labor and materials. These costs are completely fixed in relation to production volume, assuming that there is no change in the composition, number, and type of machinery and equipment that would increase or decrease the production capacity of the machining department. The cost charges themselves are determined on the basis of depreciation schedules that remain the same in amounts with respect to both volume of production and production time periods.

In the third example, what is called a "semivariable" cost is characteristic of any classification by which there is a constant expense regardless of whether the department is producing and by which there is also a variable increment in proportion to volume levels. It is difficult to say whether or not any account classifications in an operating department will correspond to this behavior pattern. Cost analysis may reveal that certain inputs such as maintenance supplies and utilities will contain both a fixed amount and a variable rate based on volume levels.

The fourth illustration shows what is called a "semifixed" or "step-cost" pattern. This classification experiences constant or fixed cost for a range of product output and then adds or drops a "layer" to this fixed cost as the range of activity increases beyond a certain level or falls below a certain level. The labor cost of supervision in a plant department may be such a classification. Supervisors are ordinarily salaried, and this labor-cost component is therefore constant in relation to activity or product levels, but within a certain range. If the range of output increases or a production shift is added, it may be necessary to add supervisory personnel to the department (table A-2).

This simple illustration assumes that for a single shift, normal or expected monthly output will not exceed 10,000 units of product in the department. For added increments of production runs that may be required for a given month to replenish unusually low inventories or to meet unexpected increases in customer orders, the schedule shows the additional requirements for supervision and the corresponding step-type or incremental cost that is fixed only within the output ranges indicated. This schedule also shows that an additional shift is required for a volume level exceeding 15,000 units. The variable or direct rate for factory labor should not change with an additional shift unless there is a change in the mix of labor, that is, a change in the number of workers employed for each labor grade.

Analysis of past operating activity for the purpose of defining cost behavior can be accomplished by means of any one of several ordinary statistical methods. These methods include the scatter graph (figure A-2), semiaverages (tables A-3 and A-4), and ordinary least squares (table A-5). In each of these examples, we will use direct labor hours (DLH) as the base activity rather than units of output.

The scatter graph (figure A-2) shows a plotting of dollar costs for utilities in

Table A-1
Variable Cost of Grade 1 Labor

Activity (Volume of Output)	Grade 1 Labor Cost
1,000	$ 700
3,000	2,100
4,000	2,800
5,000	3,500
6,000	4,200
8,000	5,600
10,000	7,000

the machining department of plant 1 that corresponds to different levels of labor-hour input. This pattern is semivariable with a minimum expense of $600 per month at shutdown. We can determine a variable rate per DLH above the minimum in this way:

$$\text{Fixed amount} = \$600 \text{ per month}$$

$$\text{Average expense} = \$5,100 \text{ per month}$$

Variable rate (per DLH)

$$= \frac{\text{average expense} - \text{fixed amount}}{\text{average direct labor hours}}$$

$$= \frac{(\$5,100 - \$600)}{7,500 \text{ DLH}}$$

$$= \frac{\$4,500}{7,500}$$

$$= \$0.60 \text{ per DLH}$$

The semiaverage method would analyze monthly data for a one- or two-year operating cycle, separating the highest expense months from the lowest expense months (table A-3).

The average difference in each column is computed for both direct labor hours and utilities expenses as shown in table A-4. The variable rate is derived through dividing the average expense difference by the average direct labor difference.

$$\text{Variable rate} = \frac{\$720}{1,200} = \$0.60 \text{ per hour}$$

The fixed amount would then be determined by way of a formula using the overall averages for direct labor hours and the classification expense together with the variable rate.

Table A-2
Production Manning and Cost Schedule: Supervision

Level of Activity (Production Output in Units Per Month)	Number of Shifts	Number of Supervisors	Supervision Cost Level Per Month
0-10,000	1	1	$1,500
10,000-15,000	1	2	3,000
Above 15,000	2	3	4,500

$$\text{Fixed amount} = \text{average classification expense} - (\text{variable rate} \times \text{average DLH})$$

$$= \$5,100 - (\$0.60 \times 7,500)$$

$$= \$5,100 - \$4,500$$

$$= \$600 \text{ per month}$$

Both the scatter graph and semiaverage methods are easy to apply and will yield sufficiently accurate estimates of cost-behavior patterns for an activity-account classification. For any classification, it is best to analyze past data trends by first pinpointing the exact amounts that are fixed and the length of time for which they have remained so. This example contains both fixed and variable components (hence, is "semivariable"). One can easily see the limitation of the semiaverage method in that the fixed amount is an approximation derived by formula rather than being isolated as the first step in the analysis.

The ordinary least-squares method (table A-5) is a common statistical technique for fitting a trend line to variable data and is mathematically more precise in arriving at a variable cost rate than the scatter graph. Its application is particularly appropriate when analysis involves several periods of past operating experience and a long series of cost data or plot points. Using the same twelve months as in table A-3, we will rearrange the data in chronological order.

$$\text{Variable rate} = \frac{\Sigma XY}{\Sigma X^2}$$

$$= \frac{3,896,000}{6,560,000}$$

$$= \$0.5939$$

$$\text{Fixed amount} = \text{Average expense} - (\text{variable rate} \times \text{average DLH})$$

$$= \$5,100 - (0.5939 \times 7,500)$$

$$= \$5,100 - \$4,454$$

$$= \$646$$

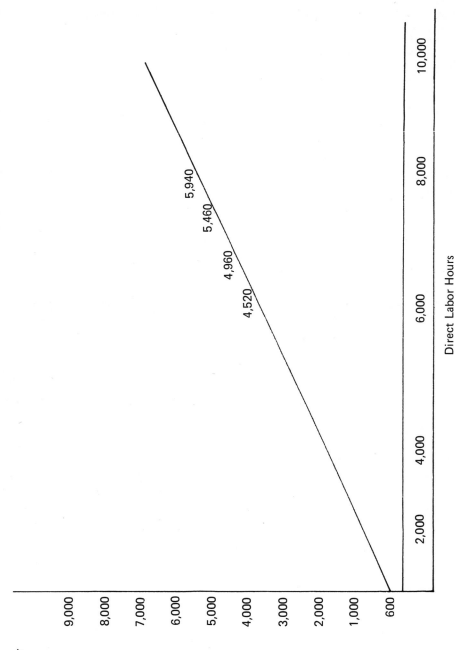

Figure A-2. Plant 1, Machining Department, Scatter Graph Analysis, Classification: Heat, Power, and Light

Table A-3
Plant 1, Machining Department, Semi-Average Analysis, Classification:
Heat, Power, and Light

Six High Months				Six Low Months		
Months	*DLH*	*Expense*		*Months*	*DLM*	*Expense*
October	7,300	$ 5,000		November	6,500	$ 4,500
March	8,100	5,460		December	6,900	4,760
April	8,900	5,940		January	6,500	4,520
May	8,500	5,700		February	7,300	4,980
June	7,700	5,240		August	7,300	4,960
July	8,100	5,420		September	6,900	4,720
Total	48,600	$32,760			41,400	$28,440
Monthly Average	8,100	$ 5,460			6,900	$ 4,740

The least-squares method is computationally more sophisticated and would require computer programs for practical application in many organizational departments. Like the semiaverage method, this illustration has the disadvantage that the fixed costs are derived after the variable rate has been set rather than being isolated prior to the analysis. Wherever possible, it is best to apply these methods to time series of variable costs after the fixed component of operating costs and expenses has been isolated in the accounts. Also the variable coefficient or rate is a self-weighting average rate for the entire twelve-month data series in the least-squares procedure.

Table A-4
Cost Differences in Semi-Average Direct Labor and Expense,
Classification: Heat, Power and Light

	Average DLH	*Average Expense*
High months	8,100	$5,460
Low months	6,900	4,740
Difference	1,200	$ 720

Table A-5
Worksheet for Application of Least-Squares Statistical Method of Cost-Behavior Analysis

Month	DLH	Expense	Variance from Average DLH (X)	Variance from Average Expense (Y)	XY	X²
January	6,500	$ 4,520	−1,000	−580	580,000	1,000,000
February	7,300	4,980	−200	−120	24,000	40,000
March	8,100	5,460	600	360	216,000	360,000
April	8,900	5,940	1,400	840	1,176,000	1,960,000
May	8,500	5,700	1,000	600	600,000	1,000,000
June	7,700	5,240	200	140	28,000	40,000
July	8,100	5,420	600	320	192,000	360,000
August	7,300	4,960	−200	−140	28,000	40,000
September	6,900	4,720	−600	−380	228,000	360,000
October	7,300	5,000	−200	−100	20,000	40,000
November	6,500	4,500	−1,000	−600	600,000	1,000,000
December	6,900	4,760	−600	−340	204,000	360,000
Total	90,000	$61,200			3,896,000	6,560,000
Average	7,500	$ 5,100				

Index

About the Author

Lewis Daniel Houck, Jr. is a graduate of Princeton University and received the M.B.A. (with distinction) and Ph.D. degrees from New York University's Graduate School of Business. In 1966 he was appointed graduate instructor in accounting and management at New York University, where he conducted a major research project on financial reporting and control systems for diversified industrial corporations, enlisting the cooperation of six major U.S. conglomerate firms. He served as educational projects manager for the National Association of Accountants in 1969 and 1970. Prior to joining the faculty at New York University, Dr. Houck was manager of special research in merchandising at Young & Rubicam, Inc., and account executive and marketing manager at Selling Research, Inc., both in New York City. He has also served as a consultant to manufacturing and service firms in the areas of management organization planning, marketing, operations planning, and financial control. Most recently Dr. Houck has been with the U.S. Department of Agriculture, where he developed the first continuing national survey to monitor consumer economic behavior.

Dr. Houck is a member of numerous professional associations and has recently been appointed a Fellow of the American Biographical Institute and a Fellow of the International Biographical Association. He has also presided at international conference seminars on marketing and communications.